COARSE FISHING

A Guide To Successful Angling

Introduction By Tom Pickering

Colour Library Books

CLB 3337
This 1993 edition produced exclusively for
Colour Library Books Ltd, Godalming, Surrey

First published in 1992 by Collins Willow,
an imprint of HarperCollins Publishers, London

Based on The Art of Fishing © Eaglemoss Publications Ltd 1992

ISBN 1-85833-056-4

Printed and bound in Italy

Contents

Introduction

We all know how crucial it is to have a wide range of effective techniques at our fingertips. As a match angler competing at international level, I certainly do. But whether you fish competitively or not, on one thing we all agree: the fishing scene doesn't stand still. And that's a healthy sign.

I can remember the time when, if you wanted a really effective electronic bite indicator you had to make your own. A few years later, boilies were a new thing; so were wagglers and the rebirth of pole fishing. With increasing numbers of anglers, the boom in new waters and a generally better organized sport, new methods are bound to crop up ever more frequently, swelling the armoury of fish-catching techniques. Some are gimmicks or just plain off-the-wall, and fall deservedly by the wayside. Others go on proving their worth season after season, and we begin to wonder how we ever did without them.

But how do you pick up these essential skills? In *The Complete Book of Coarse Fishing* a team comprising many of Britain's best fishermen have come together to help you do just that. Top names like John Bailey, Neville Fickling, Jim Gibbinson, Dave Harrell, Bob James, Peter Mohan, Andy Orme and Barrie Rickards show you, in clear, straightforward language and with colour photographs and information-packed diagrams, how to master the genuine, tried-and-tested innovations of recent years. But what they also offer, as the title of this book suggests, is a complete guide to improving your fishing, whatever your present level of expertise. Throughout the book the emphasis is on the ▶

practical approach the contributors have evolved over many years – and it has certainly paid off for them.

Techniques and Tackle, the opening chapter, gives expert advice on choosing and using the right tackle in a wide variety of situations. Baits and Lures weighs up the full range of proven baits, both natural and artificial, and offers hot tips on getting the best out of them. Know Your Fish looks at the main coarse species in depth, since you can never know too much about the ways and the habitat of the fish you're after. A Specialist Approach combines this understanding of the major species with unbeatable advice on the best methods of catching them.

So, whether you're just starting out or you've already got some sound experience under your belt, and whether your preference is for fishing in rivers, lakes or reservoirs, *The Complete Book of Coarse Fishing* tells you all you need to know to boost your success rate and get even more enjoyment out of our marvellous sport. You'll wonder how you ever managed without it!

Tom Pickering

CHAPTER ONE

TECHNIQUES AND TACKLE

Float rods

Casting, controlling the tackle, striking and playing fish are the basic functions which a float rod must do well. Top Midlands matchman, Dave Harrell, helps you to choose the right rod.

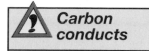

Carbon conducts

Carbon is an excellent conductor of electricity. Don't use a carbon rod anywhere near electricity power lines. The current can arc from the power line to your rod without the rod even touching it and the results could be fatal.

S ince carbon fibre replaced glass-fibre as the main rod-building material, the choice of float rods has grown dramatically. Each season, manufacturers are adding new models to the vast range – each with their own advantages and disadvantages.

Rod materials

The action, lightness and feel of a rod depend on the materials it's made of. Split-cane, greenheart, Spanish reed and glass-fibre have all been used to build rods but materials like carbon fibre and kevlar have made them obsolete.

Carbon fibre versus glass-fibre To appreciate the advantages of carbon fibre, go to a tackle shop and compare a carbon float rod with a glass-fibre float rod of the same length and action.

Before picking up the rods, notice that the carbon rod is slimmer – maybe only 10mm (⅜in) at the butt – perhaps half the diameter of a glass rod. This is a great advantage (particularly in windy weather) because it enables the rod to slice through the air, offering less resistance when casting and striking.

Notice too, how much lighter the carbon rod is. A typical weight for a 12ft (3.6m) glass rod is 8-10oz (227-283g) whereas a 12ft (3.6m) carbon rod might weigh 4½-6oz (128-170g). Apart from making the rod suitable for one-handed casting, it means you can hold it for hours without tiring.

If you take the glass rod in one hand and the carbon rod in the other and give each a gentle 'waggle', the carbon rod returns to a state of rest sooner than the glass rod – carbon fibre is a more resilient material. In

Choose the rod to suit the kind of fishing you think you'll be doing. If you expect to floatfish for powerful species like tench or small carp, go for a more powerful rod.
This angler had an enjoyable day bagging-up with roach on light float gear.

Tip *Waxing joints*

Prevent the joints on your rod from sticking by rubbing a little candle wax or pencil graphite on to the male section. You can pack out loose joints slightly by lightly coating the male section with carbon spray which also prevents sticking.

When fishing, check the joints don`t work loose.

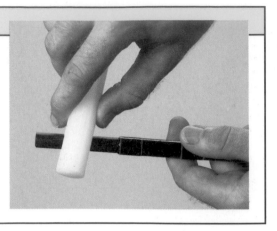

Tip *The four hand method*

If your rod gets stuck together, don't try to pull it apart by yourself. Get assistance from another angler. Each person then grips the rod on one side of the joint with one hand, and on the other side of the joint with the other hand. A steady pull should bring the rod apart without too much difficulty.

fishing terms this means that it is more responsive – making accurate casting easier and giving a crisper strike, which is useful when bites are fast.

Finally, compare the prices. Carbon fibre is a more expensive material so you must be prepared to pay more for the rod. Some manufacturers expect you to pay more for their name alone but you should buy a rod strictly on its merits.

Carbon composites Some carbon fibre float rods include kevlar in their construction. Kevlar – a combination of polymers and nylon – is a non-stretch, shock-absorbent material used for making bullet-proof vests and lumberjacks' trousers (as protection against the chain-saw). Braided around a carbon fibre core, it increases torsional strength (good for accurate long distance casting) and makes for a crisper action.

Rod length
It is possible to buy rods up to 17ft (5.2m) long but these are specialist tools and float rods usually range from 11½-14ft (3.46-4.2m). Getting the right length of rod for the job is important. As a general guide the farther out you intend to fish the longer the rod needs to be.

Ultimately, choose the length of your rod to suit the actual swim you are fishing. If there are overhanging trees you may have to use a short rod. A longer rod will give you extra control when playing large fish over dense marginal weed or snags. If you intend to do all your float fishing with one rod then a rod of 13ft (3.9m) should cover most eventualities.

An 11½ft (3.46m) float rod is a good length for short range work – such as fishing the far bank of canals and lake margins with 2 or 3BB wagglers.

Rods of 12-13ft (3.6-3.9m) are a good length for medium to long range waggler work. A 12ft (3.6m) rod is useful when not casting too far on lakes or casting to the middle of rivers like the Warwickshire Avon or middle Severn. When fishing reservoirs or the far side of rivers, a 13ft (3.9m) rod will give you the leverage to achieve extra distance on the cast and pick up the line better when striking.

Rods of 14ft (4.2m) or more are useful when fishing a stick float. They give scope for extra float control such as holding the line clear of marginal weed or keeping the float on line in windy conditions.

Action and stiffness
Rods have a certain profile when a steady pressure is applied to the tip. This is the rod's action. Don't confuse rod action with rod stiffness – rods having similar actions may vary in stiffness.

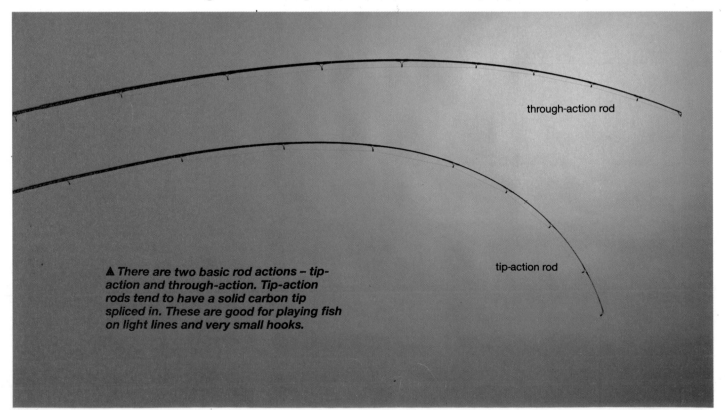

through-action rod

tip-action rod

▲ *There are two basic rod actions – tip-action and through-action. Tip-action rods tend to have a solid carbon tip spliced in. These are good for playing fish on light lines and very small hooks.*

► *For float fishing on rivers, Dave Harrell likes to use hard chrome rings. They do not wear as well as lined rings but they have a lower 'friction factor'. This helps when trotting a float because it means that the line can be paid out smoothly and the bait presented at exactly the same speed as the current.*

◄ *The most popular ring linings are made from either silicon carbide or a ceramic mixture of alumina oxide and titania oxide. Silicon carbide is a very hard, light, super smooth material but it is rather brittle and expensive. Ceramic linings are heavier and not as hard as silicon carbide linings but they tend to be more durable and are only a third of the price.*

Although there are two basic actions for float rods (tip-action and through-action) there are degrees of each. A recent trend is towards a rod which combines both actions. It is important to choose the right action for your fishing.

Through-action rods have a hollow, unspliced tip. With a through-action rod, the pliancy decreases steadily from the tip to the butt section. If you intend to do all your float work with one rod, a fairly soft, through-action carbon rod is a good choice. It will be sharp enough to hit quick bites, forgiving enough in the tip to handle fine hooklengths of 1lb (0.45kg), but also have enough power in the butt to handle heavier tackle and deal with fish like tench, carp and chub.

Through-action rods also have special applications. When fishing light wagglers of 2 or 3BB at short range for soft-mouthed skimmer bream or roach, a softish, through-action rod prevents fish from being bumped off or the hook working free.

For medium to long-range waggler work on lakes and rivers, a stiffer rod can punch the float out; and, when a long sweeping strike is needed to pick up the line and set the hook, it can absorb the shock .

Tip-action rods have nearly all their pliancy in the top section, making them very quick on the strike. Some tip-action rods have a fine, solid carbon top spliced into the top section which makes the rod even more 'tippy'.

⊗ Clean rings

Many anglers never bother to clean their rods. Rings soon become clogged with mud and groundbait which dries to a rock hard consistency. This acts like sandpaper on the line and defeats the object of lining a ring with a low friction material. Your rods will benefit from an occasional wipe down with a cloth and soapy water. Worn or cracked rings should be replaced.

► *Your rod should have the correct number of properly spaced rings. Too few rings will make the line stick to the rod in wet weather and cause the line to depart from the rod's natural curve. Too many rings interfere with the rod's action. On a 13ft (3.9m) rod Dave Harrell likes to see two rings on the butt section, five on the middle and nine (including the tip ring) on the top section. He thinks a 12ft (3.6m) rod should have one ring less, a 14ft (4.2m) rod one more.*

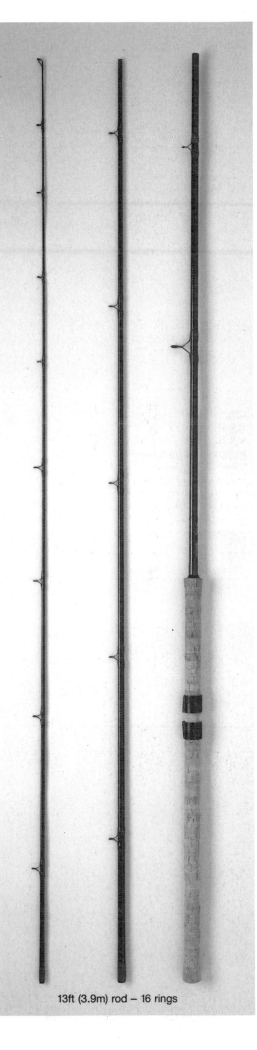

13ft (3.9m) rod – 16 rings

Tip-action rods are ideal for stick float and small balsa fishing on rivers like the Trent, Severn, Thames and Warwickshire Avon, where a fast rod is often essential for hitting quick biting roach, chub and dace.

A very fine tip will allow fish to be played out on hooklengths down to 12oz (0.34kg) and hooks as small as 24 or even 26. This is why some anglers prefer to do all their fishing with tip-action rods. However, some tip-action rods are too stiff in the middle and butt sections for certain kinds of fishing. If you expect to catch bream you should be particularly careful. A tip-action rod which 'locks up' on the strike will bump these soft-mouthed fish off.

A new action Recently the trend has been towards a rod having a 'hybrid' action. When light pressure is applied to the tip of these rods they behave as if they had a tip-action – making them suitable for stick work. As more pressure is applied to the tip, the middle and even the butt sections come into play, so that the rod is quite capable of waggler work, and able to handle larger fish too.

Fittings

Don't make the mistake of thinking that rod fittings are merely auxiliaries. The best blank won't make a good rod unless it is correctly ringed.

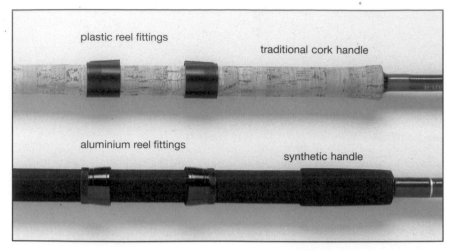

plastic reel fittings

traditional cork handle

aluminium reel fittings

synthetic handle

Rod rings The correct type, number and positioning of rod rings is crucial.

It is the job of the rings to guide the line smoothly, keeping it as close to the profile of the rod as possible. Good rings should keep friction to a minimum and be wear resistant. A wear-resistant material is less likely to damage the line.

There are only two types worth considering – hard chrome and lined rings. Hard chrome are good for trotting rods, where it is important to keep friction very low but they need changing every season. Lined rings are more wear resistant but not quite as smooth as chrome.

▲ *A handle of 21-23in (53-58cm) is about right. Cork is traditionally the material for handles and it takes some beating. It is light and pleasant to the touch. Synthetic handles are easier to keep clean but choice of material really is a personal matter.*

Aluminium is a common material for the reel fittings but new materials, such as plastic and carbon fibre, tend to be lighter and kinder on the hands in cold weather.

Using the rod

A float rod should not be thought of simply as a stick with which to cast the float out and bring fish in. Handled by a good angler, a rod can be used to encourage more bites. You can use it to sink the line in windy conditions, and to hold the line off the water on rivers so that the float is kept on course.

When playing big fish, a skilfully handled rod helps to keep the fish on the hook. Holding a rod high above the water will give you control over a fish that tries to dive for the cover of weed. If you are unlucky enough for a boat to pass through your swim as you are playing a big fish you may be able to avoid losing it by pushing your line deep into the water.

Playing a fish with the tip of the rod close to the surface of the water helps to prevent the fish from splashing about and disturbing the rest of the shoal.

Stick float magic

Stick float fishing is one of the most satisfying ways of fishing a river. Top stick angler John Allerton gives you the basics.

▼ *Until recently, if you wanted a good stick you had to make it yourself – not an easy job. Tackle shops now stock a wide range of excellent quality stick floats.*

Choose any swim on a river and it is likely that it is not of an even depth and that the current doesn't flow at uniform speed or in only one direction. Match anglers on waters such as the Severn, Trent and Warwickshire Avon have pioneered a method that can be used to search the water.

With a stick you can present a bait at various depths. You can run it through at the speed of the current and, because a stick is attached by its top and bottom, you can hold it back very hard and it won't go under (unlike a waggler). Because of its design it can register bites as the bait is sinking, making it extremely versatile.

Stick design

The top of a stick (body) is made from a buoyant material such as balsa, and the bottom (stem) is made from a much denser material such as cane, lignum (a very dense wood that actually sinks), thin wire, alloy or plastic. It is this combination of buoyant and dense materials that gives the stick its stability.

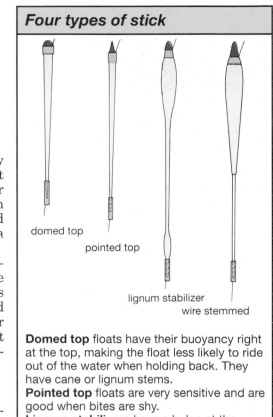

Four types of stick

domed top

pointed top

lignum stabilizer

wire stemmed

Domed top floats have their buoyancy right at the top, making the float less likely to ride out of the water when holding back. They have cane or lignum stems.
Pointed top floats are very sensitive and are good when bites are shy.
Lignum stabilizers have a bulge at the bottom of the stem, making them extremely stable. They are easy to cast and ideal for running through at the speed of the flow.
Alloy and wire stemmed sticks are sensitive and make holding back much easier.

Tip *Shirt button*

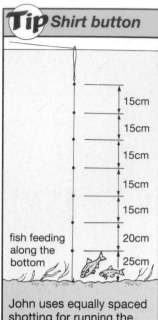

15cm
15cm
15cm
15cm
15cm
20cm
25cm

fish feeding
along the
bottom

John uses equally spaced
shotting for running the
bait through at the speed
of the flow.

Stick technique

Fishing a stick correctly is all about presenting your hookbait in a manner acceptable to a feeding fish. Whether running through, holding back or fishing on the drop, there are certain things to aim for and other things to avoid.

Float size Never use a float that is bigger than necessary. As a rough guide, for swims of 1-1.2m (3-4ft) deep use a 4 no.4 float. For swims of 1.5-2.5m (5-8ft) deep use a 5 no.4 float. For swims of 2.7-3.7m (9-12ft) deep use a 6 or 8 no.4 float. For swims over 4.3m (14ft) deep, use a different method – not a stick float at all. The pace of the swim should also affect your choice – for faster swims use a heavier float.

Plumbing up You can't use a stick to run a bait along the bottom unless you know where the bottom is. Accurate plumbing is essential.

Mending the line Never let your reel line overtake your float – keep a straight line to your float. If the wind is troublesome, put a

number 6 or 8 back shot about 30cm (1ft) above the float to sink the line.

Casting to the fish Always cast downstream – this assists float control. When fish are really feeding they tend to gather in a small area. This may be at the top, bottom or the middle of your swim. Don't waste time trotting your float all the way down to them. Casting to the feed area saves time and catches more fish.

Four ways with the stick

Although there are four basic ways to fish a stick, the skilful angler can combine these to suit the conditions on the day.

Running through at the speed of the flow is probably the most natural, though not necessarily the easiest, way of fishing a stick. It can be very effective in summer when the fish are moving about. Your bait should touch bottom or run through several inches off, so accurate plumbing is essential. It is a good method when fishing about 15m (16yds) downstream in the main flow.

Lift and drop Sometimes you can entice fish by making the bait rise and fall as it travels through the swim. Do this by setting your float to the depth of the swim and lightly shotting the bottom 60cm-1.8m (2-6ft). Checking the float every few metres down your swim and then letting it run through causes the bait to rise and fall. How often you do this and the amount of time you hold back depend upon the flow and the way the fish are feeding. The key to success is to experiment.

On the drop Use this method when fish are feeding in mid-water, under your loose feed. Fish this rig off the bottom and shot it lightly so that the bait falls slowly through the feed zone. By casting so that the shot lands in a straight line downstream of the float, the bait sinks in a smooth arc. The float gradually rights itself as the bait sinks, and is able to register a fish intercepting the bait on the drop.

Holding back When the water tempera-

Making the bait dance

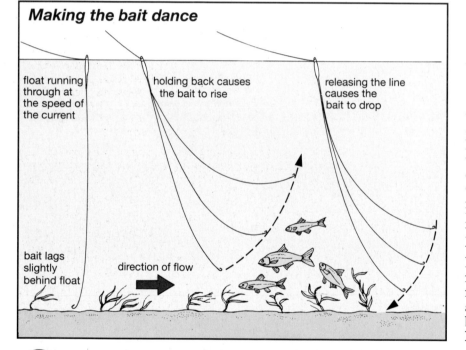

float running
through at
the speed of
the current

holding back causes
the bait to rise

releasing the line
causes the
bait to drop

bait lags
slightly
behind float

direction of flow

Tip *Stop tangles*

Be generous when cutting a piece of silicone rubber tubing for the stem of your stick – a piece about 17mm long is ideal. Wet the stem of your float before sliding the rubber over it – this makes it easier to put the rubber on and prevents the line from getting damaged.

Don't push all the rubber on – leave about 3mm overhanging. This helps to prevent the line tangling around the top of your stick when casting.

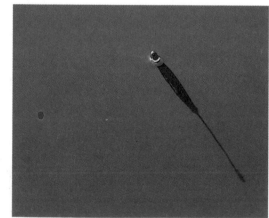

▲ *When edging a stick through at the speed of the current, keep the line behind the float and try to interfere with the float's progress as little as possible.*

▲ *Holding back causes the float to ride out of the water and lean back. Do this by using your index or middle finger on the lip of the spool to stop line from leaving the reel.*

ture is low constant holding back often scores. By setting the float 15-45cm (6-18in) overdepth, and inching it through the swim, you can steer the bait into the fishes' mouths. You may only need to fish one or two rod lengths out. A centrepin is ideal for this, though it takes some mastering.

Feeding

Feeding is not separate from, but a major part of, stick float technique. It is vitally important to get it right.

Where, when and how much The aim is to keep the fish interested and feeding in the position you want them. Feed too much and you may fill the fish up or make them chase the feed downstream. Feed too little and

Holding back

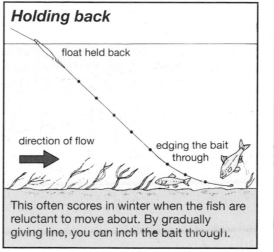

float held back

direction of flow

edging the bait through

This often scores in winter when the fish are reluctant to move about. By gradually giving line, you can inch the bait through.

On the drop

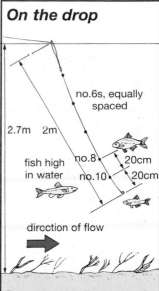

no.6s, equally spaced

2.7m   2m

fish high in water

no.8   20cm

no.10   20cm

dircction of flow

By setting the float under depth and using light shotting, the bait sinks slowly through the mid-water feed zone.

Tip Dotting down

"Sometime ago" says John, "I found that I caught bigger roach and chub by accident when mending the line. My theory was that fish often swim with a bait in their mouths although you can't always see the bites.

By using a very thin-topped stick and shotting it to a dot, I found that I could see the bites better and hit a large percentage of them.

The correct way to shot a stick is to add shot until it sinks, then remove one no.8 (or a no.6 if conditions are very poor) so that the slightest touch sinks it."

---

they may move upstream to an angler who is feeding more bait.

Always feed downstream – 2-3m (6-10ft) is about right. By feeding about 20 maggots or casters, twice a cast, you can keep a steady trickle of feed going through your swim. This often encourages the fish (particularly roach) to move up in the water, where you can get them on the drop. The windier the conditions are, the more inclined the fish are to rise. So don't be put off if it looks choppy.

If you are getting plenty of bites and fish, feed more frequently. If bites are few then cut down on the quantity of feed. Whatever you do keep feeding – even if it is only six

▼ *An angler unhooks a nice Thames chub which fell to a 'shirt button' stick rig. Some anglers occasionally bunch their shot to get the bait down quickly but John Allerton always prefers to string his out.*

Tip *Nick the bait*

If you hook too much of the maggot's skin it fills the bend of the hook and reduces the hook's fish-holding capacity. There is also a tendency for the bait to wrap around the bend when a fish takes the bait, causing the fish to be bumped off. Nick the smallest amount of skin so the maggot hangs free. This makes the bait lively and keeps fish hooked.

▼ *Stick tactics account for a fine chub on Cheshire's River Dane. Many anglers prefer open-face reels for stick float fishing because the line peels easily from the spool, but others – like the angler shown here – do all their stick fishing with a closed-face reel. Use the design you feel most comfortable with.*

maggots every other cast – or else the fish you do have there will leave.

Correct feed line When choosing a line on which to trot the float, make sure you can cast to it comfortably and feed it accurately. Once you've mastered the technique closer in, you'll be able to fish farther out with the same control.

Roach have a tendency to hang just off the feed line, so every now and again try running your float 1.8-2.7m (6-9ft) beyond the feed line. If this proves successful, keep the same line – don't start feeding farther out. Chasing the fish simply causes them to move out.

The business end

Light lines and small hooks help you to achieve perfect bait presentation.

Line On some waters the roach and chub are 'well-educated' – wise to crude, clumsily handled tackle. A reel line of not more than 2lb (0.9kg) b.s minimizes line drag and therefore does not hinder the float's progress through the swim. Choose your hooklength to suit hook size, and the size of hook to suit the bait. This gives you the best chance of fooling canny fish.

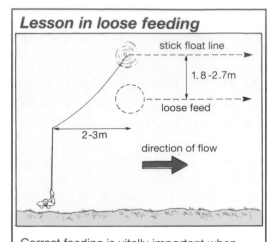

Lesson in loose feeding

stick float line

1.8-2.7m

loose feed

2-3m

direction of flow

Correct feeding is vitally important when fishing the stick. John always feeds slightly downstream of himself and runs the float down just beyond the feedline.

Use a size 20 or 22 to a 1lb (0.45kg) hooklength when using maggots for roach, dace and chub. For casters, use a size 20 or 18 to a 1lb (0.45kg) hooklength. In winter when the going is hard, a size 24 to a 12oz (0.34kg) bottom can produce a few bonus fish.

Fishing with wagglers

There is often confusion about what a waggler is. Is it a specific kind of float? Should it have a body? Why is it so special? Here are the answers.

▼ *After casting to the feed area, dip the rod in the water and give a few sharp turns of the reel to leave the line below the surface, away from any wind.*

Strictly speaking, waggler is a term that may be applied to any float attached bottom only. For this reason it comes in a variety of shapes, sizes and materials. It holds no mystery, but once you master waggler fishing you have at your disposal an extremely versatile technique and one that produces results when all else fails.

Types of waggler

There are basically two types: straight and bodied, both with or without inserts. The main stem of a waggler is usually made from peacock quill, sarkandas reed or plastic, with the body made from balsa or cork, and the insert from thinner quill, reed, cane or plastic. Some are fashioned entirely from one piece of balsa. Wagglers come in a range of sizes, from two BB (the lightest) to three SSG (the heaviest). Tackle shops stock these under different commercial names.

Why wagglers?

Without exception, you want to get the bait to where the fish are and keep it there. If the fish are a long way out you may have trouble casting to them. If the wind is strong you may be unable to keep the float over the feed. A waggler will help you to solve these problems.

Firstly, a float that is attached by its bottom, with the bulk of the shot around its base, acts like a dart as it flies through the air. It is possible to cast it a long way with great accuracy.

Secondly, because the line issues from the bottom of the float, you can keep the line (from float to rod) entirely beneath the water's surface, away from the wind.

However, there are times when you need to hold a bait back – when fishing medium and fast-flowing rivers, for example. If you use a waggler it will dive under each time you pull on the float; a float attached top and bottom – a stick float, for example – would be better than a waggler.

Which waggler?

Four things should be considered when choosing which waggler to use: location of the fish, wind strength, depth of water, and shyness of fish.

The location of the fish: as a rough guide,

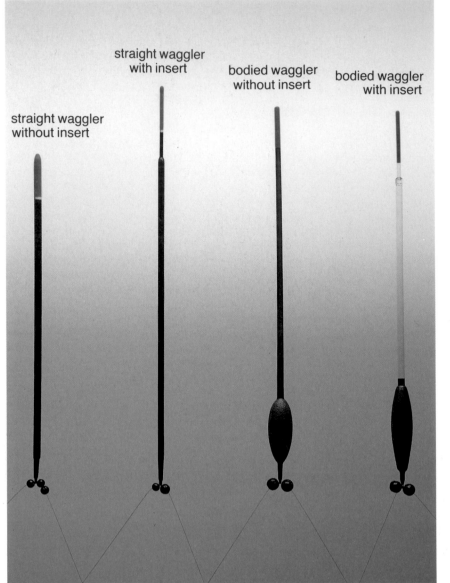

straight waggler
with insert

bodied waggler
without insert

bodied waggler
with insert

straight waggler
without insert

if the fish are three or four rod lengths out, you will need a lightish float taking only two, three or four BB. If the fish are further out choose a heavier float taking from two AAA to several SSG. When in doubt, it is almost always best to choose a float on the heavy side; this makes casting less of a strain.

Wind strength: a stronger wind demands a heavier float to get the bait out, especially if it is blowing in your face. On large, open expanses of water, where the wind is particularly strong, powerful surface drag and undertow tend to move the float out of position. Long wagglers – up to 45cm (18in) – help to counteract these effects, and using a bodied waggler increases stability.

Depth of water: the waggler's dart-like behaviour tends to make it pierce the water on entry. In shallow water a long float that dives too deeply may scare the fish away from the feed area. In this situation you can use a bodied float to good effect. With a body you can use a shorter float while retaining the shotting capacity of a straight waggler.

Shyness of fish: if the fish are biting shyly you may need an insert. Inserts are particularly useful for detecting bites on the drop. But make sure it is thick enough to see.

Attaching a waggler

The traditional method of attaching the waggler by its bottom eye makes float changing inconvenient. It is better to use ready-made, quick-change adaptors or – for small wagglers – a piece of silicone rubber tubing.

Silicone rubber is available in several diameters. Choose one to suit your wagglers. Keep a 15cm (6in) length in your tackle box and cut off pieces as you need them. Use

▲ *There are two basic types of waggler; the straight waggler and those with bodies. Both straight and bodied wagglers can have inserts which help detect shy bites. Most inserts are fixed though removable ones are available.*

Tip Accurate casting

It is hard to judge long distances over the water. When fishing at long range, Dave Berrow puts an elastic band on the spool. This enables him to cast to the same spot every time, ensuring that the hookbait is over the feed area. To do this, cast to the feed area then slip a small, flat elastic band over the spool, trapping the line at the required length.

DAVE BERROW'S FAVOURITE RIGS

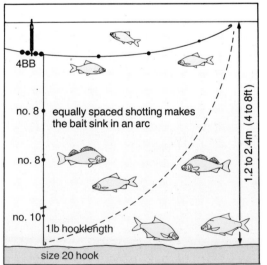

4BB

no. 8   equally spaced shotting makes the bait sink in an arc

no. 8

no. 10

1lb hooklength

size 20 hook

1.2 to 2.4m (4 to 8ft)

▲ *Lakes and rivers 'on the drop rig'. This rig will catch fish at all levels. The bulk of the shot goes round the base of the float. A fish taking the bait on the drop will cause the insert to lift or cause a slight delay in its settling.*

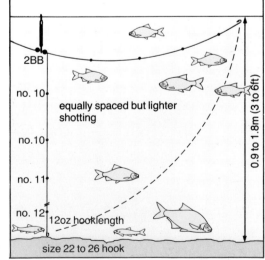

2BB

no. 10   equally spaced but lighter shotting

no.10

no. 11

no. 12   12oz hooklength

size 22 to 26 hook

0.9 to 1.8m (3 to 6ft)

▲ *Canals and ponds 'on the drop rig'. For shy canal fish use a lighter version of the lakes and rivers rig. A fish intercepting the bait causes a bite to be registered in the same way.*

scissors – this gives a cleaner cut and prevents the line from slicing through the rubber on the cast.

Float adaptors allow the float to swing more freely. When striking with a heavy waggler this is an advantage: the float is free to 'collapse' and direct contact is made between the angler and fish. To use a float adaptor simply thread it on to the line and insert the waggler.

Rods, reels and lines

To get the most from your wagglers your tackle needs to be balanced.

The rod should be powerful enough to pick up the line quickly when striking at distance but not so stiff that there is risk of snapping off, or bumping fish off on the strike.

Ideally you should use two rods. A 12 to 13ft (3.6 to 3.9m) through-actioned rod with a softish tip is perfect for handling pond and canal rigs. For waggler fishing lakes and rivers a 13ft (3.9m) rod with a similar action but with a bit of extra power in the butt is ideal.

If you only have one rod you will have to modify your striking and casting to suit the conditions.

Reel: an open-faced fixed-spool allows you to cast further than a closed-faced reel.

Line: remember that your line strength depends upon the size of fish you expect to catch and the size of float you use. Generally, for the size of float used on ponds and canals (2-4 BB) you can get away with a main line of about 1½lb (0.7kg). For the floats used on lakes and rivers (2 AAA-2 SSG) a heavier line is required; 2 to 2½lb (0.9-1.2kg) is about right.

▲ **Shop-bought wagglers come in a variety of shapes and sizes. The quality has been much better in recent years and it's no longer necessary to make your own.**

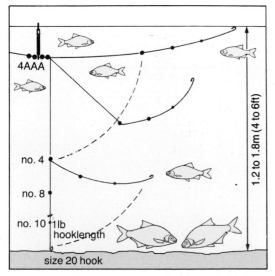

▲ **Lakes and rivers 'on the bottom rig'. The no.4 makes the hookbait sink faster, getting it through to the better fish on the bottom. When feathering on the cast, the no.4 brings the hooklength over in a nice arc, preventing tangles.**

▲ **It is important to use the correct shotting pattern down the line because this directly affects bait presentation. Bunching too much weight too close together leads to tangles when casting and makes the bait behave unnaturally.**

Locking the float

Using most of the float's total shotting capacity to lock it in place is the simplest part of shotting a waggler and yet many people get it wrong by putting too much shot down the line. This makes casting impossible.

▶ *These beautiful specimen bream fell to a waggler rig. Whether you're long range fishing for bream on lakes or fishing for chub on the far river bank, using the waggler method is very effective.*

▲ *A selection of float adaptors. To use one, thread the line through the eye at the bottom, slide the adaptor up the line to the desired depth and push the bottom of the waggler firmly into the adaptor. Lock the float with shot placed on either side of the adaptor.*

More often than not you will want a sinking line. Some brands will sink of their own accord and it certainly helps to buy one of these, but you can treat a line to make it sink by soaking it in a solution of washing-up liquid.

Fishing the waggler

When you cast, let the rod and reel do the work for you. Unless fishing at an exceptional range, a smooth cast is all that is needed. If you have to lash the float out to reach the fish it could be because your float is too light for the job.

Feathering: an important trick to learn when fishing a waggler is feathering the line just as the float is about to land in the feed area. Do this by very gently increasing the pressure of your forefinger on the line as it spills over the spool's lip.

Feathering gives you extra control over where the float lands and reduces the float's impact. It allows the hook and shot to precede the float into the water and so prevents tangles. It is essential to good waggler fishing and takes a bit of practice to perfect.

Sinking the line: a light breeze is often enough to pull the float off your feed. If you are fishing a still water you will probably want to sink your line. To do this, cast a couple of yards beyond your feed area, submerge the rod tip and give a couple of sharp turns on your reel while at the same time jerking the rod to one side. Make sure all the line is submerged; even half a metre (2ft) left floating is enough to tow the float.

Float colour: choosing the correct colour for your float tip is important – get it wrong and you won't see the bites. Your choice should be determined by the surface colour of the water. Orange shows up well in broken (choppy) water. Black shows up well in areas of calm water where the sky is reflected. White is best when fishing in the dark reflections of trees or under the far bank of canals or rivers.

One transparent pattern of waggler uses interchangeable inserts so that quick changes of tip colour can be made to suit the conditions.

Striking: a hard, sharp strike may cause the fish to be bumped off or the hook hold to loosen – resulting in the fish being lost as you bring it in. A nice sweep to the side or a steady lift will set your hook sufficiently.

Feathering your line . . . . . . for the pinpoint cast

hooklength behind float

▲ *Release the line from under your forefinger to send the float zooming towards a target slightly beyond the feed area. Your forefinger is kept close to the spool's lip, ready to start feathering. At this stage the hooklength lags behind the float.*

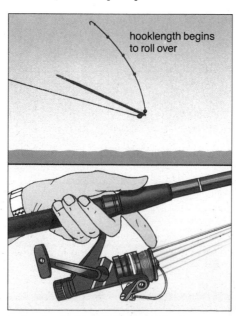

hooklength begins to roll over

▲ *As the float approaches the target area, slow the line by gently touching the spool's lip with your fingertip. Only with practice will you know just how much pressure to apply. The hooklength will begin to roll over and precede the float.*

hook in front of float

▲ *Slightly increase the pressure to land the float spot on target (just beyond the feed area) with minimum disturbance. The terminal rig should land in a straight line with hook in front of float. Wind the float backwards over your feed, sinking the line.*

Fixed-spool reels

Chosen with care, a reel should balance your tackle, suit your kind of fishing and, if it is good quality, last you a lifetime. But you must pick the right one for the type of fishing you do, says matchman Ken Collings.

There are three basic types of reel: fixed-spool, centrepin and multiplier. For coarse fishing the centrepin and multiplier are highly specialized and the fixed-spool is the most popular, all-purpose reel. Unlike centrepins and multipliers, the fixed-spool has its central axis parallel to the rod rather than at right angles to it. As the name 'fixed' suggests, the spool does not revolve when casting; the line leaves the spool by spilling over the lip instead.

Types of fixed-spool

There are two kinds of fixed-spool reel – open-face and closed-face.

Open-face On this design, the spool and bale arm are exposed. The bale arm is either disengaged with your free hand (the one not holding the rod) or, with automatic bale reels, by the hand holding the rod.

Closed-face These reels have the spool and pick-up pin enclosed in a housing. The pick-up pin is disengaged by pressing a button with the index or second finger of the hand holding the rod.

The choice between an open or closed-face reel depends on the type of fishing you want to do. Each has its good and bad points in particular situations and each is better suited to some techniques than others. Among the most important factors to think about before choosing are the line strength you'll be using and the spool capacity you want.

▼ *Effortless casting and smooth playing of big fish are tests that a good reel must pass with flying colours. Reel design has come on in leaps and bounds in recent years with the use of strong, light, corrosion-resistant materials. Graphite compounds are a typical choice for the body – as is the case with this open-face fixed-spool reel (inset).*

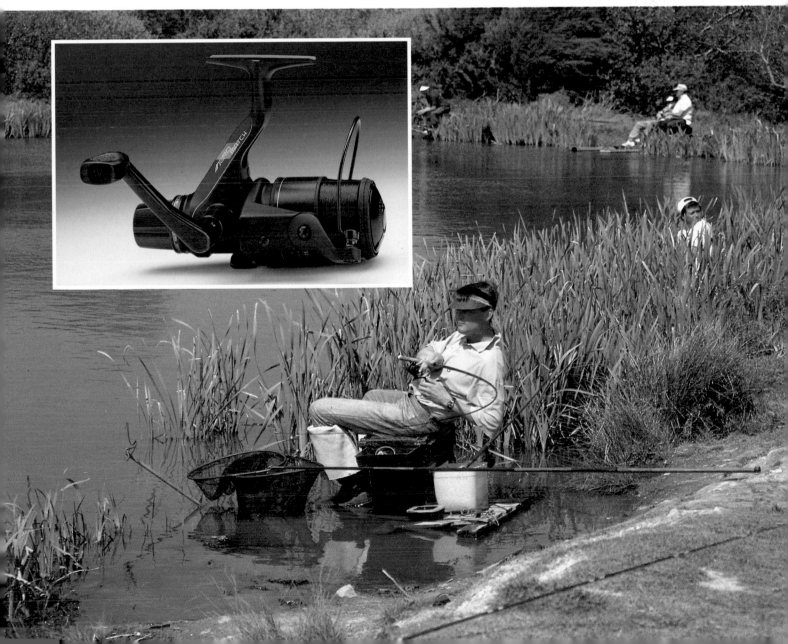

Line strength

The main disadvantage of the closed-face reel is that it has a narrow spool. Heavy line lies unevenly on the spool, causing casting problems and making the closed-face unsuitable for lines above 4lb (1.8kg) breaking strain.

If you intend to go for large, hard-fighting fish such as carp, pike, tench or barbel, you need an open-face reel. Its wider spool takes less coils to fill it and distributes the load over a greater area. This reduces pressure on the spool and, together with the reel's sturdy design, allows you to use lines of up to 20lb (9kg) b.s. At the other extreme , the open-face can handle lines as fine as 2lb (0.91kg) b.s. This capability makes it wonderfully versatile.

Spool capacity Most manufacturers provide tables telling you how many metres of a certain breaking strain will fill your spool to the correct level without backing. For most types of fishing 100-150m (109-164yd) of line is enough. Any more than this is a waste of money and leads to poor line-lay and `bedding-in'. Bedding-in is a condition where the surface coils of line (which would normally be free to leave the spool) become trapped between underlying coils. This causes the line to snatch as it comes off the spool, making it impossible to cast or trot properly.)

In general, open-face reels have a greater capacity than closed-face designs and good quality open-face models provide a wider range of interchangeable spools than closed-face models. Most closed-face models have only two spools: a shallow fine line (match') spool which takes about 100m (109yd) of 2lb (0.9kg) line and a deep spool which takes about 100m (109yd) of 12lb (5.4kg) line.

▲ *The closed-face reel's push-button line-release makes it very fast but its trotting ability is often questioned on the grounds that it is prone to bedding-in. However, many Midlands matchmen do all their fishing with them.*

▼ *When trotting with an open-face reel, a manual bale is useful. It can be engaged with the free hand ready to play the fish.*

Casting and trotting

With an open-face reel the line peels effortlessly off the wider spool. This means that you can cast much farther, with less effort, more accurately than with a closed-face reel. This same smooth supply of line also makes the open-face reel a tempting choice for trotting on rivers. In this situation an open-face is better because pressure on the spool from big fish tends to make the line bed-in with closed-face reels.

Open-face problem

However, the open-face does have some disadvantages. The finger you use to control your line when trotting is in the way when the bale is engaged to play a fish. If you remove your finger from the lip of the spool the fish is briefly given slack line and may come off. Keeping your finger on while snapping the bale down on the line is not much of an answer: the line jolts the fish and it may be bumped off, or the hook hold loosened.

One solution is to have a manual bale so that it can be brought over with the free hand, and most modern reels have these. The alternative is to risk using a closed-face reel (whose pick-up pin is inside the housing away from the finger) and hope the line does not bed-in. Your choice finally depends on whether or not you think you will take big fish.

Closed-face advantages

When there is a facing wind, the open-face reel runs into serious problems. The line can blow back behind the bale arm and, if you don't notice this happening, you may snap or tangle it as you reel in. Having to

Tip Line load

Even the best reel will not function properly if the spool is not loaded to the correct level: underload it and you will be unable to cast properly, overload it and the line will spring off. It should be loaded to within about 2mm (¹/₁₆in) of the spool's lip.

closed-face spool   open-face spool

look down at the reel all day to check the line is all right soon spoils your fishing. In this situation, closed-face reels are best as the spool is sheltered from the wind by its housing.

For speed fishing, too, the closed-face is a winner. Its push button line-release makes it fast to use and, even though some open-face models have automatic bales, the simplicity and convenience of the push button release is hard to beat and might give you the edge in a match.

Standard features

Different manufacturers' reels vary in overall design but almost all have at least some of the following features.

Gearing All fixed-spool reels have a geared retrieval so that, for one turn of the handle, the bale or pin rotates more than once. The gear ratio varies from one design to another, but on fast retrieve open-face models the ratio is usually 5 or 6 to 1. Closed-face reels have a lower gearing; 3 or 4 to 1 is typical. In general, this means open-face reels have a quicker retrieve than closed-face reels.

Drag Nearly all reels are fitted with a preset drag system. This acts as a safeguard against the sudden rush of a big fish. On modern reels the drag is either at the back (stern drag) or, on closed-face reels, on the handle.

With a preset system, the line is put under pressure, and the drag set so that the spool begins to rotate and give line before it breaks. Good drags can be smoothly adjusted while playing a fish.

A characteristic of drags is that they can cause the line to twist as it comes off the spool, weakening it. One way to make sure

this does not happen is to screw the drag down tight and play big fish by back winding.

Anti-reverse Nearly all reels have an anti-reverse switch which stops the reel from back winding. This can be useful for getting just the right amount of tension in the line when you are quivertipping on fast rivers, where the flow makes the reel backwind.

Inter-changeable quick-release spools most reels have quick-release spools so you can remove them by simply pressing a button.

Reels which take spools of different line capacities are useful. It means that you can keep a spool of different breaking strain line for each type of fishing and need fill each spool with only 100m (109yd), say, of line. So, for example, in early summer, tench might be your quarry – and a spool taking

▲ *On an open-face spool, line can peel freely from the wide spool. Tapered spools (like the one above right) reduce resistance at the front of the spool making casting even easier. Moulded concentric ribbing promotes even line-lay. Closed-face spools are narrower and suited to short-range work with lines below 4lb (1.8kg). The chenille trim at the front and back of the spool serves the same purpose as a skirt on the open-faced spool in stopping line from tangling round the inside of the reel.*

When to use each type of reel	
Open-face reels	**Closed-face reels**
Trotting when the fish want a bait presented at exactly the same speed as the current.	Trotting rivers when the fish are not particular about the bait being presented at the speed of the current.
When accurate casting is necessary.	Speed fishing with a medium-sized waggler (4 BB) when accurate casting is not important.
Fishing with light wagglers of about 2 or 3 BB.	Tangle-free casting when the wind blows line off the spool of your open-face reel.
When using heavy lines for big fish.	
Long range floatfishing with big wagglers of 2SSG or more.	

Bedding-in

You can reduce the effects of bedding-in on closed-face reels by loading them with as little line as possible. The late, great Clive Smith used to load his with just 25m (27yd) of line.

100 m (109yd) of 4lb (1.8kg) line would be ideal. But, in late autumn you may be after roach and need a shallower spool taking 100 m (109yd) of 2lb (0.9kg) line.

Automatic arm Some open-face reels have automatic bale arms for one-hand casting. These serve the same purpose as the push-button release on closed-face reels. The feature is useful when speed is important, as in match fishing, but on some the line is apt to tangle round the bale.

Bait runners These are found on some open-face models. They are useful for fishing for carp, pike, eels, or any other fish which runs with a bait. A bait runner allows the fish to take line freely while the bale arm is closed. By flicking a switch, you disengage the bait runner and you're ready to strike without having to worry about re-engaging the bale arm.

Buying a reel

Before buying a reel, think about the kind of fishing you'll be doing most. If in doubt, ask your tackle dealer to help you and check out the following points:
● As a general guide, go for the established brands as they provide the most efficient back-up service should anything go wrong or need replacing.
● The reel should be smooth running so that the handle continues to rotate a few times after a quick flick. Ball races promote smooth running and make reels particularly good for handling large fish. Manufacturers describe these as 'ballbearings' and some reels have up to three sets.
● Pay particular attention to the bale arm. It should open and close easily but positively. You shouldn't have to wind hard to get it to close over again. If it has a line roller make sure it rolls.
● Check to see that the drag gives out line smoothly.
● Try the reel on a rod. It should feel comfortable and you should be able to reach the lip of the spool easily with your fingertip.
● Check the spools carefully. Make sure they are of the right capacity for your kind of fishing. If they are open-face spools they are best if they have a skirt. This prevents the line from blowing inside the reel and tangling. Spools for closed-face reels should have a chenille trimming for the same reason. Make sure you can get spare spools and check to see if they are included in the initial price of the reel, or if you have to buy them as an extra.

▶ *Service your reel at least once a season. Major repairs should be left to your tackle dealer but if yours is a reel which can be reassembled easily it is best to strip it completely before cleaning.*

Remove the cover and pick out any sand or grit. Wash in warm soapy water. Use a good oil to lubricate the bearings and a light grease on the gears. A quick spray inside and out with moisture repellant will keep your reel in good order.

Open-face features

1. Adjustable (stern) drag
2. Bait runner setting
3. Bait runner switch
4. Anti-reverse
5. Push-button spool release
6. Manual bale option

The open-face design is probably the best choice for all round fishing.

Feeding your swim

Correct feeding, more than anything else, is what sets the consistently successful angler apart from the rest.

Many anglers can pick a good swim, choose the right method and present a hookbait properly, yet still don't catch much – usually because they don't feed correctly.

Small to medium roach, bream, dace, chub, barbel, perch and rudd...all are very different fish, but all tend to swim in shoals. Much of the time these shoals roam around looking for food. Having found some, they stop only long enough to eat it.

If you don't feed a swim you only catch the occasional fish – whenever a shoal chances by, in fact. But it's no good chucking in feed willy-nilly. To attract, hold and consistently catch fish, you must gauge *what*, *how much* and *how often* to feed.

What to feed

There are two basic types of feed. Loose feed is samples of hookbait or other baits, fed by hand or catapult if floatfishing or legering, or via a block-end swimfeeder.

Groundbait is essentially wetted breadcrumbs, fed by hand or catapult if floatfishing or legering, or via an open-end swimfeeder. Samples of hookbait or other baits can be added or, when fishing within loose-feeding range, you can feed it neat and loose-feed over the top of it.

Knowing when to loose-feed and when to groundbait is crucial. Bream and rudd are commonly very fond of groundbait, while

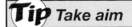
▶ *There are two main types of loose-feed catapult: mesh (top), for greater distance; and pouch (bottom), for greater accuracy close in.*

▼ *A catapult is essential to loose-feed a swim beyond throwing range. Lock your elbow and hold the catapult dead still before firing.*

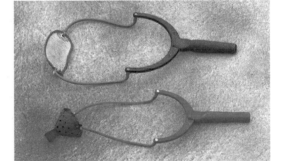

▶ *1990 World Champion Bob Nudd with the sort of catch that is well within the reach of every angler, so long as you feed correctly.*

roach, dace, chub, barbel and perch tend not to like it. Groundbait is also usually 'the kiss of death' in clear, cold water, in which all fish tend to be wary and easily overfed. It is therefore used much less than loose feed in winter.

How much and how often

The aim is to tempt fish into your swim and keep them there without filling them up. The saying 'little and often' holds true.

Little Sparing feeding forces the fish to compete for the feed. You can always step up the amount if you think there are a lot of fish there, but if you feed heavily to start with, yet only attract a few fish, you risk overfeeding them.

Start with a walnut-sized ball of groundbait or about a dozen loose-fed bait samples, or both. When bites are hard to come by, feed half this amount. If the fish are feeding really well, double it.

Often Frequent feeding ensures a steady stream of feed going into the water, increasing your chances of attracting fish – not only at the start, but throughout the session. It also encourages bites 'on the drop' in warm weather, resulting in a faster catch rate.

When trotting running water, feed every cast. On still and slow-moving waters, feed at least every five minutes.

Exceptions The main exception to the 'little and often' rule is bream fishing. Bream can be very nervous fish and don't always appreciate feed constantly landing on their heads. The standard attack when breaming is to lay a large, initial carpet of feed and catch as many of the shoal as possible before feeding again. When you do feed again, do so carefully and if the bream have their heads down they should be too preoccupied with eating to notice.

Another exception is when you find yourself being pestered with small fish. In this case often the only answer is to blast in the bait to try to feed them off.

▼ *'Little and often' applies nine times out of ten. Feed a dozen or so bait samples every cast when trotting flowing water – every few minutes when fishing still or slow waters.*

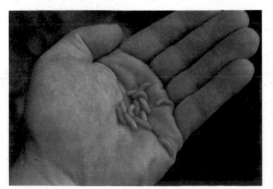

BAITDROPPER

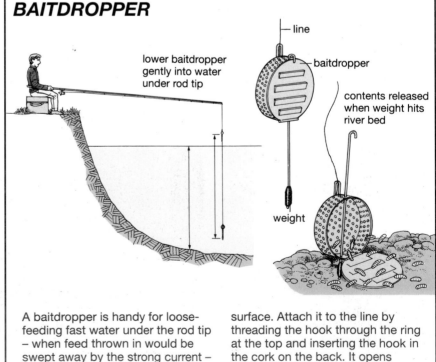

A baitdropper is handy for loose-feeding fast water under the rod tip – when feed thrown in would be swept away by the strong current – and for getting the feed down past small fish in mid-water and near the surface. Attach it to the line by threading the hook through the ring at the top and inserting the hook in the cork on the back. It opens automatically when it reaches the bottom, releasing its contents.

Mixing and using groundbait

Tackle shops sell bag after colourful bag of groundbaits, containing everything from pigeon droppings to molasses, but the real secret to successful groundbait is in the mixing.

At its simplest, groundbait is nothing more than dried and crushed bread. In recent years, however, so-called Continental groundbaits have become very popular. These contain all sorts of ingredients besides bread: binders such as ground peanuts; flavourings like vanilla; even laxatives (supposedly to make the fish hungrier!). The packaging of these groundbaits usually recommends what types of fish and waters they are for, and how best to use them, but it can still be very confusing to know where to start.

Mixing rules

Whether you use plain bread or a Continental groundbait, the basic rules of mixing and using are the same. Unless

▶ *A special groundbait catapult is essential for feeding bream swims a long way out on reservoirs and other large still-waters.*

you understand these no amount of additives will help you to catch more fish.

The first thing to consider is the kind of container you mix your groundbait in. Many anglers use a bucket or such-like, which is a mistake because the deeper and narrower the container, the harder it is to get an even mix; the groundbait at the top tends to be over-wetted, while that at the bottom is too dry. Also, any maggots you put in tend to burrow down and accumulate in a mass at the bottom. The ideal con-

▼ *When fishing close-in you can throw your groundbait in by hand, but be sure to mix it properly or the balls will break up in mid-air and land all over the place, scattering your fish.*

Mixing groundbait

1. Put some groundbait into a large, shallow mixing bowl or tray, preferably one with rounded corners. Add the water a bit at a time, mixing vigorously and thoroughly with your fingers all the while to make sure the water is evenly absorbed.

2. With the right mix of water and dry crumb the groundbait feels light and fluffy. You will know it's just the right consistency when you can easily squeeze it into balls with gentle pressure yet break it up again without it forming stodgy lumps.

3. Mould your groundbait into orange-size balls for medium range breaming, tangerine-size balls for close-in fishing for skimmers and rudd. The harder you squeeze the balls, the farther you can throw them and the deeper they sink before breaking up.

4. If you have mixed your groundbait correctly you can add quite a few casters, maggots or sweetcorn or whatever, but don't overdo it or the balls will break up in mid-air and fly everywhere. Shown here are caster 'pies' – the downfall of many bream and tench.

tainer is wide and shallow, which allows a thorough and even mix.

Next, don't mix all your groundbait in one go at the start of the session. If you do it will dry out during the course of the day. Far better to make it up a small batch at a time, as you use it.

The same rule applies to adding bait samples, especially maggots. If you put a whole lot of maggots in at the start, as well as working their way to the bottom they absorb moisture and become floaters.

Different mixes

The most important quality of a groundbait is not its colour, smell, taste or ingredients, but its texture. The same bag of dry groundbait can be put to a wide range of uses simply by varying its texture when you mix it at the waterside.

Mix it very dry and squeeze it very gently so that the balls only just hold together, and you have a groundbait that breaks up into an attractive cloud as soon as it hits the water – ideal for fishing on-the-drop in still waters in summer.

The same, very dry, mix is also ideal for open-end swimfeedering on still waters, as the groundbait literally explodes out of the swimfeeder as it absorbs more water on the bed of your swim.

Mix groundbait so it is moist but not sloppy, and it will be just sticky enough to bind together with maggots or casters and hold together in mid-air. Yet it won't be so stodgy as to stop it breaking up as it sinks to form an attractive cloud in the bottom half of the water – ideal for still-water and slow-river bream.

Throwing groundbait

Most of the time you can comfortably reach your swim with your groundbait by throwing it in by hand, either overarm or underarm. Never struggle to get distance because, groundbait being relatively light, it is all too easy to strain a muscle in your arm or shoulder. It's much better to buy and learn to use a groundbait catapult.

When using a groundbait catapult, don't try to fire in balls bigger than about tangerine-size, and give each ball a 'glaze' with water to prevent it from sticking to the pouch.

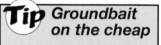

Tip Groundbait on the cheap

The cheapest way to buy ordinary groundbait is by the sackful. Store it in a plastic dustbin with a tight-fitting lid to keep it fresh and dry and out of the reach of rodents.

An even greater saving can be made by making your own groundbait. Ask your family and neighbours to save all their crusts and leftover bread. Dry the bread in an airing cupboard or similarly warm place, then grind it up in a food processor. Start this in the close season so you have some in reserve.

Fishing the slider

Many anglers try the slider once, get in a tangle, and never try it again. Fished correctly, however, a sliding float makes light work of deep water, says match ace Tony Saunders.

A much neglected method, even by otherwise quite experienced and proficient anglers, the slider allows you to floatfish deep water without having to fix the float so far from the hook that casting becomes at best difficult and at worst impossible.

How the slider works

A sliding float slides on the line by virtue of one or two small eyes, depending on whether it is a sliding waggler for still and slow water (one eye, in the base of the float) or a sliding balsa for fast-flowing water (two eyes: one at the base, the other on the side, near the top).

When you cast, a sliding float hangs only a few feet above the hook, prevented from sliding all the way down by shot.

In the water, the shot pull the line through the eye or eyes until the float is

cocked by a stop knot at the desired distance from the hook – usually the full depth of the swim.

When to use a slider

The most common misconception about the slider is that you only fish it when the water is deeper than the length of your rod. A 13ft (3.9m) rod might mean that you can fix a float 13ft (3.9m) from the hook, but you can't cast comfortably with the float jammed against the top ring. A good rule to remember, in all aspects of angling, is that if you feel comfortable your performance is enhanced. So if you are faced with a swim 10ft (3m) or more deep, consider using a slider.

Sliding wagglers

You can use any bodied or straight waggler as a slider, so long as it's semi-loaded.

Semi-loading ensures the float stays with the shot throughout the cast. If you try to use an unloaded waggler as a slider it tends to slide up the line, away from the shot, in

---

(Tip box)

Tip Loose ends

Leave 2cm (1in) long loose ends when you trim the stop knot. If you trim it any closer it can catch in the rod rings and, if the swim is so deep that the knot is on the reel, trap line against the spool.

▶ *Fail to master the slider and you could miss out on a bumper catch such as this fine bag of roach the next time you are faced with deep water. You can leger, of course, but if legering doesn't work and you can't fish the slider, you're stuck.*

▲ *Almost any waggler can be used as a slider, so long as it's semi-loaded and takes at least another 2AAA shotting, says Middlesex tackle dealer Tony Saunders – as this bream found out to its cost.*

Tip Closing the gap

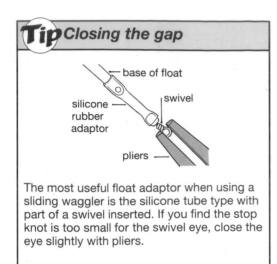

The most useful float adaptor when using a sliding waggler is the silicone tube type with part of a swivel inserted. If you find the stop knot is too small for the swivel eye, close the eye slightly with pliers.

mid-cast, affecting accuracy and distance, and causing tangles.

As a rule, use a float that takes at least a further 2AAA shotting on the line, because there has to be enough weight to pull the line through to the stop knot.

Adapting wagglers

These days you can buy a wide range of semi-loaded wagglers from your local tackle shop. Should you have any difficulty in finding them you can easily adapt an unloaded waggler yourself by twisting out the plastic peg in the base and replacing it with a length of 3mm (⅛in) brass rod. This should be from 2.5-5cm (1-2in) long, depending on the size of the float. Glue it into the base of the float, leaving about 13mm (½in) showing. On to this you can then put an adaptor.

The best type of adaptor is a silicone tube with part of a swivel inserted. The hole of the swivel is usually big enough to allow free passage of the line but small enough to catch the stop knot.

Shotting up

Once you have attached your reel and threaded the line through the rod rings, remove the last 15cm (6in) or so of reel line and use it to tie on a sliding stop knot (see *Stop knot* tying sequence 1-4) about 2.7m (9ft) above the end of the reel line. Then thread the float on the line and tie on the hooklength.

You can now shot up your float as if you were fishing a 1.5-1.8m (5-6ft) deep swim with a fixed waggler. Nip on the largest of your bulk shot immediately above the float and lock the float on the line by putting the rest of the bulk shot immediately below it. Adjust the bulk shotting until about three quarters of the float submerges, then add your intermediate and dropper shot.

Next, remove the shot immediately above the float and replace it on top of the rest of the bulk. Flick out the float, leave the bail arm off and check that the line is sliding freely through the eye of the float to the stop knot.

Check the wind

Before you test the depth of your swim, carry out the following routine. Imagine you are standing on a clock face at 6 o'clock, with where you want to cast to at 12 o'clock. Note the direction of the wind.

If it is blowing from any point from 6-3 or 6-9 o'clock, regard this as a wind from behind and use the shotting pattern shown in *Wind direction*, diagram 1.

If it is blowing from any point from 12-3 or 12-9 o'clock, regard this as a facing wind and use the shotting pattern shown in *Wind direction*, diagram 2.

Casting

You must use the overhead casting technique. If the wind is blowing from the left, cast from over your right shoulder. If it is blowing from the right, cast from over your left shoulder.

Feather the line to check the float just before it hits the water. This ensures that the intermediate and dropper shot carry on past the float in a straight line, so avoiding tangles.

Cast past where you want to fish, so that the line sinks as you wind the float into position. Then open the bail arm to allow line to peel off the reel as the bulk shot sinks your hookbait.

Plumbing up

Rather than struggle with a plummet on the hook, plumb the depth of your swim by trial and error. Make a number of trial casts, moving the stop knot a few inches up the line each time until the dropper shot just rest on the bottom of the swim and the float doesn't quite cock properly.

Then note the length of line between the hook and the dropper shot. Let's assume it's 45cm (18in). If you want the hookbait to trip along the bottom of the swim, move the stop knot down 45cm (18in). If you want to fish the hookbait overdepth, move the stop knot down 15-30cm (6-12in).

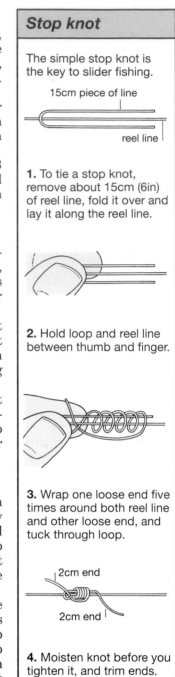
Spotting bites on the drop

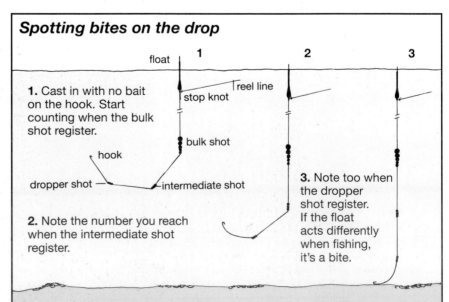

1. Cast in with no bait on the hook. Start counting when the bulk shot register.

2. Note the number you reach when the intermediate shot register.

3. Note too when the dropper shot register. If the float acts differently when fishing, it's a bite.

Wind direction and shotting patterns

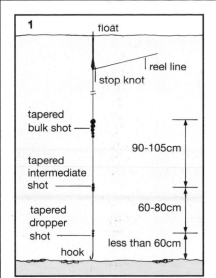

1. float, reel line, stop knot, tapered bulk shot, tapered intermediate shot, tapered dropper shot, hook, 90-105cm, 60-80cm, less than 60cm

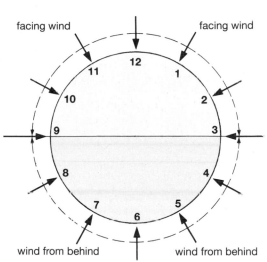

facing wind, facing wind, wind from behind, wind from behind

1. The more the wind is from behind, the less intermediate and dropper shot you need – down to one of each, even. But always taper shot size and spacings towards the hook.

Standing at 6 o'clock and casting to 12 o'clock, a wind from 6-3 or 6-9 is from behind, one from 12-3 or 12-9 a facing wind. If the wind is blowing from the right, cast from over your left shoulder, and vice versa.

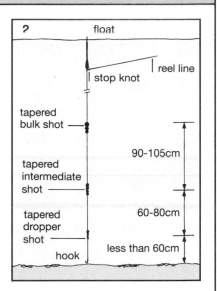

2. float, reel line, stop knot, tapered bulk shot, tapered intermediate shot, tapered dropper shot, hook, 90-105cm, 60-80cm, less than 60cm

2. The more the wind is in your face, the more intermediate and dropper shot you need to avoid tangles when you cast. Again, taper shot size and spacings towards the hook.

Counting for bites

Because the float cocks in three definite stages you can spot bites on the drop. This you do as follows.

Look carefully at the *Spotting bites on the drop* sequence of diagrams. Once the bulk shot has registered (diagram 1), start counting. After a few casts (with no bait on the hook) you will find that the setting of the float tip in diagram 2 – with the intermediate shot registering – is reached on the same number each time. Likewise the setting of the float tip in diagram 3, with the dropper shot registering, is reached on the same number each time.

Remember these numbers when you actually start fishing with a baited hook. Then, if you count to either number and the float hasn't settled in the usual manner, a fish has probably intercepted your hookbait on the drop, so strike!

Fast water

Top and bottom sliding floats for running water are rarely found in tackle shops nowadays, but you can easily adapt ordinary balsa floats yourself by glueing or whipping on small eyes.

Sliding balsas don't have to be semi-loaded, though some anglers find them easier to cast if they are. Try both, to see which type you personally get along with best. Semi-loaded or not, like sliding wagglers they should take at least 2AAA shotting on

▶ *One advantage of the slider is that you needn't worry about the float jamming in the top eye of the rod when you have played a fish to the surface and are about to land it.*

Sliding balsa

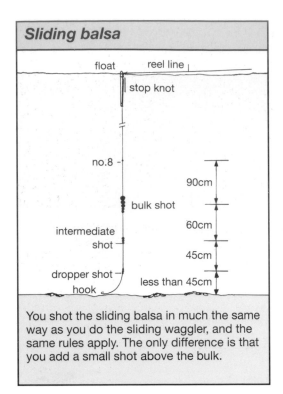

float   reel line

stop knot

no.8

90cm

bulk shot

60cm

intermediate shot

45cm

dropper shot

less than 45cm

hook

You shot the sliding balsa in much the same way as you do the sliding waggler, and the same rules apply. The only difference is that you add a small shot above the bulk.

the line for best results.

Shotting is much the same as for the sliding waggler, the only difference being the addition of a small shot above the bulk, to keep the float and bulk apart during the cast. This is essential whenever you use a float attached top and bottom, otherwise the hook tends to wrap itself around the top

of the float in mid-air.

Adjust the intermediate and dropper shot in the same way as with the sliding waggler, according to the wind direction.

The casting technique is also the same as with the sliding waggler, the only difference being that you should feather the line in mid-flight, rather than just before the float hits the water. This way, the hook precedes the float through the air, minimizing the risk of tangles. Again, you should overcast and retrieve to the desired spot, though you wouldn't usually want to sink the line.

▶ *To make an ordinary balsa into a sliding float, whip on two metal eyes, having first bent them over at right angles to prevent the line sticking to the side of the float. Whip one on at the base, and the other at the side, near the top.*

▼ *If you are a float-making enthusiast you can easily make your own sliding balsa floats and customize them to suit the waters you fish. The three floats at the top are home-made, while the two floats at the bottom are adapted shop-bought ones.*

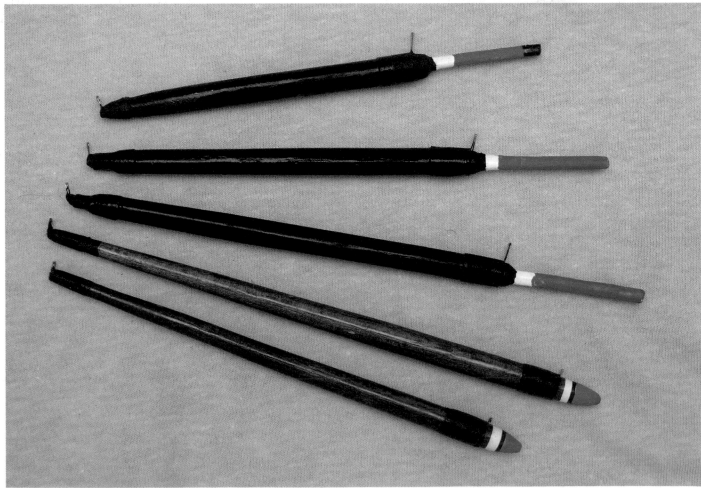

Balsas and Avons: floats to beat the flow

Balsas and Avons are the boss floats on running water whenever conditions demand the use of weight down the line, says Middlesex match angler and tackle dealer Tony Saunders.

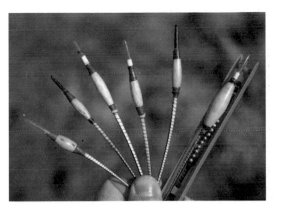

Like stick floats, you use balsas and Avons exclusively for trotting running water; their buoyancy is concentrated towards the top and you attach them to your line top-and-bottom with float rubbers. But there the similarity ends.

Stick floats basically have light shotting capacities – up to about 4BB. You use them mostly with small baits such as maggots and casters at close range (up to, say, three rod lengths out) in steady water of moderate depth – up to around 2.5m (8ft). You usually dot them right down to register shy bites and shot them shirt-button style with small shot (10s, 8s, 6s and 4s) to catch on-the-drop as well as near the bottom.

Balsa and Avon floats, on the other hand, typically have much heavier shotting capacities – up to several SSG – and are buoyant enough to support big baits such as luncheon meat as well as smaller ones like maggots and casters.

You generally use them to fish faster, deeper water farther out from the bank. Most of the shot is normally bulked close to

▲ *Home-made 'Topper' Haskins balsa and crowquill Avons. Shot them with a streamlined string of BBs as bulk. Kept on winders they're ready for immediate use each trip.*

▼ *A range of balsa and Avon floats for fast-flowing water. From left to right: three standard Avons, four balsas, two 'Topper' Haskins balsa and crowquill Avons, and two standard Avons.*

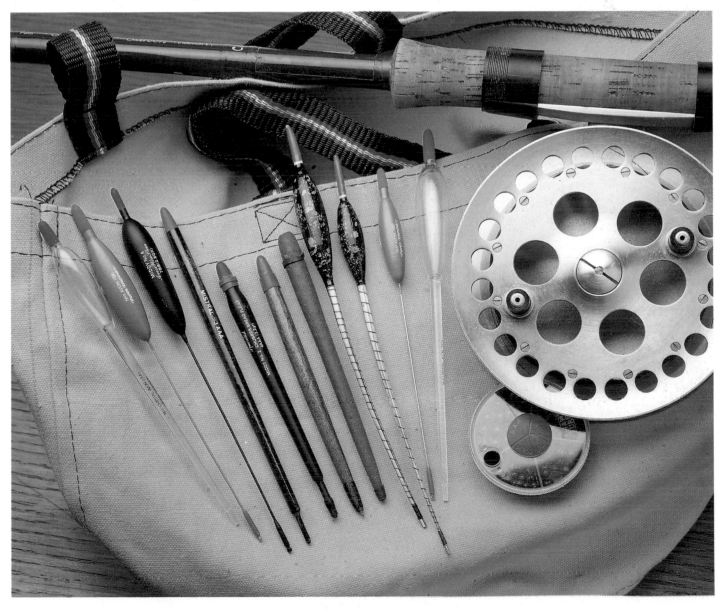

Back-shotting an Avon or balsa in a downstream wind

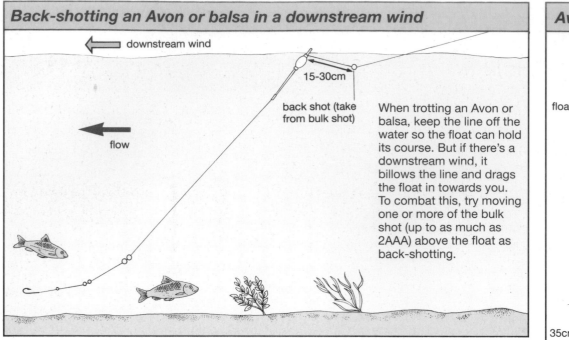

downstream wind

flow

15-30cm

back shot (take from bulk shot)

When trotting an Avon or balsa, keep the line off the water so the float can hold its course. But if there's a downstream wind, it billows the line and drags the float in towards you. To combat this, try moving one or more of the bulk shot (up to as much as 2AAA) above the float as back-shotting.

the hook – to make long-distance casting easier and to get the bait quickly near the bottom and keep it there.

Balsa floats
Though balsa floats are indeed usually made of thickish lengths of balsa wood, some manufacturers have brought out polystyrene and hollow plastic versions. Whatever the material, all have fat, buoyant tops that allow them to ride very fast and often turbulent water without being constantly dragged under the surface.

Because they carry a lot of shot for their size, balsas are ideal for fishing large, delicate baits such as wasp grub, luncheon meat and breadflake. Light floats require a

vigorous cast, which makes such baits prone to flying off the hook in mid-air. With a heavy balsa, however, you can cast these baits a long way with only a smooth and gentle underarm swing.

This is not to say you can't use balsas to good effect with smaller baits such as maggots – you can. Despite their lack of sensitivity, bites with balsa floats are usually very bold whatever the bait, because in very fast water a fish has only a moment in which to grab the bait.

▼ *The 'Topper' Avon being used to good effect on the Thames. Designed for the Bristol Avon, it has proved its worth on many other rivers.*

Avon rigs

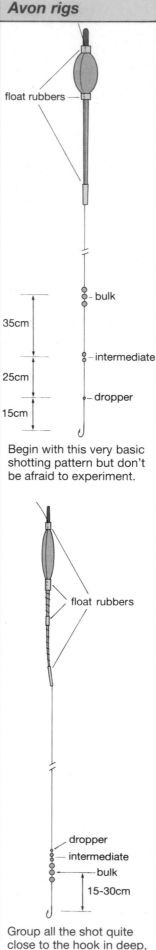

float rubbers

bulk

35cm

intermediate

25cm

dropper

15cm

Begin with this very basic shotting pattern but don't be afraid to experiment.

float rubbers

dropper
intermediate
bulk
15-30cm

Group all the shot quite close to the hook in deep, slightly 'boiling' swims.

▲ *An Avon is often the first choice float on the swift, gravelly streams and rivers favoured by grayling. Small baits work best for these fish and the Avon, with its bulbous body and slim top, has the buoyancy needed to ride the flow without offering much resistance to biting fish.*

Tip Attention to detail

A longish (20mm) bottom float rubber that overhangs the end of the float eliminates a potential tangle point and allows better bait presentation and a cleaner strike.

Down the line, leave a 1-2mm gap between each shot in a group to make the line hang straight.

Using a 'Topper' to avoid small fish

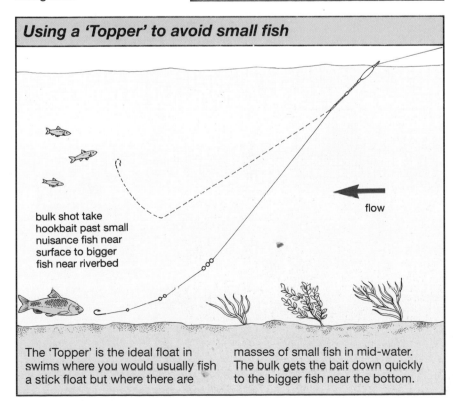

bulk shot take hookbait past small nuisance fish near surface to bigger fish near riverbed

flow

The 'Topper' is the ideal float in swims where you would usually fish a stick float but where there are masses of small fish in mid-water. The bulk gets the bait down quickly to the bigger fish near the bottom.

Shotting for balsas

Bunch most of the shot (SSGs, AAAs, BBs) below halfway between float and hook. Over a clean riverbed where the water isn't turbulent you only need one or two dropper shot. Indeed, you sometimes find you can get away with bunching all the shot as close as 25cm (10in) from the hook.

Where the bottom is rocky, use several closely spaced droppers to combat the turbulence – spread them out below the bulk at intervals of about 5cm (2in), stopping around 15cm (6in) from the hook. In either case there is no need to use droppers smaller than size 6.

Avon floats

Avon floats have slim stems below bulbous bodies, and long, slim tops. Traditionally made from cane and balsa, they are now also available with polystyrene or hollow plastic bodies and wire or plastic stems.

In many ways Avons bridge the gap between sticks and balsas. Their bulbous bodies give them buoyancy and, combined with their denser stems, allow you to hold them back slightly to slow down the bait.

Their long, slim tops, meanwhile, give a degree of sensitivity and allow you to see them clearly right to the end of a very long trot.

The 'Topper' Avon

A variant of the standard Avon is the 'Topper' Haskins balsa and crowquill Avon. This superb float was developed and perfected some years ago by south-west matchman 'Topper' Haskins for his local Bristol Avon. He is still winning matches with it to this day.

On much of the Bristol Avon a prevailing upstream wind makes it difficult to present a bait at the steady speed of the flow with a waggler or stick, because there isn't enough shot down the line with these floats. High banks and deep water, meanwhile, make tangle-free, long-distance overhead casting very awkward.

The 'Topper' was the answer. It has a slimmer body than a standard Avon and a longer, slimmer top, making it that bit more sensitive. It carries a lot of shot, however, allowing easy underarm casting and effective fishing of deep, steady water.

The 'Topper' is now established as an excellent float for any river where there is steadily flowing water of more than 1.5m (5ft) deep. In fact, the deeper the water the better it seems to work.

It's the ideal float in swims where you

▲ *A swim on the Hampshire Avon – the river that gave its name to the Avon float.*

Tip Casting lesson

With bulk shot down the line, you can use an overhead cast for distance work. But feather the line in mid-cast to straighten the rig before it lands. When fishing close in, an underarm swing is all you need and is much less likely to result in tangles.

would usually fish a stick float but where there are masses of small, nuisance fish near the surface and in mid-water. The bulk shot takes the bait straight down to the better fish near the bottom, but no sensitivity of bite registration is lost (see diagram, *Using a 'Topper' to avoid small fish*).

Shotting for Avons

Use the same basic shotting pattern for both standard and 'Topper' Avons. Start with the bulk (a string of BBs is more streamlined than a few AAs or SSGs) about 75cm (30in) from the hook with one or two intermediate and dropper shot (see *Avon rigs*, diagram 1).

As with most shotting patterns, however – perhaps even more so with these floats – it doesn't pay to be too rigid. The key to success is versatility and experimentation.

Say you're fishing a 'Topper' in a swim that's 'boiling' slightly. You'll need to move the bulk right down to within 15-30cm (6-12in) of the hook, switching the intermediate and dropper shot to immediately above the bulk.

This forms a large but aerodynamic bunch of shot (see *Avon rigs*, diagram 2). If you think about it, all there is then between the float and a point very close to the hook is a length of thin, relatively taut line which is hardly affected by the turbulence at all.

◄ *Master the basics of fishing balsa and Avon floats and you are ready for bumper catches of fast-river fish – like these prime chub.*

Waggler fishing on rivers

Whatever rivers you fish, the versatile waggler is your best friend, says top matchman Dave Hinton.

Whether you fish wide rivers, narrow rivers, fast rivers or slow rivers, carry a selection of wagglers with you every time you go. No other float can cope with such a range of swims and conditions.

Top-and-bottom floats (sticks, balsas and Avons) are basically restricted to pacy water, not too far out, on days when the wind is favourable – preferably a gentle upstream breeze.

With a full set of wagglers you are equipped to fish very slow as well as fast water at any distance up to about 40m (44yd), even on days when the wind is a wicked downstreamer.

It has to be said, too, that the basics of waggler fishing – shotting and casting but above all float control   are easier to master than the basics of top-and-bottom float fishing.

The only real limitation of the waggler is that you can't use it to slow the bait in running water in the way you can with the stick or pole. Winter roach especially often want the bait held back hard at just half the speed of the flow.

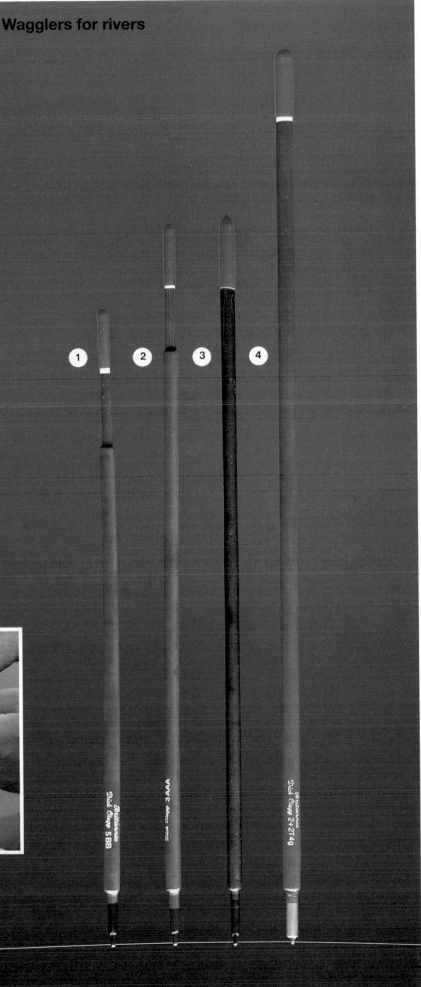

Wagglers for rivers

① ② ③ ④

▲ *In summer it's worth moving some of the droppers up to the float to make the bait sink slower when fish are taking on the drop.*

▶ *Use straight wagglers for river fishing. Those with inserts (1, 2) are mostly for slow water in summer. Those without inserts (3, 4) are mainly for fast water in winter. Dave Hinton prefers unloaded floats (1, 2, 3) – you might like semi-loaded ones better (4).*

Tip *Waggler rods*

Dave Hinton doesn't agree that you need different rods for different types of float fishing. Whether a rod has a spliced tip or more of an all-through action, he believes the important thing is finding the rod that suits *you*.

Much more important than which rod you use is how you actually use it.

River wagglers

You can buy wagglers made from balsa, sarkandas (Indian reed) or hollow plastic but most top anglers favour ones made from peacock quill. It's very much a subjective thing but peacock quill is an extremely light material and wagglers made from it do seem to cast and to ride the water better – provided they have no more than one or two *thin* coats of paint. Time was when you couldn't buy a decent peacock waggler for love or money but now there are many excellent ones on the market and you are almost spoilt for choice.

For river fishing you need a range of straight wagglers – with and without peacock inserts – taking from 2-4AAAs. You can use bodied wagglers but they are really designed for distance fishing on still waters and drains.

Wagglers without inserts have thickish tips that don't show up bites on the drop very well but which make them excellent for fishing a bait on the bottom in pacy water. They don't drag under easily (except when you get a bite!) – even when fished overdepth, if you undershot them. Therefore you mainly use them in winter, when river flows tend to be faster and fish are likely to be caught near the bottom.

Wagglers with inserts have thinner tips that clearly register bites on the drop but which make make them prone to pulling under if fished overdepth in pacy water. Therefore you mostly use them in summer, when rivers tend to be slower and fish are more likely to be caught up in the water.

Waggler size depends on three things. The stronger the wind, the farther you have to cast and the more shot you need down the line, the bigger the float you need.

Four simple waggler rigs for rivers

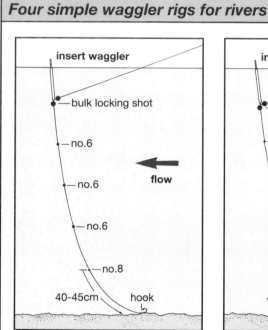

For pacy rivers such as the Trent or Severn in low summer flows. It's light enough to attract bites on the drop from fish in mid-water.

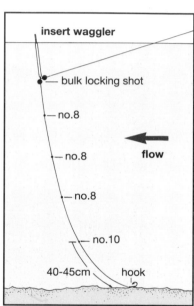

For slower rivers like the middle Thames or Warwickshire Avon in low summer flows, when you are looking to catch predominantly on the drop.

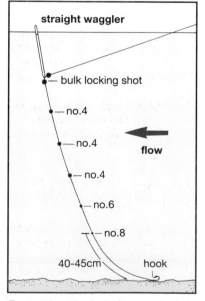

For getting the bait down quickly in fast rivers such as the Trent or Severn when they have extra water on – as they usually do in winter.

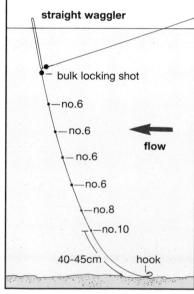

For getting the bait down in slower rivers like the middle Thames or Warwickshire Avon when they have extra water on – winter, mainly.

▲ *The advantages of an open-face reel over a closed-face reel for waggler fishing are that you can cast farther and the line doesn't bed in on the spool after playing a big fish.*

▲ *Dave Hinton prefers a closed-face reel as it rarely tangles, even when it's very windy, and fewer fish are lost when engaging the pick-up pin than when closing a bale arm.*

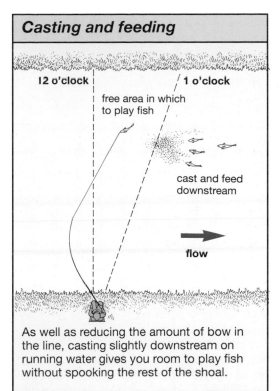

Casting and feeding

12 o'clock

1 o'clock

free area in which to play fish

cast and feed downstream

flow

As well as reducing the amount of bow in the line, casting slightly downstream on running water gives you room to play fish without spooking the rest of the shoal.

A good rule, however – and this applies equally to stillwater fishing – is to err one BB on the heavy side. Then, unless you are fishing tight to the far bank, you can overcast and draw the float back into your swim. This helps you to sink the line when necessary (see below). Erring on the heavy side also gives you weight in reserve if the wind gets up or the fish move farther out – but never hesitate to change to a heavier float if the situation demands it.

Waggler length is important. Generally, the stronger the wind, the longer the float when you need to sink the line – up to 30cm (12in) long. A long float hinders striking when fishing shallow, however, so you sometimes have to compromise.

Casting wagglers

Feather the line before the float hits the water, so the float, droppers and hook don't all land in a tangled heap. When fishing tight to the far bank, feathering the line also stops the float from landing with a splash and plunging down into the water – a sure way to scare off fish.

Sinking or floating line

Whether to fish a sinking or a floating line is governed by wind conditions.

Use a sinking line on all but the calmest days on rivers with little or no flow, as even a slight breeze catches a floating line and moves the float.

On flowing water only use a sinking line when there's a downstream wind. In a downstreamer a floating line bows in front of the float, dragging it through too fast. Even a sinking line tends to form a bow in a 'downgate' wind. To minimize this problem, cast downstream – the stronger the wind, the farther

▲ *Steve Gardener swings in a summer dace from the Thames. He's actually using a slim balsa waggler here but a straight peacock with a fine insert does the same job.*

◄ *A straight peacock waggler with a thin insert shows up a bite on the drop very well on slow rivers as the fish holds up the dropper shot.*

Tip Line tips

To make a sinking line sink faster, soak the spool for a week in a solution of fuller's earth and washing-up liquid.

To make a floating line float better, run it through a cloth smeared with line grease or spray it with line/fly floatant.

▶ *A fine bag of roach. In summer, when rivers tend to be low, slow and clear, the fish can often only be caught way out from the bank in the fastest water. This is when the good waggler angler can really score.*

downstream you should cast. And use a heavier float than usual, to give you greater control.

After casting and sinking the line, leave the bale arm open (if fishing an open-face reel) or the pick-up pin disengaged (if using a closed-face reel) and let the line peel off as the float moves downstream. This way the float goes down in a straight line and doesn't arc in towards the bank.

Use a floating line on running water when there's no wind or when there's any kind of upstream wind. Cast slightly downstream and let line peel off the reel as before. You can allow a slight bow to form but mend the line regularly to stop the bow becoming so big that you can't pick up all the line when you strike. Mend the line to a point a metre or so above the float to avoid moving the float and hence the bait.

Shotting river wagglers

Use simple but flexible shotting patterns. Always put 90% of a waggler's total shot loading around the base as locking shot, leaving a small gap so the float collapses cleanly on the strike.

The faster the water, the more shot you want down the line. The four simple rig diagrams shown cover most situations.

Start by fishing the exact depth with the droppers spread evenly between float and hook, leaving around 40cm (15in) between the last shot and the hook. You can then vary the depth and move the droppers around according to how the fish are biting.

In summer it can pay to go shallower, or move some of the droppers up to the base of the float so the bait sinks slower. If small fish such as bleak prove a nuisance, smashing the bait near the surface or in midwater, try bulking most of the droppers just below halfway between float and hook.

In winter it can pay to go overdepth. In pacy water, use a waggler without an insert and remove one or two droppers so it is undershotted and doesn't drag under.

The basic leger kit

Roy Marlow, who has legered his way to hundreds of competition wins, gives his own choice of tackle for a basic leger kit.

In very simple terms legering means fishing on the bottom without a float, but using some form of bite indication.

Legering is by no means a new technique. It has been popular for hundreds of years. Yet in just the last decade there have been enormous developments.

A vast range of equipment is readily available – but to purchase every item would cost the earth. Fortunately it is not too expensive to buy a basic outfit that can do a little of everything and start you off on the right track.

Quivertips

Today the choice of rod and bite indicator is inseparable. Modern legering rods include provision for bite indicators as an integral part of the design.

The two main types of bite indicators are swingtips and quivertips. Swingtips have been around for 40 years and quivertips about 20 years. Most people use quivertips because they have many advantages as bite indicators – especially the fact that you can use them in fast-flowing waters where swingtips would be useless. If you are buying your first leger rod it should certainly be a quivertip.

Quivertip rods come in two forms, with either a screw-in end eye that will take a variety of bite indicators, or with quivers which can be pushed in and still be interchangeable. Quivertips that push in are preferable. They vary in sensitivity so choose the right one for your conditions.

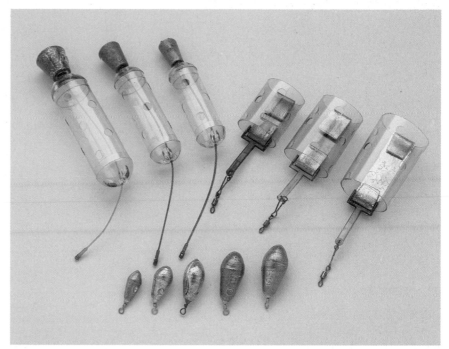

▲ *A selection of open and block-end swimfeeders, and a range of essential weights.*

The basic kit

1. Target board – for easing bite identification.
2. Rod rest with multi-position head.
3. Sturdy fixed-spool reel with 3-4lb line.
4. Leger rod rest.
5. Leger rod butt – containing extra quivertips.
6. Leger rod – main section.
7. Leger rod – quivertip section.

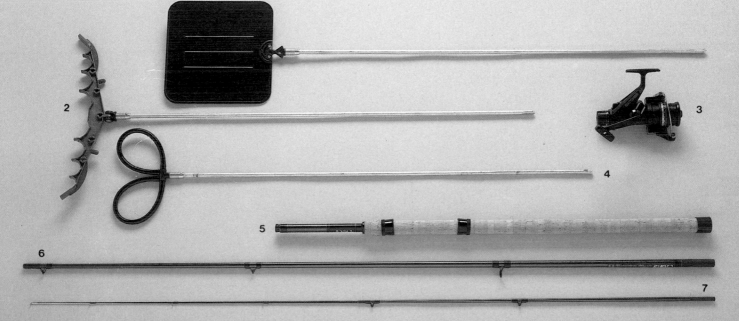

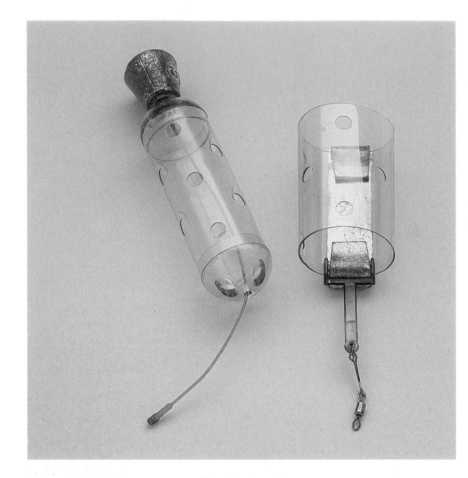

A basic mistake many beginners make is to buy a rod that is too short. If you buy one, say, 10ft (3m) long – including the quiver – then in effect you are fishing with a rod of only 8½ft (2.5m). This is too short. You need a rod with a total length of around 11ft (3.3m) – and if it comes with a variety of interchangeable tips, so much the better.

You should choose a rod made of carbon or a carbon composite – the difference in price between carbon and glass-fibre is negligible. Buy a rod manufactured by a top company, from the current catalogue. Ask your tackle dealer or local anglers for advice on which model to go for. It is a good idea to make sure you can get replacement joints for the rod in case you have an accident.

Reels and line

Your reel should be slightly bigger and stronger than a float-fishing reel. It needs to work harder – particularly if you use it for feeder-fishing. For most conditions a fixed-spool reel with at least 100yd (95m) of 3-4lb (1.4-1.8kg) line is strongly recommended. The reel should be filled to capacity, using old line as backing. Avoid the new 'super' lines – they may be excellent for float-fishing but most are rubbish for legering. It is important to remember that some lines sink and some lines float – you need a line that sinks.

Special equipment

You will also need a number of other items: one or more rod rests, a choice of swimfeeders – to attract fish to your patch – and a target board to show up bites on your quivertip more clearly. Target boards show up the shyest of bites, but allow you to concentrate when fish are slow to feed.

▲ *In action a block-end swimfeeder (left) releases the bait through holes in the feeder. To fish an open-end feeder (right), partially fill it with your hookbait and then plug the ends with groundbait. The bait is released through the holes and through the ends as the groundbait plugs dissolve.*

Leger rods

The length and stiffness of the rod is governed by the waters you are going to fish. For example, a rod ideal for fishing the lower Severn would not be ideal for use on a lake.

It would be nice if everyone could start out with a number of different rods, but since this is probably beyond most pockets you will have to accept a compromise with your first rod.

Tip *Idleback*

Rod rests were once nicknamed 'idleback' because it was thought they were used only by lazy fishermen eating their sandwiches! Now leger fishermen rely on them.

When fishing longer rods two adjustable rests can be used for support. A rest with a multi-position head means you can alter the rod angle with the minimum of fuss, or use two rods where permitted.

▶ *Quivering excitement – the sensitivity and robustness of a quivertip can be seen clearly here. An open-ended swimfeeder helped account for this roach. A wealth of species can be caught on basic leger tackle.*

Basic knots

A fish lost because the hook pulls out or because the fish gets into a snag is something that can't be helped. Fish lost because of knot failure is a result of poor angling.

There are no 'strong' knots – no matter how well-tied and reliable a knot is, it's still a weak link in the tackle. Unfortunately, even in the simplest rig you need at least one knot – to tie the hook on – so we're stuck with them. But by choosing the right knot for the job, tying it correctly and avoiding granny knots you can cut your losses.

A good knot

Two of the commonest ways in which knots fail are when the knot slips and comes undone and when the line breaks next to the knot as it is put under pressure. These can have several causes.

A slippery customer Nylon monofilament isn't the easiest stuff to knot. Firstly it is extremely smooth so there is always a natural tendency for the knot to slip. (A slightly curly 'pig's tail' at the end of the line is a sure sign that this has happened.) Secondly, line damages easily. Surface abrasions, kinks, twists and general deformation of the cross-sectional profile all reduce line strength. In the higher breaking strains – above 10lb (4.5kg) – this may not be a significant reduction but light hooklengths can be weakened by 50% or more. Merely tying a knot and pulling it tight damages the line but some knots do more harm than others.

The old faithful It is surprising how many anglers pile one granny knot on top of another in the hope that the join won't yield. It only takes one encounter with a sizeable chub, carp, tench, pike or barbel to realize that this faith is misplaced. Grannies are not designed to do any job in particular. They give a poor return in terms of knot strength – badly deforming the line so that it snaps well before its recommended breaking strain is reached.

Friction Easing a knot tight causes the line to slide against itself or another item of tackle, under considerable pressure. This generates heat. Excessive heat weakens the line and can even cause it to melt. It is essential to lubricate the knot **before** making it tight – you can do it with water or saliva – but it must be lubricated in some

▼ *Knots are the weak links in your tackle but there is no need to make them any worse by tying them badly. Make sure each knot is secure.*

▲ *There's a thin line between you and your fish. Don't ignore an unwanted knot in your hooklength – replace the hooklength.*

Six frequently used knots

1. Half blood knot

A simple knot for attaching swivels, legers, hooks etc. But do at least six turns to stop it from slipping.

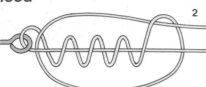

2. Tucked half blood

A variant on the blood knot, this knot has the same applications but is less likely to slip.

3. Double overhand loop

This is a reliable knot for making a loop in hooklengths or mainline – ideal for the loop-to-loop method.

4. Loop-to-loop

A simple and popular method of attaching hooklengths to the mainline. Its only drawback is that it has a tendency to pick up weed.

5. Water knot

A small, neat versatile knot for joining line to line – good for attaching hooklengths and making paternosters.

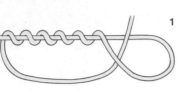

6. Whipping knot

a. This is for tying on spade end hooks. Make a loop and lay it against the hook shank leaving a 6cm (2 ¹/₂in) free end.

b. Wrap the free end around the loop about eight times and pass it through the loop. Moisten the knot.

c. Hold free end and apply steady pressure to the hooklength so the knot slides tight. The line should come off inside of spade.

Stop knot

reel line

1. Make a loop in a 15cm (6in) piece of line or cotton and lay this against the reel line.

15cm (6in) piece of line or cotton

2. Wrap one free end around reel line and over other free end six times, then pass through loop.

2cm (3/4in)
reel line
2cm (3/4in)

3. Moisten knot and pull the free ends to tighten it. This knot is ideal for stopping sliding floats.

► *If you have trouble tying spade end hooks, then try using a hook tyer.*

way. Not only does this help the knot to snug down properly but it prevents the line from weakening.

Tightening the knot Don't pull a knot tight by tugging it. Line has a certain amount of elasticity but a sudden shock loading causes permanent deformation and weakens it. Ease it together slowly under an even pressure.

Twists and turns Give your knots a generous number of turns if this is appropriate. If you are advised to do at least half a dozen turns then make sure you do at least half a dozen or else the knot may slide undone when under pressure.

Knot gone wrong Most of the well-known knots look neat if they have been tied correctly. If the finished result looks untidy then it has probably gone wrong. Don't take chances – break the line off and start again. This may be a difficult task if your hands are wet or cold but it is worth it. A knot that has been badly tied doesn't function properly.

Trimming off When you've tied a knot you need to trim off any loose ends. Just how close you trim a knot depends on what it is being used for. Before trimming hook knots latch the hook on to something – such as scissor handles – and pull the knot tight. Use the scissors to trim within 1mm of the knot. With other knots – such as those used to tie on swivels – you can afford to leave 3-4mm. Always allow a little for slippage.

Keep knots to a minimum. Knotted line may be only 80% of its recommended breaking strain.

Fishing with feeders

The swimfeeder is used for all species of coarse fish on all waters and is an excellent method for feeding accurately at long range.

A swimfeeder is a bait-holding container attached to your line that gradually allows its contents to escape. It is weighted so that it sinks quickly to the bed of the river or lake and stays there.

You can fill the feeder with the same type of bait that you are using on the hook and, because of its closeness to the hook, this gives a very accurate means of feeding the swim. This is particularly useful for fishing deep waters and fast-flowing rivers, where it is difficult to ensure that hookbait and loose feed end up in the same place.

When to use a feeder

Whether to use a feeder or not will depend upon the fishes' feeding habits on the day and how far away the fish are.

Feeding habits Because the feeder is fished as a leger, presenting a static bait on the bottom, there is no point using a feeder if the fish are only feeding on the surface. Similarly, if the fish want a bait that moves with the current it is better to floatfish.

▶ *Small feeders are good for a 'defensive' approach when fishing is hard. This bream fell to worm fished with a little, block-end feeder.*

Distance With the right tackle you can cast a feeder 46–55m (50–60yd) or more. This is an advantage if fish are feeding at long range on lakes or wide rivers (especially when conditions make it difficult to feed accurately with other methods – such as catapulting).

Types of feeder

There are two types of feeder: the open-end (with variations) and the block-end. They can be used on still and running waters.

Open-end feeders are open at both ends. They are partially filled with maggots or casters, or particle baits (hempseed or sweetcorn, for example) and the ends plugged with groundbait. The bait is

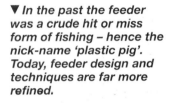

▼ *In the past the feeder was a crude hit or miss form of fishing – hence the nick-name 'plastic pig'. Today, feeder design and techniques are far more refined.*

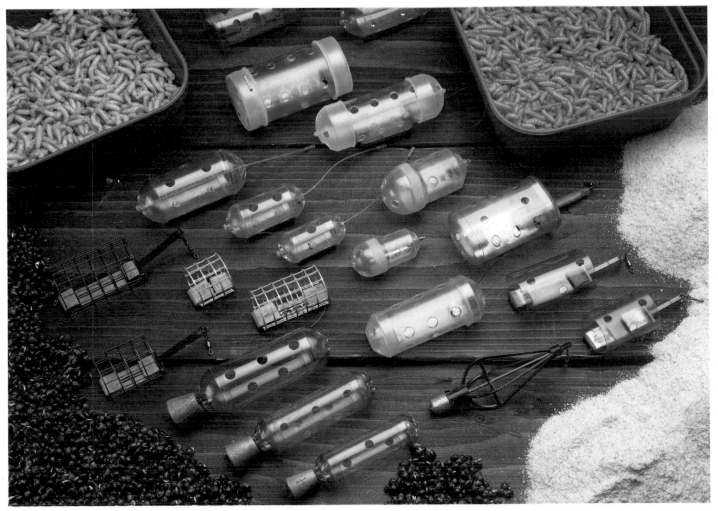

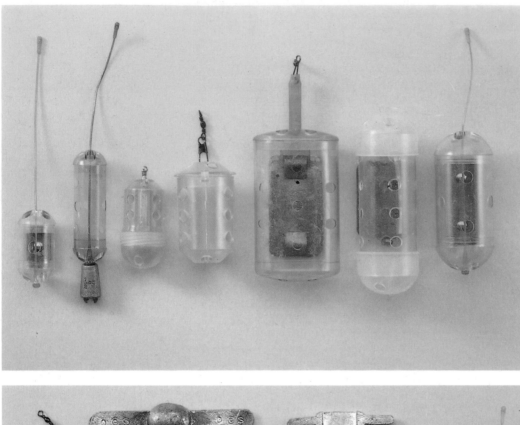

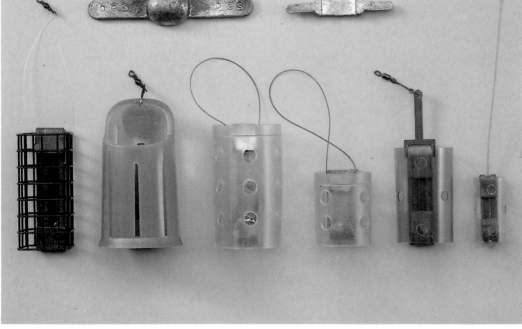

◀ Block-end feeders come in many shapes, sizes and colours. Some have quick change, clip-on, non-toxic weights. Others can be made open-end by unscrewing the end cap. They are attached to the line by swivel, stiff nylon link or a loop of heavy line. As a general guide, you should choose the smallest, lightest feeder you can get away with.

⊗ Making sure it empties

Winding in a feeder that has not emptied properly is bad practice. It deposits bait around the swim and disperses the fish, thereby defeating the feeder's main object. When filling an open-end feeder do not compress the groundbait too much, and avoid stodgy groundbait, which tends to stick to the inside of the feeder.

◀ Of the range of open-end feeders, the cage feeder is a good choice for groundbait. Another recent design, made of soft moulded plastic, planes to the surface quickly on the retrieve – a good choice over weedy or snaggy bottoms.

released in two ways: some escapes through the holes and the remainder is released as the groundbait plugs dissolve.

More recent variations are the cage and frame feeders. These are packed with a mixture of groundbait and loose feed and are ideal for bream, which always appreciate a bit of groundbait.

Block-end feeders are closed at each end. The feeder is filled by removing a cap at one end, and the bait is released solely through the holes. Block-enders are normally filled with either squatts, pinkies or big maggots which are able to crawl out of the holes. Casters and hempseed can be used if the flow is strong enough to wash them out, but on slow waters you may need to enlarge the

holes in the feeder and twitch the rod occasionally to coax the bait out.

Choice of feeder

Both types of feeder come in a range of sizes and weights from ¼ – 3oz (7 – 85g).

Whether you use the block-end or open-end variety will depend upon the type of bait you want to put in it. The important thing is that the bait is able to get out.

It is worth bearing in mind that there are days (particularly in the winter) when the fish are finicky and will not be tempted by groundbait. However, they may still be attracted by a few maggots delivered by way of a block-ender rather than an open-ender, which needs to be used with groundbait.

Tip Enlarging the holes

The holes in block-end feeders can be enlarged to let the bait out freely. Use a pair of scissors or a sharp blade to join two holes together. Individual holes can be enlarged using a special tool. These are available from tackle shops.

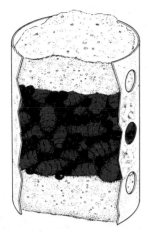

▲ *Fill an open-end feeder with hemp and caster, and plug each end with groundbait. This is ideal for chub, barbel and big roach.*

Weight A feeder should carry enough weight to get the bait where you want it and keep it there. On rivers, a stronger flow requires more weight but don't overdo it. The golden rule is to use just enough weight to hold bottom.

Some feeders have fixed weights while others have interchangeable weights which just slide off, making it easy to add or subtract weight to suit the conditions.

Size The size of feeder you choose usually depends on how much bait you want to put out on each cast. But remember, bigger feeders are more likely to shift with the current.

Bite indication
The feeder is fished as a leger and you can use any of the usual bite indicators. Quivertipping is the most popular and probably the simplest.

Most rods designed especially for feedering (called 'feeder rods') have built-in quivertips.

Rods and line for feedering
It is essential to get the right combination of rod and line for feedering.

Rods Fast rivers, slow rivers and still waters make different demands on the rod.

A feeder rod of 11 or 12ft (3.3 or 3.6m) is good for all three types of water. Shorter tip rods are available but a longer rod enables you to cast with less effort and greater accuracy. It picks up line quicker on the strike and gives greater control when playing fish (especially over troublesome weedbeds).

A fast-river rod should be fairly powerful (having a stiffish butt) and be capable of casting feeders from 1½ – 3oz (43 – 85g). It usually has a straight-through (unspliced) tip section or a heavyish quivertip.

For slow rivers you need a rod with a softer action and a spliced tip section capable of casting feeders of about ½ – 1oz (14 – 28g) or just over.

Stillwater feeder rods have an even softer action with a soft quivertip capable of casting leads, or feeders from ¼ – ¾oz (7 – 21g).

▲ *The feeder is only an accurate method of feeding the swim if it is cast to the same spot each time. Inconsistent casting spreads feed all over the swim and so disperses the fish.*

Tip *Tempting trail*

A few minutes after the feeder has settled, give a half turn of the reel handle. This pulls the feeder and hooklength back, leaving a trail of attractive loose feed around the hook bait.

The feeder empties better if you get the right mix of groundbait. The trick is to mix it fairly dry. then when you cast it in, the bait readily absorbs water and virtually explodes from the feeder.

bottom-feeding fish are attracted to loose feed

emptying feeder

pull

feeder inactive

Tip Holding bottom

Remember that increasing the line's diameter increases the line's resistance to the flow, making it likely that your feeder will be dragged out of position. Often, a lighter feeder and lower breaking strain line, such as 1½ oz (43g) feeder to 5lb (2.3kg) line, holds bottom as well as a heavier rig of 2oz (57g) feeder to 6lb (2.7kg) line.

Feeder rigs

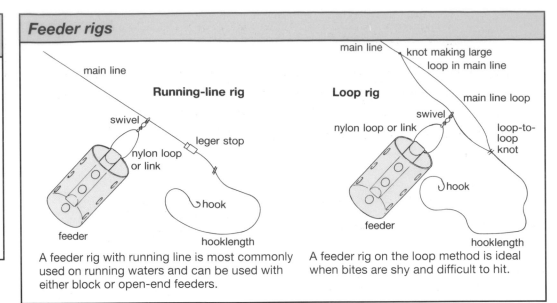

Running-line rig

main line — swivel — nylon loop or link — feeder — leger stop — hook — hooklength

A feeder rig with running line is most commonly used on running waters and can be used with either block or open-end feeders.

Loop rig

main line — knot making large loop in main line — main line loop — swivel — nylon loop or link — loop-to-loop knot — hook — feeder — hooklength

A feeder rig on the loop method is ideal when bites are shy and difficult to hit.

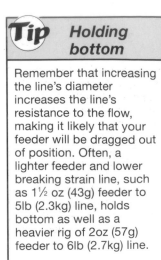

feeder rod with selection of push-in tips

◄ *For feeder fishing you have a choice of two types of feeder rod. Some rods have several top sections with a quivertip permanently spliced into each. Others take a selection of push-in tips, allowing you to cope with a range of conditions (left). This system means you don't need to pay for a whole section each time you need a new tip.*

▼ *Keep a range of tips of varying stiffness: a soft tip for shy biting, canal and lake fish, and stiffer tips for when the flow is stronger. Feeder weight and casting distance affect the choice of rod more than tip.*

Sometimes a heavier rod with a fine tip is useful. For example, on big reservoirs long distance casting may require feeders of 1oz (28g) or heavier to achieve the distance and get the feeder down quickly. This is where an extra top section with a fine quivertip is useful. When casting, the tip will fold over and the 'meatier' part of the rod provides the long range casting power. The fine tip is then ready to register shy bites.

Line You need a variety of breaking strains from as low as 2½lb (1.1kg) for ultra-light feeders, to 6lb (2.7kg) for feeders of around 3oz (85g). Your choice of breaking strain depends upon the weight of feeder but you should aim to get away with the lowest without the feeder cracking off on the cast. When you are deciding on the line strength, remember that a bait-filled feeder may weigh twice as much as an empty one.

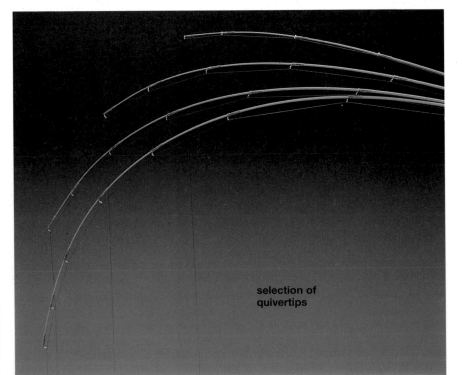

selection of quivertips

Fishing the bomb

Straight legering is something of a dying art in general coarse fishing, thanks to the spread of the swimfeeder. There are still days, however, when 'the bomb' beats both feeder and float says England star Dennis White.

Tip Count down

If you are unfamiliar with a water, make a few trial casts to different spots first, to find any changes in depth. As soon as the bomb hits the water, tighten up. Count the seconds till the tip springs back, showing that the bomb has hit bottom. A bomb sinks at 1m (3¼ft) or so a second, so if it takes four seconds, the depth is about 4m (13ft).

Forty years ago, legering was widely regarded as a crude, 'chuck it and chance it' method, fit only for catching eels, and with tackle to match: short, stiff rods (also used for piking); thick line; big hooks; badly designed weights; and inefficient bite indicators.

All that changed with the invention of the Arlesey bomb, the swingtip and the 'donkey top' (the forerunner of the quivertip). In the 1950s and 1960s, big fish anglers such as Dick Walker and class match anglers like Ivan Marks proved that, far from being crude and ineffective, legering is, in some circumstances, a deadly method of fishing requiring as much skill as any other.

Today, legering is the most popular technique for catching specimen fish, using specialised rods, rigs and methods of bite indication.

In general coarse fishing, however, straight legering – or fishing the bomb, as it is called – is something of a dying art, thanks to the spread of the swimfeeder. But there are still times when the bomb outscores both the feeder and the float.

When to fish the bomb

Basically, you fish the bomb or feeder when the fish are out of range of a float or when

▼ *The swingtip is a very sensitive bite indicator and is preferred by many anglers for shy-biting still-water roach and bream.*

▲ *Large Arlesey bombs are popular with big fish anglers. You can paint them different colours to match different types of lake bed.*

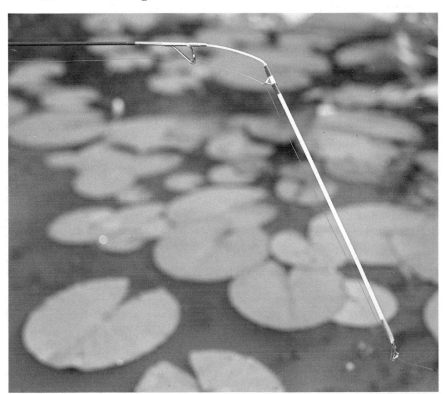

you need to present a still bait on the bottom but conditions make this impossible with a float.

The main advantages of the bomb over the feeder are that it lets you try different spots in your swim without spreading feed everywhere, and lets you determine a feed pattern without having to cast in every time you want to feed.

Canals Most canals are very shallow so are not suited to fishing with a feeder as the splash of it hitting the water can frighten fish away. The bomb is rarely the first-choice method on canals either, as you can usually fish a still bait hard on the bottom with a pole. But the bomb may be the answer on canals when you wish to fish the far bank and the wind is too strong to use a waggler or a long pole, or the spot you wish to fish is beyond the reach of your pole.

Still and slow-moving waters The bomb is usually better than the feeder in shallow, still waters and slow-moving waters (less than, say, 1m/3¼ft deep) because the fish can be frightened away by the splash of a feeder.

▲ *Arlesey bombs are streamlined weights with built-in swivels. Invented by the great Dick Walker, they cast well and rarely tangle.*

▼ *These screw-bombs (variants of the Arlesey) are flattened to hold bottom better in fast flows. They have plastic anti-tangle links instead of swivels.*

▼ *Before the invention of the Arlesey bomb, anglers had to use drilled bullet and coffin weights, which were not aerodynamic, caused tangles and created a lot of resistance to biting fish.*

Water knot

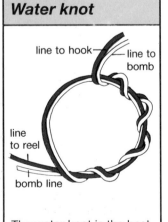

The water knot is the best knot to use to tie a bomb link to your reel line.

after a frost and when the water is clear in winter. Usually in these conditions the fish don't want a lot of feed and will not take a moving bait, factors which rule out the feeder or float.

In high and coloured, even flooded, rivers, often only the occasional big chub or barbel feed. If so, fishing a big bait like lobworm or luncheon meat with a heavy-action rod, strong line, big hook and a heavy bomb can be the only way to catch.

Bomb/feeder rods
A single 9 – 10ft (2.7 – 3m) rod with a threaded end-ring for screw-in swingtips and quivertips – and sometimes a spare top section with a permanently spliced-in quivertip – has traditionally covered most of the general coarse angler's bomb/feeder requirements.

In recent years, however, the trend has been towards carrying a range of bomb/feeder rods of different actions and lengths, each with a selection of two or three push-in quivertips of varying stiffnesses. For instance, different rod actions are needed for different sized bombs and feeders – the bigger the weight, the heavier the rod action. Different rod lengths are also needed for casting different distances – the greater the distance, the longer the rod. And when it comes to quivertips, different ones are needed for different flow speeds. Soft (usually glass fibre) quivertips are used to detect shy bites on still and slow-moving waters. Stiffer (usually carbon fibre) quivertips are needed on faster waters to counter the flow.

Push-in quivertips are better than screw-in quivertips and swingtips in that they do not affect the casting and fish-playing action of a rod. Swingtips in particular make casting awkward, as they flap about and sometimes wrap themselves around the rod top.

However, many anglers still believe that swingtips give better bite indication than even the softest quivertip when fishing for shy-biting stillwater roach and bream, because they offer less resistance.

Choosing a rod
If you fish every kind of water, you need a full range of bomb/feeder rods. If you only fish certain kinds of water, you obviously don't need them all.

Light-action rod For distances up to about 40m (44yd) on still waters and slow-moving rivers, for small fast-flowing rivers and for close-in work on larger fast-flowing rivers, you need a 9 – 11ft (2.7 – 3.3m) light-action rod with a range of push-in quivertips.

This is the rod nearest in action to the traditional general-purpose leger rod, and does indeed cover most anglers' legering requirements.

Such a rod is suited to 2 – 3lb (0.9 – 1.4kg) main line, 12oz – 2lb (0.34 – 0.9kg) hook-

Whatever the depth of the water, the leger will always outcast the feeder and fly through the air more accurately, so is often the better choice in very windy conditions.

Assuming the fish will take groundbait, use a groundbait catapult to feed your swim. Make the balls a little bigger than golf balls, and try to land them within a 4 – 5m (4½ – 5½yd) area. You must hit this area with your bomb, so to ensure accurate casting, line up a permanent feature such as a tree or house on the far bank and use a knot of cotton on the line to show the distance cast.

Before putting the groundbait in the catapult cup, wet the outside of the ball to form a 'skin': this will prevent it breaking up in flight. If your first ball does break up in mid-air it may be because you mixed it too dry or too wet, or because you put too much feed (maggots, casters, etc) in it.

If the fish won't accept groundbait you have no choice but to use a block-end feeder – the type made specifically for maggots and casters. Even then, you can switch to a bomb when you feel you have put in enough feed.

Fast-flowing water Fishing maggots with the bomb close-in down the side, combined with meagre loose feeding, can be a good method in fast-flowing rivers, especially

lengths, bombs up to about ¾oz (21g), and small feeders.

Medium-action rod For distances of about 40 – 60m (44 – 66yd) on still waters or slow-moving rivers, and for medium-sized fast-flowing rivers, you need an 11–12ft (3.3 – 3.6m) medium-action rod, again with a range of push-in quivertips.

The extra length is needed to pick up the line for a positive strike when fishing at a distance on still waters and slow-moving rivers, and to keep as much line as possible out of fast-flowing rivers when propped or held upright.

Such a rod is suited to 3 – 4lb (1.4 – 1.8kg) main line, 1 – 3lb (0.45 – 1.4kg) hook-lengths, ½ – 1½oz (14 – 43g) bombs, and medium-size feeders.

Heavy-action rod For large fast-flowing rivers you need an 11–12ft (3.3 – 3.6m) heavy-action rod. Usually these come with two top sections, one with a stiff spliced-in quivertip and one with an ordinary rod tip.

Such a rod is suited to main line of about 6lb (2.7kg), 2 – 4lb (0.9–1.8kg) hooklengths, and 1 – 3oz (28 – 85g) bombs and feeders.

On such tackle fish either hook themselves against the weight of the bomb or feeder, or give unmistakable drop-back bites as they dislodge the bomb or feeder.

Arlesey bombs

For straight legering you cannot beat the Arlesey bomb. Invented in the 1950s by Dick Walker, this aerodynamic weight with a built-in swivel casts well and rarely tangles the line. Other bombs you may see in tackle shops are variants of the Arlesey bomb.

Previously, leger anglers used drilled bullet and coffin weights, but these were not aerodynamic. Also, because they were threaded on the line, they caused tangles and created resistance to biting fish.

You need a selection of bombs in the following sizes: ⅛oz (3.5g), ¼oz (7g), ½oz (14g), ¾oz (21g), 1oz (28g), 1½oz (43g), 2oz (57g) and 3oz (85g).

Which size to use depends on rod

▲ Legering is now the most widely used technique for catching specimen fish like carp, but in general coarse fishing straight legering is something of a dying art.

Paternoster rigs

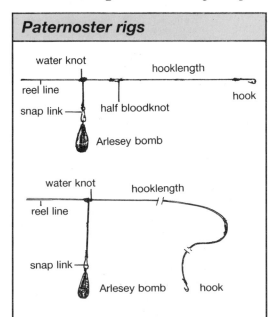

A simple paternoster is the best rig for shy-biting fish on still and slow-moving waters. The lengths of the tail and bomb link depend on the depth of the water being fished and how the fish are feeding.

When fishing at long range it pays in any case to use a short tail and link to minimize tangles and to magnify bites.

Sliding link rigs

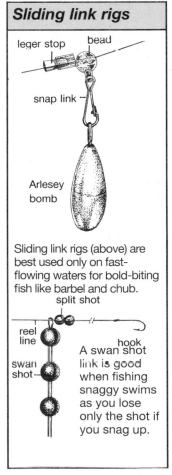

Sliding link rigs (above) are best used only on fast-flowing waters for bold-biting fish like barbel and chub.

A swan shot link is good when fishing snaggy swims as you lose only the shot if you snag up.

strength, distance to be cast, strength of flow (on rivers) or tow (on still waters), and wind strength.

Bomb rigs

Keep rigs simple to avoid tangles. The two basic rigs are the paternoster and sliding link. The paternoster is better for shy-biting fish on still and slow-moving waters as it offers less resistance. The sliding link is best used only on fast-flowing waters for bold-biting fish such as chub and barbel.

Paternoster Tie a 15 – 20cm (6 – 8in) piece of line (the bomb link) about 90cm (3ft) above the end of the reel line with a water knot. Tie the end of the reel line to the hook-length loop with a half blood knot. Tie a snap link to the end of the bomb link with a half blood knot. The snap link lets you change the size of bomb, or change from bomb to feeder.

The tail (from the hook to the water knot) can be shortened or lengthened according to how the fish are feeding. The shyer the bites, the longer the tail needs to be so that the biting fish feel less resistance.

On canals and very shallow still and slow-moving waters, start with a 2.5 – 5cm (1–2in) bomb link tied 2.5 – 5cm (1–2in) above the end of the reel line, and use a 30cm (12in) hooklength rather than the usual 45cm (18in).

Sliding link Thread a sliding bead with snap link on to the reel line, followed by the plastic sleeve of a leger stop. Tie the end of the reel line to the hooklength loop with a half blood knot. Attach the bomb to the snap link. Fix the leger stop sleeve in place with the leger stop peg. You can lengthen or shorten the distance between bomb and hook by moving the leger stop up or down the line.

Alternatively, use two no. 4 shot instead

▼ *When fishing the bomb on still and slow-moving waters, set the rod roughly parallel to the bank and level with the ground.*

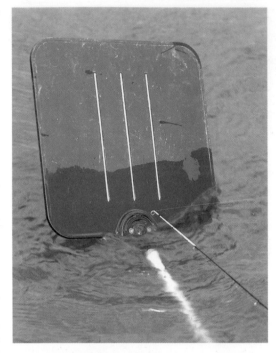

◀ *With the quivertip positioned in front of the target board, the stillwater angler is ready to spot the slightest of bites.*

◀ *No mistaking this bite! Even when the fish are biting boldly, though, a target board is useful because it acts as a wind break and stops the tip bouncing around in the wind.*

> ✕ **Deciding distance**
>
> Before you make your first cast, bear in mind that conditions can change. If you start too far out, you could have difficulty reaching the same spot in the wind.

of a leger stop, and swan shots pinched on a short, folded-over piece of line in place of the bomb and bead. Use two no.4s because one tends to slip. You can add or take away swan shots as needed.

Rod positioning

A bite registers most clearly with the quivertip at right angles to the hook.

In fast-flowing water you also need to keep as much line out of the water as you can, so cast slightly downstream and position the rod rests so that the rod tip points up and out over the river at an angle of about 45°.

In still and slow-moving waters the priority is to keep the rod tip out of the wind, to make it easier to spot bites. Position the rod rests so that the rod is parallel to the ground and almost parallel to the water's edge.

Fishing the rolling leger

This is an exciting technique that catches the fish other methods can't reach. Barbel, chub and roach expert Andy Orme tells how to fish it to deadly effect.

▼ *This angler just knew there had to be a barbel or chub lurking under the overhanging bush at the end of the clear far bank run. All he had to do was roll his baited hook into place.*

An active and versatile way of fishing a moving bait in running water, the rolling leger can be deadly for chub, barbel and roach. It's suitable for all strengths of current, from the rush of the Hampshire Avon to the sedate flow of the Nene.

But for some strange reason the rolling leger is rarely – if ever – used by most anglers these days. Don't be one of them, or you'll miss out on some great sport!

Where it scores

A rolling leger allows you to trundle a hook-bait in a natural fashion along the river bed. In many swims it's impossible to do this with a float, perhaps because the depth is very uneven, or the current near the river bed is slower or faster than that at the surface – or even, as in parts of weirpools, mov-

About Andy Orme

Andy Orme has many big fish to his credit including a 13lb 7oz (6.1kg) barbel, a 5lb 5oz (2.4kg) chub and a 2lb 12oz (1.25kg) roach. He is marketing manager for Ryobi Masterline and the author of many articles. His other interests include scuba diving.

ing in a different direction. Or it may be because the fish are sheltering under the cover of water weed, or trees or bushes trailing in the water.

Where the river bed is covered in weed or boulders the rolling leger is difficult or impossible to use, because the current continually sweeps your rig into snags.

The ideal swim for the rolling leger is a clean run of more or less even-sized gravel – with a shoal of hungry fish at the end!

When to roll

It sounds obvious, but a rolling leger only scores when the fish are in the mood to take a moving bait. In general terms, therefore, it works best in summer, when water temperatures are higher and the fish actively searching the river bed for food.

In winter it's more likely to catch in mild spells than on the coldest days when a static bait is generally more effective. That said, on cold days it can be an excellent way of searching a swim for fish: once you've found where they are it takes but a moment to add a bit of extra weight to convert the rig to a static leger.

Equally, it's a simple matter to take a bit of weight off a static rig and set it rolling. So be flexible in your approach and try both a static and a rolling rig until you find the best method for the day.

No special tackle

You don't need any special tackle to fish the rolling leger – just the same rods, reels and lines you use when quivertipping a static bait for barbel, chub and roach.

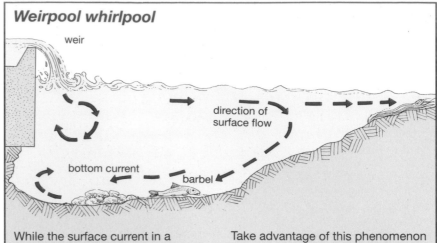

Weirpool whirlpool

weir

direction of surface flow

bottom current

barbel

While the surface current in a weirpool is obviously away from the weir, the bottom flow may well be in quite the opposite direction.

Take advantage of this phenomenon by using the bottom flow to roll your leger and bait right up to the noses of any resident barbel.

Nor do you need any special rigs. The only thing that's special about the rolling leger is the attention you must pay to the size of the weight.

Get it right

Using exactly the right size of weight is the key to fishing the rolling leger. For any particular swim, you have to experiment until the weight is just light enough not to hold bottom yet just heavy enough not to be swept away by the current.

Carry plenty of different sized Arlesey bombs, therefore, plus some BB, AAA and swan shot. In a fast current you may need a 1½oz (43g) Arlesey bomb, while in a slow flow you may need only a couple of BB shot.

Tip Break out

As well as allowing fine-tuning of weight, shot are less likely to snag up if a hooked fish gets weeded. Pinch them on gently and with luck they'll pull off in the weed, leaving you attached only to the fish.

▼ *Andy Orme loves diving into rivers to photograph his favourite fish. He found these barbel holed up among boulders – not a good swim for fishing a rolling leger!*

Undercover barbel

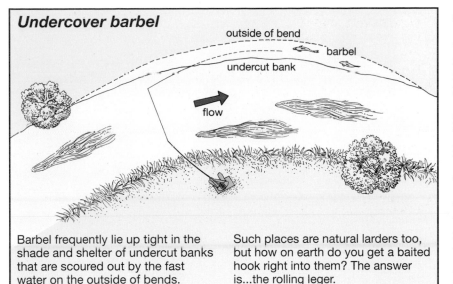

outside of bend

barbel

undercut bank

flow

Barbel frequently lie up tight in the shade and shelter of undercut banks that are scoured out by the fast water on the outside of bends.

Such places are natural larders too, but how on earth do you get a baited hook right into them? The answer is...the rolling leger.

Sometimes adding one or two shot to the line just above the bomb can make all the difference between the bomb trundling correctly along the bottom and being swept away with the current.

Arlesey bombs sometimes roll too easily, so carry a range of duplicates that have been flattened slightly in a vice.

Best baits

The best baits are those that enable you to bury the hook in them. If you fish with the hook point sticking out of the bait then it risks getting caught up as it moves along the river bed. Therefore baits such as maggots, hemp, worms and sweetcorn are better floatfished or fished on a static leger or

▼ *Berkshire's River Kennet. Find a clean gravel run before you opt for the rolling leger on such a heavily weeded river.*

swimfeeder rig.

Old traditionals that work superbly with the rolling leger include breadpaste for roach and chub, cheese and cheese paste for roach, chub and barbel, and luncheon meat for chub and barbel.

Whichever bait you use, don't forget to introduce feed samples on a regular basis. This is just as important as when you are floatfishing. For example, if you are after barbel and are fishing luncheon meat then chuck in a few chunks before every cast.

The beauty of the rolling leger is that if there is a natural bait holding area where the current deposits the free samples then it is very likely your hookbait will end up in the same spot.

How to do it

The rolling leger is an active form of fishing that's equally suitable for roving from swim to swim or for for sitting tight and thoroughly searching out one swim.

It must be fished by holding the rod as if trotting a float. You cannot fish it effectively simply by casting out and sticking your rod

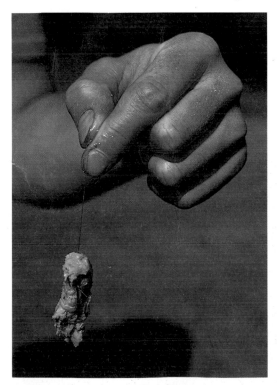

▲ *Best baits for the rolling leger are ones like luncheon meat in which you can bury the hook to avoid catching up on strands of weed.*

in a rest. Try to hold your rod well up, pointing at about 45° towards the sky. This helps you to control the rig and detect bites.

Once you have found a clean gravel run, cast the rig to its head, leave the bale arm open and control the release of line with the index finger of the hand holding the rod and reel.

Provided your rig contains exactly the right weight it will sink to the bottom and set off on a long trundle down the swim. You may find that the rig occasionally gets lodged in one spot. This spot may be a natural bait holding area, so let your rig rest

▶ ▼ It's often best to adopt a mobile, roving approach when fishing the rolling leger. Carrying the bare minimum of tackle – but not forgetting your landing net (right) – allows you to wander the bank, exploring likely lies in many different swims. Dress drably, tread quietly and cast accurately and eventually you'll be rewarded with a fight to remember and a fish like this cracking chub (below).

there a minute before twitching the rod top and sending it on its way again.

Reading the bites

Bite detection can be difficult at first. A rolling leger itself causes all sorts of pulls and twitches that can be mistaken for bites. If you are lucky a real bite is a strong, positive pull that's easy to identify and hit. Barbel often bite like this but chub and roach don't.

These fish often pick up the bait very gently and so your bite may consist of a very slight pull or twitch or the rig may simply stop rolling. Sometimes the rod top drops back and the line goes slack as a fish moves upstream or towards you with the bait. With experience you learn to read bites until it becomes almost a sixth sense. A good rule to start with is to hit any unusual indications.

You can identify bites using three methods. You can watch the quivertip, you can watch the bow in the line from the rod top, and you can hold the line above the reel and feel for bites with your fingers.

Under cover

All fish, but especially big ones, love shelter. They feel secure from predators and anglers when hidden beneath undercut banks, overhanging bushes and trees and underwater weedbeds. Casting a leger straight at such fish, or even trotting a float down to them, is often impossible.

This is where the rolling leger really scores, because you can cast slightly upstream then trundle your rig right into the fishes' lair. It may take several attempts to get right but it's worth it because fish that feel secure usually give very positive bites. Many specimen barbel, chub and roach have been caught in just this way. Master the method and you've added an invaluable string to your bow.

Freeline your way to success

It sounds simple... and it is! Yet freelining – fishing with no weight or float – is a sadly neglected method in this age of high-tech tackle and complicated rigs, says Bob James.

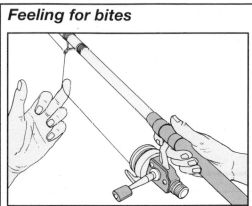

Feeling for bites

When freelining a sinking bait such as cheese for barbel and chub, use your sensitive fingertips to feel for bites.

Freelining is fishing with nothing on the end of your line except a baited hook. This usually means fishing at fairly short range, because the only casting weight is provided by the bait. But don't look on this as a restriction – more fish can be caught close in than many anglers realize.

In favour of freelining

Freelining has several advantages over more usual methods such as fishing with a swimfeeder and electronic bite alarm.

First and foremost, there's nothing on the line near the hook to cause any resistance, resulting in more positive bites.

Second, having no terminal tackle other than a hook is a great advantage when fishing near weeds or other snags, because there's no weight, float or swimfeeder to get stuck and lose you fish.

Third, your tackle needn't be so powerful. When fishing at distance with a heavy weight, float or swimfeeder the rod and the line have to be overly powerful to cope with the casting. When freelining you can get away with a less powerful rod and finer line – but never go so light as to risk being repeatedly smashed up.

Fourth, you don't need huge amounts of tackle – just your rod, bait, landing net, disgorger or forceps, spare hooks and perhaps a rod rest. This allows you to be mobile – you don't have to stay in one spot, but can move quickly and easily from swim to

▲ *John Wilson freelining for chub and barbel on a river at the height of summer.*
One of the great advantages of freelining is that you need only the minimum amount of tackle, which means you can move easily from swim to swim. But remember to wear drab clothing, tread quietly and keep off the skyline.

▲ Carp like nothing better than to bask in the sun in the sanctuary of weeds and snags. This is no place for bolt rigs and heavy weights. Your best chance is to freeline a floating bait such as dog biscuits. And because you have no weights or float on the line, there's nothing to catch in the weed or snags during the fight.

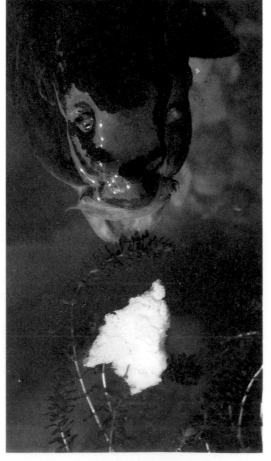

► Many carp anglers regard freelining as old fashioned, but the proof of the pudding – or in this case, the proof of the breadcrust – is in the eating. Too often, carp anglers cast heavy rigs to the horizon when they would be more successful – and get more enjoyment – freelining floaters in the margins.

swim, so covering much more water.

Fifth and finally, you can cast without causing a great deal of commotion and scaring away the fish.

A stealthy approach

Stealth and concealment are crucial whatever type of fishing you do, but doubly so when freelining because usually you are fishing close in and stalking visible fish – and if you can see them, never be in doubt that they can see you! Wear drab clothing, tread carefully and keep off the skyline. If you can, try early mornings or late evenings, when you are less visible.

From carp to catfish

Freelining can be a deadly method for many coarse fish, and for catfish and specimen eels is arguably the best.

Carp Many carp anglers today regard freelining as old hat. How often these days do you see a carp angler fishing without a huge lead and some fancy rig? Yet back in the 1960s and 1970s freelining was by far the most popular method for carp. Jim Gibbinson and Jack Hilton, celebrated carp anglers both, considered it to be THE method for this fish. It wasn't until the 1980s that bolt rigs and hair rigs – and therefore the use of heavy weights – came to

◄ *A shoal of chub gathers on the upper Bristol Avon. When a river is low and clear it's all too easy to scare away chub with one clumsy footfall. Even if you do creep up on them without being seen or heard, they are quite likely to bolt at the sight or sound of a float or weight. Freelining, of course, is the answer.*

Tip Freelining farther out

Should the need arise to cast farther than is possible with just the weight of the bait, or should you wish to freeline very light baits such as maggots, then simply tie a small stone or some other disposable (non-toxic) weight on to your line with PVA string.

This gives you the necessary casting weight, yet the PVA string soon dissolves in the water, freeing your hook and line from the stone or weight.

the fore in carp fishing.

During the 1980s the number of carp anglers increased tenfold, so pressure on waters increased dramatically. The first reaction of the carp was to move out of the margins, to get as far away from the madding crowd as they could. Since then the constant bombardment of heavy weights at such features as islands and gravel bars has led to the margins being the least disturbed areas on many lakes!

This is where the thinking angler can score, with freelined dog biscuits or other floating baits when the carp are up top, or freelined sinking baits – boilies, pastes, particles and so on – when they are rooting about down below.

Chub and barbel are two species for which freelining can be deadly, and in times of low flow there is no finer method. Shallow, clear water really does need a gentle approach, the minimum of splash with the cast and no float, weight or swimfeeder to arouse the suspicion of the fish.

It can come as a surprise to many anglers just how readily a shoal of chub responds to a steady stream of floating bait drifted over it. Crust is the obvious choice, but try dog biscuits as well – chub love them.

Stay well back from the chub to start. Then, as they become more confident about

taking the free offerings, you can creep a little closer. But never be in too much of a hurry because chub, though greedy, are wary creatures.

Having got into a position from which you can both see and fish for the chub, try to pick out the biggest, then run your hookbait down to it. You may only get one fish before the shoal spooks, so put some more bait out then try a different swim for a while. With luck you'll get one from there, and then the first shoal may be back on the feed when you return. This is not just a summer

▲ *One of the deadliest summer chub baits of all – a big, juicy black slug. The best way to fish a slug is freelining. Swing it out and up over the water so that it hits the surface with an audible plop, and be ready for an immediate take – chub seem to recognize the plop and home straight in on it.*

method; it often works in winter too – try it on a still, sunny day.

Perhaps the most exciting form of freelining is for barbel. Put a big lump of luncheon meat or cheese, or a couple of worms, on the hook and cast upstream into a promising looking gap in the weeds or a steady glide over clean gravel.

Cast well above your chosen spot to allow for the slanting of the bait as it sinks in the current. Take a little slack line and gently hold it across your fingertips. Bites when fishing like this can be almost imperceptible plucks and twitches, but more often are vicious tugs – you won't miss many but you may lose your rod if you don't hold on to it tightly.

Chub also respond well to this approach (sometimes too well when you are after barbel). Cheese and cheesepaste are excellent baits throughout the year, while in summer few chub can resist the plop of a big, juicy black slug.

Rudd Traditionally, one of the best methods for fooling big lake rudd on balmy summer evenings is to freeline floating breadcrust in the margins. Certainly, it can be very effective, but try dog biscuits too; big rudd woof them up!

Pike, zander and perch anglers often freeline both deadbaits and livebaits, especially on hard-fished waters where the fish have grown wary of rigs offering even only slight resistance.

Big eels and catfish Neither of these fish seems willing to tolerate any resistance when taking a bait, so fishing with no encumbrances on the line is common.

Bite detection

Some anglers are put off freelining because they are worried about bite indication. There's no weight for the fish to pull the line through, or float for the fish to pull under, so

▲ *With a stealthy approach it is surprising how many fish can be caught close in on freelined baits. This angler has a camouflaged jacket but is also using the trunk of the tree to hide himself from the fish. Remember this simple rule – if you can see the fish, the fish can see you.*

◀ *A fat lobworm is one of the most natural baits of all and is heavy enough to cast a fair way with no weight on the line. Try it when freelining for barbel.*

they aren't confident about what's going on at the end of their line.

Confidence is important to every angler, but it's equally important for the fish to have confidence in the bait offered them, and herein lies the answer. With many of the takes you get when freelining – notably from barbel – you would have to be at home to miss them, so boldly do they bite.

When surface fishing you see the take, so there's no need for any indicators here.

When freelining sinking baits in still waters, use a rod rest with the type of head that allows the line to run through it freely, then place a washing-up bottle top (with an artificial illumination device attached if you're fishing in the dark) – or cylinder of kitchen foil – on the line between the butt and first ring. Leave this hanging slack then sit back and wait for the action to start. On still days you can even just watch the line between the rod and water – what could be simpler?

Buying a pole kit

To reap the benefits of pole fishing - including the fun of playing fish on elastic – keep things simple.

Pole fishing has really taken off in recent years and is now almost as popular with pleasure anglers as it is with matchmen. Poles are used to catch small to medium fish close in on a fixed length of line. Their main advantages over running line (rod and reel) are better float control and bait presentation and an improved fish-to-bite ratio. There are two basic types.

Whips are short, telescopic poles with fine, flexible 'flick-tips' for casting and playing fish. You use them with line slightly shorter than the pole and attach the line direct to the tip so that hook and fish come direct to hand.

Whips come in lengths from 2-7m (6½-23ft), but one of 4m (13ft) covers most of the beginner's requirements. Such a whip usually has four sections, including the

The basic kit

To start, you need the following kit, says 1990 World Champion **Bob Nudd**:

1. A telescopic flick-tip pole 4m (13ft) long.

2. A take-apart pole 8m (26ft) long.

3. A pole rest.

4. Medium pole elastic.

5. A 0.75g cane-stem **pole float** with a 'teardrop' balsa body.

6. A 0.75g cane-stem **pole float** with an inverted 'teardrop' balsa body.

7. A 1.25g wire-stem **pole float** with a 'teardrop' balsa body.

8. A 1.25g cane-stem **pole float** with an inverted 'teardrop' balsa body.

9. Four pole float winders.

10. Rubber pole float winder anchors.

11. A length of silicone pole float rubber.

12. Weights: some 0.7g and 1g non-toxic Olivettes.

13. Size 10 shot.

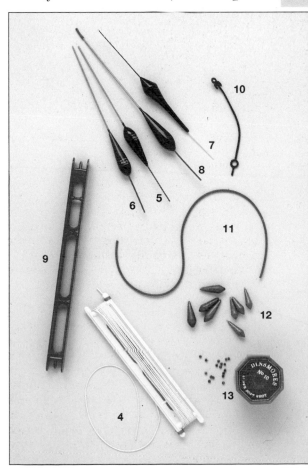

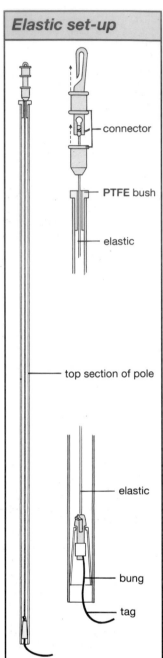

Elastic set-up

- connector
- PTFE bush
- elastic
- top section of pole
- elastic
- bung
- tag

Special pole elastic is run through the top one or two sections of the long pole and fixed in the base by a plastic bung. At the tip it passes through a low-friction PTFE 'bush'. It is kept under tension by a plastic connector, to which the line is fixed.

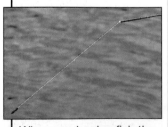

When you hook a fish the elastic stretches out of the pole tip. The bigger and stronger the fish, the farther it stretches.

tip. You can fish with it at full length or, by using only the top two or three sections, at 2m (6½ft) or 3m (10ft).

Long poles have stiff tips with elastic fitted through the top one or two sections. The line is attached to the elastic, which then takes the strain of the fish. Having take-apart – not telescopic – sections you can fish a long pole at various lengths simply by adding or taking off sections. You can also fish it with any length of line up to its full length – you just take off the necessary number of sections to net fish or rebait the hook.

Long poles come in lengths from 6-14m (20-46½ft), but one of 8m (26ft) covers the requirements for a beginner. Anything longer and you must spend a lot to get a good one, though it is a worthwhile investment as you can learn to handle, say, an 11m (36ft) pole at 8m (26ft) before progressing to using it at full length.

Buying poles

The cheapest poles are made of glass-fibre and the most expensive out of carbon fibre. In between are carbon-glass composite poles. The higher the carbon fibre content, the lighter and thinner the pole.

Look for a whip that is stiff in the bottom sections but has a soft tip. If it is sloppy all through you'll have trouble using it on windy days and will miss bites. Conversely, if the tip is too stiff you'll bump fish off on the strike and have problems with bigger fish.

When buying a long pole, look for lightness, stiffness and balance. All long poles sag slightly towards the tip, but avoid ones that sag near the butt. The sections should take apart smoothly and not stick. For this reason, choose one with 'put-over' joints – where the top of one joint fits inside the bottom of the next.

Buy from a dealer who will fit the elastic for you and show you how to do it yourself when you need to replace it.

Pole floats

Pole floats are smaller and more sensitive than ordinary floats. Most have bristle tips which offer biting fish minimal resistance. Those with 'teardrop' balsa bodies are for still water, those with inverted 'teardrop' bodies for flowing water. All are attached top and bottom, by passing the line through a tiny metal eye at the top of the body and fixing it on the stem with small pieces of silicone rubber.

Pole float rigs are shotted exactly so that only the float tips show. You store the rigs on winders, winding them on from the hook first. Each rig has a loop at the top (for attaching to the pole): a rubber anchor secures this loop to the winder.

▼ *The long pole has take-apart sections, allowing you to fish with a length of line that is shorter than the pole. After you have hooked a fish you simply take off the necessary number of sections to land it.*

Pole craft

Kevin Ashurst, the England team's most experienced member, maintains that when it comes to poles the simple things are important – and yet they are often overlooked.

▼ *This angler is using the long pole with a short line for perfect float control on the far side of the Kennet and Avon canal. The pole is excellent for this kind of fishing because you can drop the bait just where the fish want it and keep it there.*

You may know the basic differences between whips and long poles but do you know about the limitations of each approach – where and when to use a whip and how to handle the long pole, for example? If you don't then you might run into problems. Since the pole is the most expensive item you'll ever buy, it pays to take care of it.

Fishing the whip

Whips are poles having very fine, flexible solid carbon fibre top sections – to which the line is attached.

Use the whip when there are small fish fairly close in – at about 3-5m (10-16ft) from the bank. It is most effective when there are a lot of fish because it is primarily a speed method.

It is faster than running line because the length of line from the top of the whip to the hook is kept constant – fish can be swung directly to hand every time. Although the long pole also uses a fixed length of line, the whip can be much faster because it does not involve elastic: it's a simpler, more direct method. Ideally the line should be about 30cm (1ft) shorter than the whip.

Control Whips are not exclusively for

▲ *Wielding a pole for the full five hours of a match takes a lot of effort, so it is important to be as comfortable as possible. This angler is using his knee as a pivot and taking the pole's weight with his left forearm – a method that Kevin recommends.*

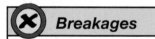

Breakages

"One thing that inexperienced pole anglers often do," says Kevin Ashurst, "is pick the pole up at the 3m point and try to hold up 10m behind them. Then they'll take it back to the shop and say it's broken. This isn't suprising because a pole isn't meant to take that kind of treatment. We've all done this kind of thing, though, and it is often the only way to learn."

▶ *In very windy conditions poles become difficult to manage and can break, so on days like this it is better to leave it to the experts.*

This angler is feeding the pole behind him to land a fish. You should do this smoothly so that you don't jerk the fish. Keep the tip of the pole out of the water so that you can see where the fish is.

speed. They are good for controlling rigs on slow rivers, canals and lakes with a slight pull. If a swim is not too deep – about 1.8m (6ft) at 4-5m (13-16ft) from the bank – then you might be able to run your float through about 2-3m (6-10ft). Within this region you'll have enough line out to control the float but if the flow is too strong you won't get a decent run through.

The float needs to be heavier than you would fish on a long pole but still light compared to those for running line – so you can cast it easily. When fishing at 5m (16ft) you need a float taking a minimum weight of 0.5g. If it's windy then you'll have to go even heavier.

Limitations It may sound obvious but the whip is only a fast method if you are catching. It is no use staying with it if you are missing bites. That's the time to try something else.

Big fish can present problems for the whip, too, because the flexibility of the flick tip is the only means of providing a running fish with line – and that may not be enough.

Long pole, short line

The term 'long pole' is misleading because you could use the top three sections of a 14m pole to fish a couple of metres out. More often than not, though, you'll be fishing at 7-8m (23-26ft) or beyond. It is usual for the length of line to be much less than the length of the pole. This means you have to dismantle – 'unship' – the pole to reach the hook.

The line is attached to elastic which runs through the top one or two sections of the pole. This serves a unique function – somewhere between that of a reel and rod top or flick tip – enabling a fish to take line but only up to a point and subject to increasing tension.

Buying a pole Poles are expensive and it pays to think carefully before parting with your money. You don't have to spend vast amounts – there are some very, very good poles for a perfectly reasonable price. It is up to you to go to a shop and haggle with your tackle dealer for a good price.

Materials Anything other than carbon fibre is not worth considering. Don't be tempted to get a glass-fibre pole. They are a thing of the past.

Length If you are at all serious about angling, you must buy one of at least 11m. Don't think: "Oh, I'll get a cheap one at 9 or 10m to learn with," because you'll see other anglers catching just a bit farther out and want a longer one. It is quite likely that any pole shorter than 11m will end up as nothing more than a landing net handle. There

Shipping-up

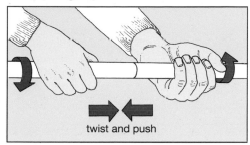

twist and push

When shipping-up, twist rather than push the sections together. This way you can control the amount of pressure and the sections are less likely to stick together.

is, nevertheless, a practical limit to the length of poles. Anything above 15.5m is difficult to handle.

Lightness and stiffness are related. Generally, an increase in lightness means a decrease in stiffness – though a good quality pole will be both light and fairly stiff.

Nevertheless, a good quality, light pole suffers when it is windy – bending, bouncing about and making good float control extremely difficult. (These kinds of conditions should in any case be left to the experts.) So to begin with it is a good idea to get a fairly light pole and to fish it when conditions are favourable. Only when you have mastered the basics should you think about fishing a heavier, stiffer pole in adverse conditions. One of between about 800-900g at 12.5m can be managed comfortably by the average angler.

Spare top sections Certainly for matches,

it is essential that you have at least one, if not two spare sets of the top three sections to your pole. This enables you to set up several different rigs at the same time. So for example, you can change from a 0.5g float to a 1.0g float just by picking up other sections of your pole, or you might want to fish identical tackles with different size hooks so that you can try a bait change. With a spare you can do this in a matter of seconds. This makes the pole an exciting method; you can try many different things within a matter of half an hour or so – you can't do this with the running line.

Joints Most modern poles have put-over joints. They make shipping-up (putting the pole together) easier – you don't have to fiddle around, struggling with unwieldy lengths of pole, trying to find the hole. You can do it without looking.

Shipping-up When you piece your pole together make sure that it doesn't join up with a 'chunk', otherwise it will jam and you'll be taking it home in a 2m length. Twist – screw – the joints rather than pushing them directly together. If the joints are

▲ *When you are landing a fish, just where you take-off (unship) depends on the size of the fish. If it is big – above a couple of pounds, say – you'll need to unship a section closer to to the tip of your pole than you would without a fish on. This is so that you can draw the fish towards you.*

Be prepared to use your landing net on fish that are much smaller than you would net on rod and line. This is because a fish of only 6oz (170g) will stretch the elastic and make it extremely awkward, if not impossible, to swing in.

Pole rollers

Use a roller to take the weight of the pole and guide it when you are pushing it back. This removes the temptation for you to lift it by the end sections (something which you should never do) and prevents the end from getting damaged. A wide roller is easier to use because you don't have to keep looking to see where the end of the pole is.

Sometimes a hedge or fence behind you serves just as well as a roller.

Tip *A gritty problem*

Putting a pole together with grit in the joints can cause great damage. A very simple and effective way to get rid of grit – especially if it is on the section that you are putting over – is to stab it in the water to a depth of 20cm (8in). This clears it and helps the sections to meet smoothly.

sections of your pole aren't rattling about. If your pole does get damaged then whip over the damaged area to reinforce it – your tackle shop will probably be willing to help.

How to sit One method is to sit with your legs at a slight angle to the water, the pole resting across your knees and the end of it trapped firmly under your forearm. This way you don't need any pole behind you to balance it – you can use the full length of the pole for the job it was intended.

Casting is simple with a pole. All you need to do is push the tackle out with the pole and lay it on the water.

Striking A lot of anglers don't strike hard enough when fishing the pole. You need to pull it hard upwards. If you strike to one side then the float tends to 'clonk' out of the water like a stick float.

Pole on the water It isn't advisable to rest the pole on the water but it can be a help to sink the line when conditions are very windy by submerging the top two sections.

The only time that a pole seems to scare fish is on a clear water when you've got them feeding on rod and line. If you put a pole over them you'll stop getting bites – either because they move off or just stop feeding. At other times they'll come right under the pole and feed. There is a canal in Liverpool that is so clear you can actually see the fish doing this.

It takes practice to get used to fishing a pole. The change from using a rod of 3 or 4m to a pole of 10 or 11m is a big one, and at first you'll probably feel a bit awkward. But after a few good catches you'll soon feel more at ease.

supposed to overlap by 8cm (3in) make sure that they do overlap by that amount. If you lift a pole when the joints are not properly overlapping it will shatter.

The joints on the sections which are not unshipped should be tight so that they don't come apart when they are not meant to.

When you are catching fish and you are unshipping and shipping-up there is always a chance of picking up grit on the end of a section. If you try to push a pole together with grit between the joints you'll do irreparable damage to it. So always make sure the joints are clean.

Avoiding damage When handling a pole be careful not to knock it against rocks or stones. Although carbon fibre is strong for its weight it is also an extremely brittle material. Even the slightest nick in the pole's surface weakens it.

It is often the case that a pole shatters and the angler concerned insists that he wasn't mishandling it. The chances are that the damage had already been done and it was only a matter of time before the pole broke. So if it is windy make sure that loose

▲▼ *Here are two methods of feeding while holding the pole. Gripping the catapult pouch with the hand holding the pole (above), and leaning on to the pole and trapping it under the belly to leave the hands free (below).*

An introduction to fishing the whip

Whip fishing harks back to the origins of angling, when someone first thought of tying a fishing line to the end of a stick. Alain Urruty outlines the basics of a method that is indispensable to the match angler.

▼ *England International Steve Gardener fishing the whip for tidal Thames dace. In the right hands the whip is an unbeatable method for building a match-winning bag of small fish close in.*

A whip is a kind of pole specifically designed for catching small fish quickly close in, fishing 'to hand' with the line attached directly to its flexible tip: no elastic is used and no line can be given.

Don't use a whip if you expect big fish such as chub or bream. Although with skill, patience, a good whip and a slice of luck you can land fish up to 3-4lb (1.4-1.8kg), more often you lose them. Worse, you leave a hook in the fish's mouth if the line breaks. When after big fish, use a rod and reel, or a pole with elastic, and save the whip for what it does best.

▶ *Hand-size roach like this are good fun on whip tackle and always a welcome bonus in a match when you are fishing for 'bits' – much smaller fish that you can swing straight in.*

Whip rigs

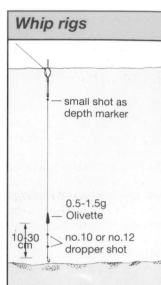

- small shot as depth marker
- 0.5-1.5g Olivette
- 10-30 cm
- no.10 or no.12 dropper shot

1. Rig for bottom-feeding fish such as gudgeon and ruffe. Cast it with a smooth underarm swing.

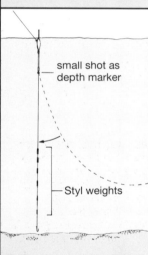

- small shot as depth marker
- Styl weights

2. On-the-drop rig. The Styls get smaller but farther apart the closer they are to the hook.

⊗ More haste...

Building a big bag of small fish on the whip isn't just a matter of all-out speed. You should aim to catch smoothly and steadily throughout the session or match, rather than go flat out at the start, get in a tangle and end up losing your way.

▶ *Dick Clegg – manager of the England team and a top-flight matchman – about to put the net under a bonus perch during a 'gudgeon-bashing' session with the whip on the Trent in winter.*

Compromise action

A whip has several conflicting jobs to do and finding an action to deal with them all involves a certain amount of compromise.

On one hand it needs to be soft and 'whippy', to allow light rigs to be cast overhead and to absorb the weight and pull of a hooked fish. On the other hand it must be fairly stiff, to enable you to swing heavy rigs out underarm and hit fast bites.

A good compromise is a whip with a stiff butt and a softish tip that bends smoothly into the middle.

Different lengths

Whips are most commonly available at lengths between 2m (6½ft) and 6m (20ft). If you buy a 6m (20ft) whip made up of six 1m (3ft) sections you can obviously use it at any length between 1m (3ft) and 6m (20ft). This is a good way to get the feel of whip fishing before investing in a whole range of whips.

However, the top 2m (6½ft) of a 6m (20ft) whip have an inferior action to a purpose-made 2m (6½ft) whip – the former being the top of a longer whip, the latter being a complete whip in itself. Ideally you should buy whips purpose-made for the lengths you fish.

All whips up to 4m (13ft) long should be telescopic, since this allows them to be of slimmer diameter and smoother action. It is common to find longer whips with take-apart bottom sections – for example, 4m (13ft) telescopic plus one, two or three 1m (3ft) extensions. These are very useful on waters where the odd big fish can come along since putting on an extra joint or two gives you leeway to play the fish.

Full range

Matchmen often set up a range of whips of different lengths, to cover every eventuality. Having the right whip set up for the right time can mean the difference between winning and framing.

For example, they might set up identical rigs on 2m (6½ft), 2.5m (8ft), 3m (10ft) and 3.5m (11½ft) whips for a gudgeon match on a canal. They may start on the 2m (6 ½ft) whip and finish on the 3.5m (11½ft) one, having caught at various times in the match on all four lengths of whip.

How many whips you buy depends on how seriously you take your fishing. You can fish at 3.5m (11½ft) with a 3m (10ft) whip and an outstretched arm. Equally, you can fish at 2.5m (8ft) with a 3m (10ft) whip and 0.5m (1½ft) tucked behind you. But it's more efficient to use whips of the exact length.

When to whip it

Fishing for gudgeon or ruffe on the near side of a canal or at the edge of a river are classic examples of when a short whip – 2-4m (6½-13ft) – comes into its own.

On still waters or slow-flowing rivers where the target species are small roach, skimmers or dace, 3-6m (10-20ft) whips can be unbeatable for building big bags.

slipping the fish into your keepnet. This
saves valuable seconds for each fish you
catch. Considering some matches are won
with 300 fish, if you save five seconds a fish
you gain 25 minutes fishing time.

Basic methods

The whip really comes into its own when
the fish are feeding well and don't require
perfect bait presentation.

When fishing for bottom-feeding species
such as gudgeon and ruffe, use a rig that
gets your bait down quickly (see *Whip rigs*
diagram 1). Have the Olivette as close to the
hook as you can. You are wasting time if you
present a naturally falling bait when the
fish are feeding on the bottom.

When after fish feeding up in the water,
use a light, on-the-drop rig (see *Whip rigs*
diagram 2). Try to establish what depth
they are feeding at. If your bites are coming
in the last 60cm (2ft) or so of water, don't

▲ *Another 'netter' – a roach
this time – for Dick Clegg
on the Trent. Note the stiff
butt of his whip and the
way the tip bends smoothly
into the middle.*

Tip Cane stem

Light-bodied floats with
cane, not wire, stems make
casting much easier when
fishing the whip, because
they follow the weights
through the air. This is true
for both types of rig and
both casting styles.

Length of line

Smoothness and efficiency are essential if
you are to amass a lot of small fish on the
whip. You must set the length of line so that
when you swing a fish in it comes exactly 'to
hand'. To be able to unhook the fish without
having to put the whip down or tuck it
under your arm, the length of line must also
allow you to bring the fish to the hand holding the whip.

There should be a slight bend in the tip at
this stage to stop the line and float wrapping around the whip. If the line is too tight,
however, the hook catches in your fingers as
you try to recast.

In a match, getting the length of line
exactly right and unhooking fish this way
enables you to put your baited hook back
into the swim at the same time as you are

Ways of attaching the line

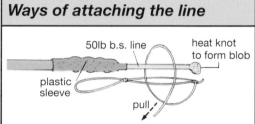

This is a quick-release way of attaching the
line to the tip of a whip. First knot a piece of
50lb (22kg) line and melt it to form a blob.
Glue the piece of 50lb (22kg) line to the tip
of the whip and cover it with a plastic
sleeve. Tie two loops in the end of your rig
line. Form a third loop in the line and pass it
through the middle loop and over the blob.
Pull tight. To release the rig, simply pull the
top loop.

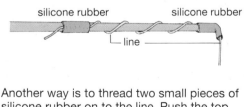

Another way is to thread two small pieces of
silicone rubber on to the line. Push the top
piece along the tip of the whip until it traps
the line. Rotate the tip so the line spirals
round the tip. Trap the line at the end with
the second piece of rubber.

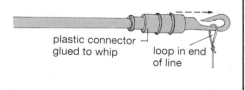

A third, very simple method is to use a
commercially available plastic connector.
Glue the connector to the tip of the whip
with epoxy resin. Tie a loop in the end of the
line. Slip the loop over the plastic hook and
slide the plastic cover over it.

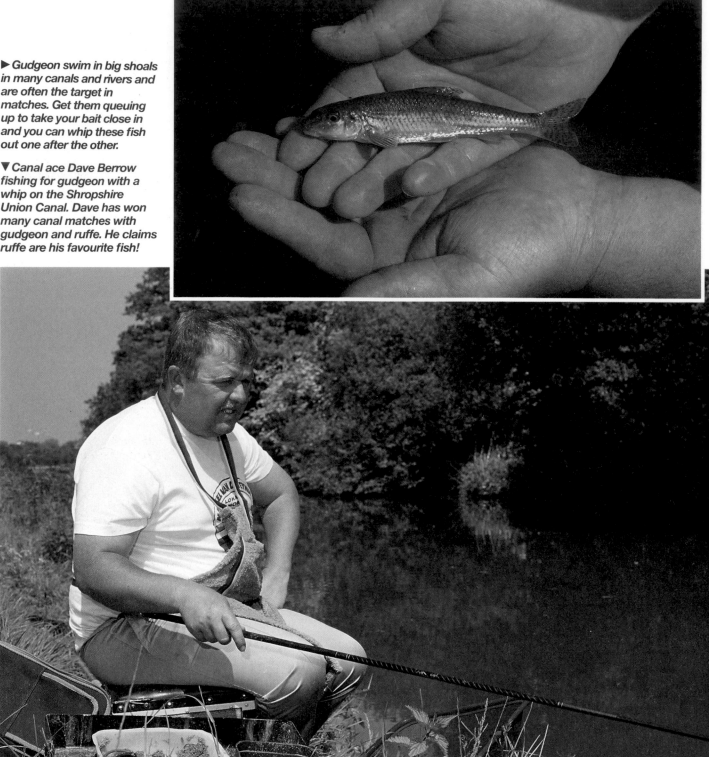

► *Gudgeon swim in big shoals in many canals and rivers and are often the target in matches. Get them queuing up to take your bait close in and you can whip these fish out one after the other.*

▼ *Canal ace Dave Berrow fishing for gudgeon with a whip on the Shropshire Union Canal. Dave has won many canal matches with gudgeon and ruffe. He claims ruffe are his favourite fish!*

spread your Styls all the way from float to hook. Concentrate them to get the bait into the feeding area quickly.

Casting with a whip

When fishing with an Olivette, the bulk of the casting weight is in one place on the line, so an underhand swing is all you need. Casting this way is extremely fast and accurate and, unlike an overhead cast with this sort of rig, makes little splash.

When using an on-the-drop rig, the weight is spread along the line so you need some force to cast it. An overhead cast using the flexibility of the whip lays the rig on the surface in a straight line.

Whip rewards

Remember that the whole point of the whip is to catch fish quickly. Keep thinking how to improve your catch rate. A change of a centimetre or two to your depth or a slight adjustment to your feeding pattern can make a big difference to your final bag. Catching a lot of small fish requires a great deal of hard work, thought and concentration. Get it right and the results can be spectacular.

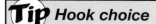

Tip Hook choice

Dace and skimmers are notorious for slipping the hook so use microbarbed hooks for these fish.

For other fish, barbless hooks save time. They allow you to bait up quickly without damaging the bait, and to unhook quickly without hurting the mouth of the fish.

Long pole/short-lining on still waters

This method can work so well for roach, skimmers and bream that it may become addictive, warns Tri-Cast Barnsley match star Alan Scotthorne.

▼ *Alan Scotthorne practising what he preaches – fishing the long pole/short line. In 1990 he used the method to win the first European Supercup.*

When roach, skimmers and bream are the target on still waters, drains and slow rivers, long pole/short-lining can be unbeatable, simply because it allows such good bait presentation.

Poles apart

Ideally you need two poles: one very light, the other as stiff as possible.

Light When fishing with a light rig (0.15-0.75g) in fairly shallow water (up to say 1.5m/5ft) at distances up to 12m (39ft), a very light pole is best as it allows you to manoeuvre the rig more delicately.

Stiff With heavier rigs in deeper water at distances up to 14m (46ft) you need the stiffest pole you can get because it takes a much smarter strike to set the hook.

Flick-tip or elastic?

You rarely see British anglers using flick-tips for long pole/short line work – but for roach to 8oz (230g) and skimmers to 2lb (0.9kg) a flick-tip is much more positive than elastic for hooking the fish and landing them quickly.

The only drawback with flick-tips is that they don't cope very well with bigger fish on fine line and small hooks. Where roach over 8oz (230g) and bream of more than 2lb (0.9kg) predominate, or where such bonus fish are a strong possibility, you're better off using elastic.

Get the elastic right

Many anglers use far too much elastic inside their poles. Years ago, before the advent of internal elastic, you used a crook at the end of your pole, with 15-30cm (6-12in) of elastic attached to it. This handled fish with no problems, so why go over the top with yards of internal elastic that hinders hooking, stretches all over the place and makes landing fish difficult?

You rarely need more than 45cm (18in) of elastic. Tighten it up by about 8cm (3in) so that it doesn't hang loose out of the end of your pole after you catch your first sizeable fish.

It's no good using light elastic with a 2g float in 3.5m (12ft) of water – it won't set the

Alan's favourite floats

▶ *These are the type of floats that Alan uses. The more bulbous sort (1) is for Olivette rigs. The slimmer kind (2) is for Styl rigs.*

1

2

Alan's basic rigs

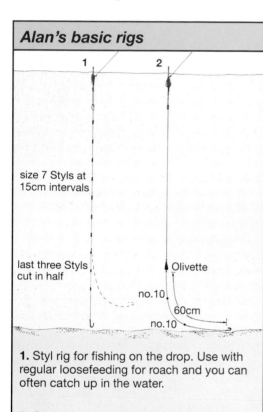

size 7 Styls at 15cm intervals

last three Styls cut in half

Olivette

no.10

60cm

no.10

1

2

1. Styl rig for fishing on the drop. Use with regular loosefeeding for roach and you can often catch up in the water.

2. Olivette rig for fishing on and near the bottom. It can work very well when fishing with groundbait for skimmers and bream.

hook properly. Equally, it's no good using heavy elastic when fishing 1m (3ft) deep with a 0.25g float – you just bump fish after fish.

As a guide, when fishing shallow – in, say, the top 1m (3ft) of water – with light floats up to 0.5g or so, use Zim No.3 ('Moyen') elastic or its equivalent.

With floats from 0.75-1.25g in swims up to about 3.5m (12ft) deep, Zim No.4 ('Gros') or its equivalent is adequate.

When stepping up float size for deeper water with a strong tow, use Zim No.6 ('Très Fort') or its equivalent.

▶ *Only a small roach for Alan this time but the elastic is there ready to come into play the next time he hooks into a better fish.*

How Alan attaches a rig to a flick-tip

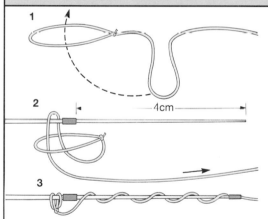

1

2

4cm

3

Glue a small piece of silicone tubing in place 4cm from the end of the flick-tip. Thread a second piece of tubing on to the line. Tie a loop in the line. Pass a second loop through the first (**1**), slip it over the tip and draw it tight behind the glued tubing (**2**). Spiral the line round the tip and trap it with the second piece of tubing (**3**).

▲ *Keep the pole tip low or the fish surfaces too soon – and don't cross hands or you risk jerking the fish off the hook, says Alan.*

the photograph on page 74).

Match the size of the float to the conditions. Say your swim is 2.5-3m (8-10ft) deep and you want to fish the full depth. A 1g float is adequate when there is only a slight surface ripple but in windy conditions you should step up to as much as 2g to combat swell and undertow.

Down the line

Shotting for the two basic types of rig – Olivette and Styl – should be kept simple.
Olivette rigs Two dropper shot below the

From pole to float

Never fish too tight to your float. The more line you can get away with the better. Fish have good eyesight and can see your pole in shallow water if it is too close overhead. Also, the longer the line, the fewer sections of pole you need to unship and so the faster your catch rate. Try not to have less than 1m (3ft) of line from pole tip to float, going up to 2m (6½ft) or even 3m (10ft) if conditions allow.

Floats for the job

The right shape of float for the conditions is essential for good bait presentation. A float that is too slim rides out of the water, but one with too round a body rides with the waves. (Two good basic shapes are shown in

▶ *You can get excellent bait presentation with a pole but it counts for nothing if you don't feed your swim correctly, says Alan.*

▲ *The 1990 European Supercup saw some of the best pole anglers in the world tame bream up to 5lb (2.3kg) on the long pole and short line at Holme Pierrepont. Here another slab hits the net.*

apart do the job well. Towards the hook, use no.7 Styls cut in half to give the hookbait a slower fall.

Hooks for the job

Hooks can be argued about forever. Certainly, when using maggots with the long pole and elastic you lose fewer fish with round bend hooks than crystal bend ones. Perhaps this is because a maggot hangs farther below the point on a round bend hook, allowing deeper penetration.

Playing fish on the pole

Elastic tends to kill the fight of a fish quicker than rod and line so use this to your advantage. Steer the fish away from the shoal, keeping the pole tip low to the surface and pushing the pole back at the same time, then unship the pole to the required length to swing the fish in or net it. Don't raise the pole and bring the fish to the surface until the fish is in netting range. If you get the fish to the surface too early and far out it thrashes about and the hook can bounce out of its mouth.

Olivette are plenty, giving you the option of catching fish on the drop in the last 60cm (2ft) or so of water or presenting a steady bait on the bottom. In good conditions use no.10s as droppers but step these up to no.8s or no.6s when there's a strong bottom tow.
Styl rigs Number 7 Styls spaced 15cm (6in)

▼ *Long pole/short-lining accounted for this impressive net of small roach – the sort of catch that wins many matches every season.*

DAVID SMITH FISHING TACKLE

Fishing the long pole to hand on rivers

Match star Jan Porter is an acknowledged expert at fishing the long pole to hand on rivers. Here he explains how to get the best out of this highly effective method.

When you are able to draw fish up a river swim on an inside line, swapping your stick float rod for a long pole to hand set-up can greatly improve your catch rate. This is especially true when there is a slight downstream breeze, because the pole allows better float control and, therefore, better bait presentation.

If you have never tried it before, fishing a long pole to hand – fishing with the same length of line as length of pole – is a daunting prospect. However, by working up in stages from, say, 7m (23ft), you soon find it relatively easy to fish comfortably and confidently at 11m (36ft).

Conditions musn't be windy, however, otherwise you cannot hope to control your tackle properly. When there's anything more than a breeze, you are better off using a rod and reel set-up.

'Casting' poles

When after roach, dace, skimmers and small chub in fairly open water, the ideal pole for long-lining is a fully telescopic one with a fine, soft flick-tip. Fish up to 3lb (1.4kg) or so *can* be landed with this kind of pole, but it's really best suited for fish up to about 1lb (0.45kg).

Such poles are very popular on the Continent (where they are called 'casting' poles), but they are very hard to obtain in Britain. They are extremely light and have a lovely soft action that is perfect for casting light float rigs.

Really they are like giant whips, and on days when small fish are feeding on the drop and flashing at the bait, they are the perfect tool. Being so light, they are easy to handle and a joy to use.

▼ *Jan fishing a long 'casting' pole to hand. Note how he is using both hands to steady the pole for maximum control over the float and for a smart upwards strike.*

For fish up to 1lb (0.45kg) or so in fairly open water, use Zim No. 2 or 3 (or their equivalents) through the top section only. For bigger fish – chub, usually – in snaggy swims, use anything from Zim No. 4 to 8 (or equivalents) through the top two sections.

Line strength must balance the elastic. With No. 2 or 3 elastic, 1½lb (0.68kg) main line is not too light. With heavier elastic, use at least 2lb (0.9kg) main line. As ever, always use a hooklength that is weaker than the main line.

◄▼ Jan makes it look easy to use a catapult when standing to fish the long pole to hand (left) – but it takes practice. When you're sitting, hold the pole between your legs to leave both hands free for feeding (below).

Generally you use 1½lb (0.68kg) main line with this type of pole – with, of course, a weaker hooklength, so that if you get broken up on a fish or snag you only lose the hooklength, not the whole rig.

Poles apart

Assuming you can't get hold of a 'casting' pole, you can still successfully fish to hand with a take-apart pole with internal elastic – and because of the elastic, you can use it for fish of all sizes up to around 4lb (1.8kg).

The nature of the swim and the size of fish you expect dictate the strength of elastic to use, and whether to have it running through just the top section of the pole or through the top two sections.

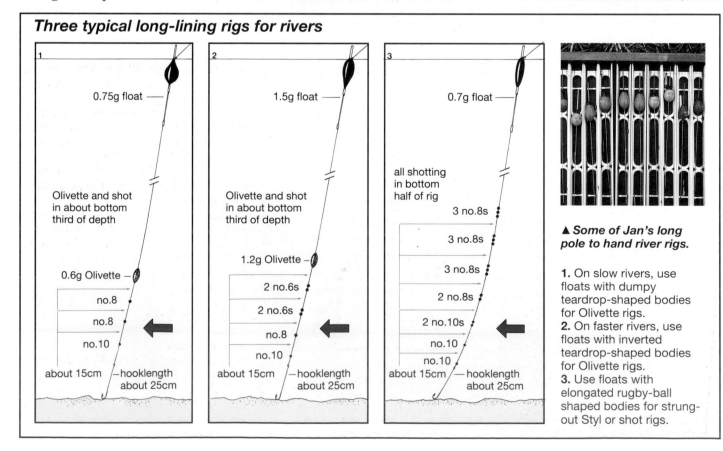

Three typical long-lining rigs for rivers

1
0.75g float

Olivette and shot in about bottom third of depth

0.6g Olivette

no.8
no.8
no.10

about 15cm — hooklength about 25cm

2
1.5g float

Olivette and shot in about bottom third of depth

1.2g Olivette

2 no.6s
2 no.6s
no.8
no.10

about 15cm — hooklength about 25cm

3
0.7g float

all shotting in bottom half of rig

3 no.8s
3 no.8s
3 no.8s
2 no.8s
2 no.10s
no.10
no.10

about 15cm — hooklength about 25cm

▲ *Some of Jan's long pole to hand river rigs.*

1. On slow rivers, use floats with dumpy teardrop-shaped bodies for Olivette rigs.
2. On faster rivers, use floats with inverted teardrop-shaped bodies for Olivette rigs.
3. Use floats with elongated rugby-ball shaped bodies for strung-out Styl or shot rigs.

The ideal take-apart pole for this method has put-in rather than put-over joints, as such a pole tends to be much slimmer, and therefore more manageable.

Put-in joints don't locate as smoothly as put-overs, but this doesn't matter when long-lining because it isn't necessary for you to unship the pole each time you catch a fish or rebait the hook.

▲ Another way of holding a long pole when standing is two-handed, with the butt of the pole jammed into the pit of your stomach.

◄ Fishing the long pole to hand can give you the good bait presentation needed to tempt roach like this.

⚠ Safety code for poles

● Before choosing a swim, remember to check first that there are no cables overhead. There have been several tragic accidents in recent years, and this simple procedure could save you from serious injury or death. Even if you think the cables are only telephone wires, it just isn't worth the risk – fish elsewhere!
● Never use any carbon fibre rod or pole *anywhere* in very thundery weather, because of the danger of being struck by lightning.

◄ When standing, netting a fish is easier if you lower the pole butt between your legs. This also leaves both hands free for unhooking.

Floats and rigs

Sometimes you can catch on the drop; at other times the fish want the bait near the bottom. To cover both eventualities, set up two rigs: one with an Olivette (accounting for around 75% of the total loading) plus a few droppers; the other with shot or Styls strung out shirt-button fashion.

Usually it pays to fish with the float very slightly overshotted and held back to slow the bait slightly.

Olivette rigs On slow rivers such as the Warwickshire Avon, use 0.5-1g floats with dumpy teardrop-shaped bodies. On faster rivers like the Trent, use 0.5-3g floats with dumpy inverted teardrop-shaped bodies.

Shot or Styl rigs On both fast and slow rivers, use 0.5-0.7g floats with elongated rugby ball-shaped bodies.

Pole prowess

It's very important to be comfortable when fishing a long pole to hand, otherwise you won't fish effectively. Depending on the nature of your peg, you sometimes feel most comfortable – and fish most effectively – standing rather than sitting.

▼ *Nice and easy does it... Jan about to net a river roach that fell for long-lining pole tactics.*

The biggest mistake you can make is trying to fish too far out. Let's assume you are fishing 8m (26ft) to hand.

If you try to fish 8m (26ft) out, your float can only run down the swim for a few feet before it starts to arc in towards the bank across the line of feed, presenting the bait unnaturally. It's much better to fish some 4-5m (13-16ft) out, so you can run the float and bait down the swim in line with the feed for much farther.

Feed them up

In fast rivers it pays to feed slightly upstream, to concentrate the fish about halfway down the swim, within easy reach. In a match, though, don't feed too far upstream, or you risk losing your fish to the angler on the next peg up! Every now and then, drop the float in upstream too – it's surprising how often you can pick up a fish in front of you, ahead of the main shoal.

Casting techniques

Telescopic 'casting' poles are flexible and relatively easy to cast with. Take-apart poles are much stiffer, which makes them much harder to cast with. Some anglers have even snapped their take-apart poles when trying to cast with them, but this shouldn't happen to yours as long as you don't try long-lining with it when it's windy, and you don't try to force your rig out with a great 'whoosh'.

The overhead cast is easiest. Hold the pole vertically in front of you, wait until the float rig is hanging still, then smoothly push the pole forward so the rig loops out over the water. This is usually the best

▲ *Jan unhooks a small roach caught on long-lining pole tactics. As when feeding the swim, hold the pole between your legs.*

method to use with Olivette rigs.

The underarm cast is more difficult. It requires a deft flick of the pole at just the right moment to punch the float rig out. This is usually the best technique to use with Styl rigs.

If you cannot master either of these techniques, you can sometimes get away with swinging the rig out sideways.

CHAPTER TWO
BAITS
AND LURES

Whites, pinkies and squatts

Almost all species and sizes of fish take maggots. They're the matchman's favourite bait and first choice for beginners and pleasure anglers.

Three kinds of maggots are sold, in their natural state or dyed various colours:

Large whites – the larvae of bluebottles – are the most widely used, as both hookbait and feed. They are usually sold in maize meal, and sometimes bran or sawdust.

Large whites can be loose fed accurately by hand up to 10m (11yd) or so, but for greater distances up to about 25m (27yd), or when there's a facing wind, you need to use a catapult or mix them in groundbait.

Pinkies – the larvae of greenbottles – are small, pinkish maggots. They too are usually sold in maize meal.

Pinkies are good as hookbait for small fish at all times and for larger fish when bites are shy and hard to come by, especially in winter. Being smaller than large whites they are less likely to overfeed the fish. They are livelier, too, and wriggle well on all but the coldest days.

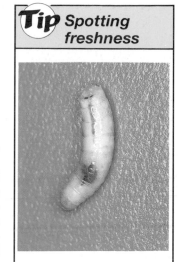

When very fresh, large whites have obvious black spots of food inside them; the bigger the spot, the fresher the maggot.

Large whites are particularly suitable for running water. Being about 13mm (¹/₂ in) long and 3mm (¹/₈ in) thick they are big enough to be seen easily by the fish and heavy enough when fed into the water to reach bottom quickly.

Pinkies are small, light maggots best suited to canals, still waters and slow-moving rivers. When fed into still or slow water they fall slowly and enticingly, but are too easily swept away by fast currents.

Squatts are used mainly as feed on canals, still waters and slow-moving rivers, especially for bream. Being slow moving as well as very small, they can be packed into balls of groundbait in larger quantities than large whites or pinkies without them breaking up in mid-air.

▶ *This small lake roach fell to a single maggot, waggler fished on a size 21 hook early in the season.*

Pinkies also make good feed but they are too small to be accurately loose fed as far as large whites.

Being lively, pinkies tend to burrow out of sight into the bottom when fed into the swim. So feed them little and often to attract fish as they fall through the water.

Squatts – the larvae of houseflies – are smaller still. They are usually sold in slightly dampened red sand.

Squatts are traditionally used as feed and only tried on the hook when all else has failed. Because squatts are sluggish, they stay on the bottom in full view when fed into the swim. This makes them good for holding passing fish, especially bream.

Buying and storing

Maggots aren't cheap but, with care, fresh large whites and pinkies can be kept in good condition for two or three weeks. Squatts unfortunately don't usually keep for more than a week.

Fresh maggots are lively and soft to the touch, not leathery. Tough, old maggots are only good in very cold water, which makes fresh maggots stretch and die. With pinkies you want to see only a slight tinge of pink; a

strong tinge is a sure sign of old age.

Maggots are sold in pint and half-pint measures. They are best kept in purpose-made plastic bait boxes with perforated lids that let the maggots breathe. Keep the boxes clean and dry and the holes in the lids unclogged. To prevent spillage, the boxes should ideally only be filled halfway – so for half a pint of maggots use a one-pint box.

The best place for storing maggots is a fridge. Failing that, choose a cool, dark, well ventilated place such as a garage floor, but bear in mind that they won't keep as long – only a week at most in summer, a bit longer in winter.

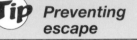

Tip **Preventing escape**

All maggots, but especially pinkies, are excellent climbers when wet, so shield them with your brolly when it rains. If they do get a bit wet, make sure you shut their bait box lids properly when you pack up, and transfer them to dry maize meal when you get home.

Cleaning large whites and pinkies

Large whites and pinkies should be cleaned at least once a week to reduce sweating and smell, so making them more palatable to fish. Squatts are best left in their original sand, though this may need slight dampening occasionally.

1 To clean large whites you need: a 3mm (⅛in) riddle; a container to fit under the riddle; some clean, dry maize meal; a clean, dry bait box. For pinkies use a 1.5mm (¹⁄₁₆in) riddle.

2 Tip the maggots on to the riddle, quickly shake it until all the old maize meal, sawdust or bran has fallen through, then immediately place it over the container.

3 After a few minutes the maggots wriggle through, leaving the dead skins and rubbish behind.

4 Transfer the maggots from the container to the clean bait box. Finally, add half a cup of maize meal per pint of maggots.

Hooked on maggots

Maggots in their uncoloured, unflavoured form are often highly successful but a bright, enticingly flavoured bait will sometimes give you the edge.

hempseed

special balance

aniseed

super fruit

nut

It's obviously important when fishing that the fish can see the bait and that they like what they see. For example, when fishing on murky waters a plain maggot may be hardly visible, whereas a bright red or yellow specimen may show up clearly. There are several things you can do to maggots to enhance their appeal.

Flavourings

Some anglers claim to have great success with flavoured maggots, arguing that fish prefer some tastes and smells to others. Whether true or not, unclean maggots have a strong smell of ammonia which certainly seems to put the fish off. This smell is greatly reduced by cleaning. Any remaining odour can be masked with flavourings. Handling maggots can also leave an off- putting smell, especially when handled by smokers who taint the bait with nicotine. These effects, too, can be reduced by using flavourings.

But how do you know which smells will be appealing to fish? Some anglers argue that sweet flavours – like vanilla – are best during the warm months and spicy ones – like turmeric – are best during the winter. The only way to find out which flavours suit your kind of fishing is to experiment.

Tackle shops stock a bewildering range of flavourings in little bottles and atomizers. On the whole these are used by carp anglers to flavour boilies but on

vanilla flavouring

bream attractor

bloodworm flavouring

roach attractor

waters where these flavourings have been introduced, anglers have found that other species (such as roach and bream, for example) sometimes show a preference for them. Flavourings in powder form that are specially formulated for adding to loose feed and groundbait are available. Popular ones are: vanilla, caramel, coriander and aniseed. Clean the bait,

▲ *All sorts of flavourings are available in liquid or powder form and some of them smell good enough to eat. But do the fish like them? There is only one way to find out which suits your fishing: experiment.*

◄ *Red, bronze, yellow and the humble white are all successful colours. A colour change often works when the going is tough. A catapult with a mesh pouch is ideal for firing out a few loose offerings each cast.*

Hooking maggots

The aim is to present a lively bait. To avoid bursting the maggot, choose a fine or medium wire, barbless or microbarb hook and gently nick the maggot just under the flap of skin at the blunt end. A crystal pattern hook is best as the maggot hangs directly beneath the point, helping you hook more fish. As a general principle, the choice of hook size depends on bait size, and the bait size depends on the size and species of fish you are hoping to catch.

Method for making maggots float

To make maggots float, the bait should be fresh – no more than three days old.

1 Put about 6mm (¼ in) water into a bait container to just cover the bottom.

2 Add a palmful of maggots. Then put the lid on so the maggots can't crawl out.

3 Leave them soaking for 20 minutes to absorb enough water to float.

then riddle off any maize or bran before sprinkling on the flavouring, or else the aroma and flavour will be absorbed by the cereal. Two teaspoonfuls are enough for a pint of maggots.

Colouring

Maggots can be dyed various colours. The most usual are yellow, bronze and red. Other maggots you may come across are green and blue, and the 'discos' in fluorescent orange, yellow and pink.

Anglers can dye their own maggots but the dye that is currently available does not 'take' so well and is easily washed off. It is better to buy ready coloured maggots. These have had the dye introduced during breeding, at the 'feed' stage, so the maggot is coloured internally.

Yellow and bronze During the Seventies, yellow and bronze were popular with matchmen (particularly on the Trent). It was then found that the particular dye used to colour these maggots causes cancer, so a ban was imposed on all such dyes. Safe alternatives have been found and yellow and bronze are widely used again.

Fish are able to differentiate between colours, and certain species do seem to prefer certain colours. Anglers have used yellow and bronze maggots to take large bags of roach, chub and dace.

Red One of the deadliest baits in the matchman's armoury is the bloodworm – the small red larvae of the midge. This highly effective, but controversial, bait has been banned at many venues. Anglers have tried to imitate it by using red squatts. Whether the fish are taken in by the substitution is doubtful, but the bait has certainly been used with considerable success for bream.

Large red maggots, red pinkies and red squatts are good for taking perch and carp, and tench sometimes show a preference for a red maggot.

Sinkers and floaters

The rate at which a maggot sinks through the water is an important factor in loose feeding. In some situations – when loose feeding on fast-flowing rivers, for example – you need to get the bait down quickly. At other times a slow sinking bait is best.

Whether your maggots are slow or fast sinkers will depend on their diet. Maggots which have been raised on meat sink quicker than those fed on fish (which have a higher water content). Most commercially bred maggots are fed meat offal, but it is worth asking your dealer what type he stocks.

Both fish-fed and meat-fed maggots can be made to float (see above right). Floating maggots can be fished on the surface to take surface feeding fish like carp, bleak, dace and chub.

Floaters can also be used to slow down the fall of the hookbait. When the bait is falling through the last foot or so of the water, it is important that it should look as natural as possible. The extra weight of even a small hook is enough to make a bait sink faster than your loose feed. You can counteract this by using a maggot that has been turned into a floater.

Bait, hook size and hooklength strength

Bait	Hooksize	Hooklength
Single large white	22 or 20	1-1½lb (0.45-0.68kg)
Two large whites	20 or 18	1-1½lb (0.45-0.68kg)
Three large whites	16 or 14	2-3lb (0.9-1.36kg)
Single pinkie	22	12oz-1lb (0.34-0.45kg)
Two pinkies	22 or 20	12oz-1lb (0.34-0.45kg)
Three pinkies	20 or 18	1-1½lb (0.45-0.68kg)
Single squatt	24 or 22	12oz-1lb (0.34-0.45kg)
Two squatts	22	12oz-1lb (0.34-0.45kg)
Three squatts	20	1-1½lb (0.45-0.68kg)

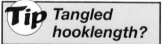

Tip Tangled hooklength?

With two or three maggots on the hook you sometimes find that the bait spins like a propeller on the retrieve, twisting and tangling the hooklength. This is especially common with fast-retrieve reels and on running water.

You might find you can solve this problem by simply winding in more slowly. Alternatively, some anglers find that hooking one maggot in the pointed end and the other in the blunt end can help to prevent twisting.

Experiment to see which works best for you.

Caster gold

**Unlike maggots, casters don't wriggle.
Nevertheless, fish find this crunchy, golden,
protein-packed bait irresistible.**

The caster on the left is an example of a good caster – plump and of a uniform colour. The one on the right is stunted, has rings around the body and probably comes from a much smaller maggot.

Buy a pint of maggots, leave them in a bait box for a few days and they'll start to pupate – to change to the next stage before becoming adult flies. At this stage the insects are known as 'chrysalids' or 'pupae'. Anglers call them 'casters'. Casters are excellent for quality roach, big bream, chub, barbel, tench, carp and even big perch, and they often out-fish maggots.

A fresh caster from a white maggot is creamy coloured but gradually darkens through pale orange, orange-brown, dark brown and finally black before hatching into a fly. During this change the shell becomes crisper and the caster less dense. This means that a freshly turned caster is a soft sinker while one that is about halfway through its development is a crunchy floater. Both sinkers and floaters are useful.

Turning your own

Good quality casters should be fresh, big and contain no skins, dead maggots or rubbish. If you buy them the quality varies from one shop to another, but it is generally pretty poor compared to casters turned at home. It isn't difficult to turn your own; all it takes is a bit of planning.

Time and temperature If you want some casters for a match or pleasure session at the weekend, when should you buy the maggots?

Take temperature into account: the warmer it is, the quicker they turn. In summer it is easier – you can get a good yield by keeping maggots in a garden shed – but in winter it is more difficult and you may need to bring them into a heated room.

As a rough guide, in summer buy the maggots about five or six days in advance. In winter allow at least eight to ten days. But bear in mind the stage the maggots are at when you get them. The times above are for **fresh** maggots – ones which still have the black feed spot clearly visible. Sometimes maggots are sold at a more advanced stage. In this condition they start to turn sooner and some tackle shops sell them as 'caster maggots'. These can be useful if you need casters in a hurry. Otherwise, get fresh bait – it gives you more control over quality.

Quality and quantity It is impossible to get big casters from small maggots. Use the biggest and best maggots you can find. Remember that you never achieve a 100% yield – two pints of casters from three pints of maggots is typical. The yield is higher when maggots are turned very slowly – ideally in a fridge. Unless you need casters urgently and have to turn them very quickly you should not try to force them as this produces inferior casters.

Sawdust Riddle the maggots and put them in some fine, slightly dampened sawdust in a shallow tray. Under no circumstances allow them to 'sweat' (go wet and slimy). If they do then the result is very small, crinkly casters which are next to useless. It is better to keep the maggots in a lid-less container on a stone floor. Provided they don't get wet

▼ *Most of these casters are floaters. It is not a good idea to feed the swim with them because the wind and current disperse them, taking the fish away. But fished as bait on the hook they are excellent.*

► *Find a riddle that rests in the top of a bowl. Don't fill it – this makes it harder for the maggots to get through. Separate maggots from casters in several stages.*

or hot they won't escape. If they do get wet they'll crawl up the sides of the container and on to the floor.

Riddling Once the maggots turn you need to separate the casters from the maggots. Do this by tipping maggots and casters on to a riddle with holes large enough for the maggots to force themselves through. The casters are left behind on the riddle. It is important to use the right gauge of mesh. If it is too fine the maggots have difficulty getting through, too coarse and the casters drop through with the maggots.

In the early stages riddle them once a day, but as the number of casters increases

Hooking a caster – two methods

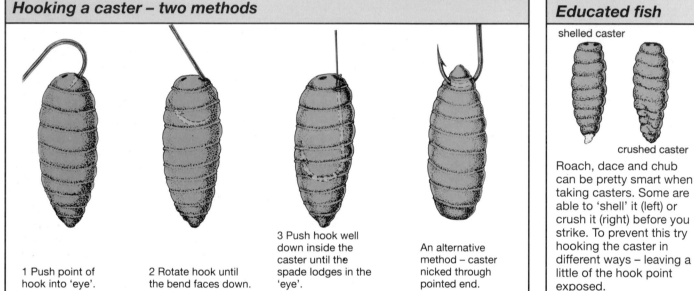

1 Push point of hook into 'eye'.

2 Rotate hook until the bend faces down.

3 Push hook well down inside the caster until the spade lodges in the 'eye'.

An alternative method – caster nicked through pointed end.

Educated fish

shelled caster

crushed caster

Roach, dace and chub can be pretty smart when taking casters. Some are able to 'shell' it (left) or crush it (right) before you strike. To prevent this try hooking the caster in different ways – leaving a little of the hook point exposed.

riddle them two or three times a day.

Keeping them cool When the first few batches of casters come off, put them into a plastic bag, leaving plenty of air. Lightly knot it and put it in a very cool place. At this stage the casters are sinkers. By keeping them cool you retard their development and stop them from becoming floaters. A fridge is ideal for this and, if you are to produce a pint or more of casters, or if the weather is hot, it is essential.

Don't put a lot of casters into an air-tight bag because even in the fridge casters still 'breathe'. Once they have used up all the air they develop 'burn' marks – ugly brown stripes – and may die.

Washing When you are ready to use the casters take them out of the bag, put them in a sieve and swill them under the cold tap. You can sort out the floaters by putting the casters into a bowl of water and skimming the floaters off. When fished on the hook floaters help to cancel out the weight of the hook and make the bait behave more naturally, so they are worth saving.

In hot weather sinkers turn to floaters within a couple of hours if they are exposed to the full force of the sun. You can prevent this by keeping them in a little water.

▼ *With casters, you may have to wait for the bites but a catch like these roach makes it well worth while.*

Lobs, reds and brandlings

Worms are one of the most deadly, versatile and readily obtainable baits and yet they are often neglected in favour of more 'fashionable' baits.

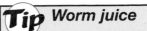

Tip Worm juice

Nipping off the end of the worm after hooking it will allow its attractive juices to flow into the water more quickly.

lobworm   brandling   redworm

◀ *Many anglers spurn the worm as an unfashionable bait. But from the biggest lobworm (far left) to the smaller brandling (left), to the red worm (above), worms catch fish. So don't neglect them.*

▶ *When first extracted from their tunnels lobs tend to be a bit slimy. Putting them into moss or grass cuttings will leave them clean and lively.*

▶ *Washing-up gloves are handy for easing lobs out of their holes. Hang on to the worm and wait until it contracts – it will pull itself out of the hole.*

During the summer months worms are a good bait for taking specimens; the matchman will often be pleasantly surprised by the bonus fish which a worm has produced. When the going gets tough, worms come into their own. On flooded rivers they often score when more conventional baits (such as maggots) have failed.

Types of worm

The three main types are: lobworms, brandlings and redworms.

Lobworms The big fat worm which you will have seen having a tug o' war with the bird in your back garden is the lobworm. It is a light reddish-brown and its tail is flatter and slightly broader than the rest of its body. These worms vary in length from 5 - 8cm (2 - 3in) to the real 'snakes' of 15 - 18cm (6 - 7in) but their average size is 13 - 15cm (5 - 6in). Lobs can be dug from the garden or collected from a wet lawn at night. Tread lightly, using a torch with a weak beam; lobworms are highly sensitive to bright light and vibrations.

You can keep lobs in the soil in which they were found or, better still, in sphagnum moss or grass cuttings. This cleans and toughens the worm's skin – making it more attractive to the fish – and helps it to stay on the hook better. Lobs can also be kept in

damp leafmould or damp newspaper.

Brandlings These have a red skin, which is softer than the lobworm's, and average 10 – 13cm (4 – 5in) in length with a series of yellow rings around the body. They are smaller than the lobworm.

When hooked, an unpleasant yellowish body fluid is released but this is only off-putting for the angler, not the fish.

Tackle shops sell pots of brandlings but they can be gathered quite easily from manure and compost heaps. Keep them in their original compost or manure and they'll stay lively for weeks.

Redworms These are deep red in colour – similar to the brandling but without the rings. They are the smallest of the three types of worm, growing up to about 5 – 8cm (2 – 3in), and are a favourite with the matchman. A single offering on a small hook, either by itself or as a 'cocktail' with caster or pinkie, is a most attractive bait for bream and perch.

This worm is fond of pig manure and can be found living alongside the brandling. Be sure to collect plenty – redworms make an excellent attractor when chopped and added to groundbait. Keep either in the substance in which they were found or in leafmould.

Storing the worms

All worms should be stored in a well ventilated box, in a cool place. Keep them damp but not wet (an atomizer is useful for applying a fine spray). Check them regularly and remove any dead or damaged worms to prevent contamination. Don't store them for longer than about two weeks.

Presentation

Worm will catch all species. Big tench, carp, chub and barbel are partial to a lob. These fish have big mouths so do not be afraid to use a big bait. Hook size depends on bait size. A bunch of two or three lobs on a size 4 or 6 hook, or a single offering on a 6, 8 or 10 is about right. Use a lob tail on a 14 or 16 to

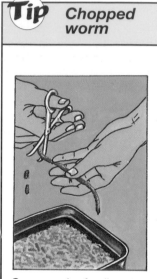

◄ You might wonder whether a fish could swallow such a mouthful, but to large-mouthed fish such as barbel, carp and chub, baits like this are most appealing.

tempt roach, perch and eels.

Big bream can often be taken on a brandling or redworm when other baits have failed, and perch love these smaller worms. Present doubles on a size 14 or 16 and singles on an 18.

Hooking It is the worm's attractive wiggle and appealing scent that make it effective. Bear this in mind when hooking it. A common mistake is to try to 'staple' a worm to a hook that is too small by piercing it several times; this results in a lifeless lump of insipid looking 'worm meat'. After a couple of casts the bait tears as the hook pulls out, and soon becomes useless. Even if a fish is desperate enough to take a bait in this condition, it is likely that you will miss the bite because the hook will not be in the correct place.

Whether presenting whole baits, part baits or cocktails, hook the worm with great care, threading it on to the hook rather than piercing it.

Tip **Chopped worm**

Carry a pair of nail scissors for cutting up the worms. Chopped worms make an excellent attractor when added to groundbait.

▼ This big bream is typical of the kind of fish that often falls to a worm bait when other baits have failed. It always pays to take a few worms with you.

▲ Redworms are very lively, and when fished with a caster on a small hook, they make a good bait for skimmer and 'slab' bream – particularly during the winter months.

Bloodworm and joker

The combination of bloodworm on the hook and joker as feed can bring huge bags of roach and bream. Dave Berrow recommends that you give them a go.

B loodworm and joker have the reputation of being an effective part of the matchman's armoury, but of little interest to the ordinary angler. While there is some truth in this, it does not do justice to two of the most effective of all natural baits. They are unbeatable in a match because they can attract and catch loads of small fish when the going is very hard. But used properly, there is no better combination for catching large numbers of bream, and other big species such as carp and tench.

Relative differences

Both bloodworm and joker are the larvae of closely related two-winged flies. Bloodworms become non-biting midges (buzzers) and jokers turn into gnats. They are both aquatic and live in the bottom sludge. Bloodworms only live in still, sometimes stagnant water, lightly polluted by, for example, farm run-off. Jokers, on the other hand, are only found in running water lightly polluted with sewage.

Both are worm-like and usually red, though you may come across other colours from time to time. Bloodworms tend to be sluggish and grow up to ¾in (19mm) long. Jokers are smaller, only reaching ⅓in (8mm), but they are much livelier. It is these variations that make their uses in fishing so different and so complementary. Bloodworm, being bigger, are an excellent hookbait, whereas jokers, which dart around in water, are an unbeatable fish attractor, holding fish in a swim like magic.

Untangling the mess

Neat (pure) bloodworm and joker form a tight ball from which it's almost impossible to extract single specimens.

Bloodworms are going to be your hookbait, so you need to separate them. This is done by dropping the tight cluster on to some finely sieved peat or compost (one pint of bloodworms needs about half a pint of peat). The bloodworms instantly begin to separate and crawl into the peat.

▲ *One of the best bream or roach hookbaits you could wish for, bloodworm fish best when hooked properly. Hook them gently in the head segment and fish them half an inch off the bottom, so their tails touch the mud.*

▼ *The matchman's best friend – bloodworm have become popular in Britain only fairly recently. Here at the 1990 European Supercup, it was easily the most commonly used bait.*

◄ *Neat bloodworm seen highly magnified don't look like they'd be all that difficult to separate – but they certainly are. Fortunately, they do all the hard work themselves – all you have to do is add finely sieved peat and wait.*

► *Bloodworm after they've been separated (above), and a load of neat joker (below). Without leem, neat joker form a sticky, compact ball. Keep a bag of it handy to sprinkle over them just before use.*

After about five minutes, put the mixture on to a sheet of damp newspaper, and fold it carefully so they cannot escape. Fold another sheet over the first but don't wrap them up tightly or you may kill them. Store the parcel in a cool place in winter (don't let them freeze) and in the fridge (at 34-36°F/1.1-2.2°C) in summer. You can keep them for up to a week this way.

Jokers are feed rather than hookbait, so separating them is not so important. Getting them into a state which the fish find irresistible is what counts. However, there is still some separating to be done – unless you fancy using the whole expensive ball at once. A substance called leem (or leam), made of finely ground clay, is perfect for separating jokers. Sprinkle it over your jokers, a teaspoonful at a time, until they have separated. They mustn't be too damp at this stage or the leem clogs up, which can make them even stickier.

In the summer you can now add the mixture to your groundbait – they mix in far more

evenly when separated. You can also use finely sieved earth from a mole hill instead of the leem. This acts both as a separator and as groundbait, adding colour to the water. In either case your jokers are now ready for use.

In winter, fish respond far less to groundbait, so it is better to loosefeed. Simply take some of the separated jokers, dampen them and roll them into a ball. The damp clay binds them together in a perfect loosefeeding ball. Store them in newspaper as you do bloodworm, though when neat they die more quickly. Never keep them in bait boxes as they will suffocate.

▲ *Leem is essential for loosefeeding jokers. Sprinkle a couple of teaspoons of it over the jokers and mix by hand. In about five minutes they should all have separated out.*

Deadly bloodworm

A size 20 or 22 fine wire hook is just right for bloodworm. Hook them in the head (which is the swollen greenish end, not the branched end), but be careful as they are pretty fragile. They are deadly fished either on the drop in a cloud of jokers and groundbait, or hard on the bottom with a groundbait and joker carpet.

To take advantage of joker, you don't actually need bloodworm on the hook. Such is their fish-holding power, they'll keep them biting and in your swim, almost whatever the hookbait.

▼ *A small ball of joker is easy to roll once you've added the leem, making it perfect for loosefeeding in the depths of winter.*

Tip Change tactics

● Sooner or later when fishing bloodworm you'll start to miss bites. When this happens, either hook the bloodworm a few segments below the head, or change to joker, fished about 8in (20cm) off the bottom. Both seem to do the trick and changing to joker may help sort out the bigger fish.

● In winter when it's very cold it sometimes pays to use joker as hookbait. They are much livelier and can take fish all day.

Seeds of success

Cheap, clean and easy to prepare, hempseed is a superb summer hookbait for roach and an excellent attractor for dace, chub, barbel, tench and carp.

Tip **Black & white**

Add a teaspoon of baking powder (bicarbonate of soda) to the water before cooking hemp. It turns the seeds a uniform black, so the white shoots show more clearly.

▲ *The most economical way to buy hemp is raw and in bulk. Raw hemp lasts almost indefinitely if it is stored correctly. Keep it in airtight bags in a dark, dry place away from mice.*

Hemp was introduced to British coarse fishing by Belgian refugees during World War I. Based in London, they used it to catch large numbers of good-sized roach from the tidal Thames.

By the 1930s, hemp was so popular and successful throughout the country that many angling clubs banned it. Some people said it drugged roach into a feeding frenzy, others that it took root and grew under-water! Fortunately, common sense pre-vailed and there are now very few places where hemp is banned.

Preparing hemp

You can buy hemp ready cooked from most tackle shops, but it is much cheaper to buy it raw and prepare it yourself.

Simply put about four parts water and one part raw hemp in a saucepan. Bring to the boil. Then turn down the heat and leave it to simmer. After about half an hour the seeds will start to split, and white shoots emerge from many of them.

Take the saucepan off the heat and strain off the water into a container. Keep the oily, hemp-flavoured water to use the next time you mix groundbait.

Hold the strainer under a running cold tap for a minute or so to cool the hemp and prevent further cooking. If you cook hemp for too long it splits open too far and becomes too soft to stay on the hook.

Stored in the fridge in an airtight con-tainer, cooked hemp stays fresh for up to a week or so. Cooked hemp also freezes well, allowing you to prepare batches in advance and to keep whatever you have left at the end of each outing. Use airtight polythene bags for freezing.

Fishing with hemp

Once cooked, hemp is ready to use and needs no further preparation at the water-side. The only thing you have to remember is to put it in plenty of water at the start of the day, because it floats if allowed to

---

Cooking hempseed

Don't overfill the saucepan when cooking hemp, but make sure there is enough water or it will boil dry. And open a window, or the whole house will smell of boiled hemp!

When cooked, most of the seeds split open slightly and white shoots sprout from many. Squeeze a few with your fingers – they should feel firm, not mushy, as they crush.

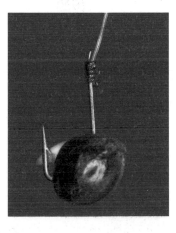

▲ *Insert only the bend of the hook into the split. If you bury the point it sticks in the shell on the strike. Use a 3mm (⅛in) maggot riddle to separate the largest seeds for the hook.*

▲ *When after tench, carp and barbel, try tying a couple of short pieces of dental floss to the hook, then stick on as many seeds as you like with instant glue.*

▼ *You may have to wait a while for your first bite when fishing with hemp for roach, but persevere and you could be rewarded with a bumper catch of big redfins.*

dry out – and you want it to sink.

Roach Hemp is a supreme summer and autumn hookbait for floatfishing for roach, attracting bites on the hottest of days when other baits fail. For some reason it rarely works as a hookbait in winter, though it still pays to feed it then.

Use a single seed on a fine wire 18 or 16 hook. Squeeze the seed gently to open the split and insert the bend of the hook, leaving the point exposed.

To prevent false bites from roach mistaking split shot down the line for hemp, pair the shot up or use rectangular Styl weights instead.

A pint of hemp is usually enough for a day's roach fishing. Loose feed a dozen grains at most each cast, and be prepared to wait an hour or two for your first bite. When the bites do start, though, they can come every cast, with the fish often rising up in the water to intercept the free offerings.

Many anglers complain that roach bites with hemp are too fast to hit. The secret is to ignore the first fast dips and wait for a more definite bite.

It is worth taking a few tares as a change hookbait as well, as they often attract the bigger roach. Tares are large, brown seeds that swell and soften when cooked, but don't split. To prepare them, soak in cold water for 24 hours to help swell and soften

them before cooking in the same way as hemp. To fish a tare, use a 16 hook nicked through the skin.

Dace and chub Hemp is rarely used on the hook for dace and chub, but it is common to feed it with your chosen hookbait, especially in summer and autumn.

Barbel, tench and carp all love hemp. A large carpet of hemp on the river or lake bed gives off an enticing, oily smell, which attracts the fish into your swim. Once there, the fish become preoccupied with picking up the seeds and stay until they have eaten them all. So top up the swim with more hemp from time to time to hold the fish. On the hook you can either fish 6-12 grains of hemp threaded with a needle on to a hair rig, or stuck to the hair with instant glue. Alternatively, try a larger, more prominent bait such as a piece of luncheon meat.

Ground hemp

It was once thought that fish mistake hemp for freshwater snails. Actually, they simply like the smell and taste of it. This is borne out by the fact that ground hemp is an excellent groundbait additive. Hemp can be bought ready ground, or you can grind it up yourself in a food processor. Half cook it first to soften it so the processor doesn't take too much punishment.

Using tares

You need a bit of confidence to use this bait but once you've caught on it you'll want to use it again and again.

Have you ever fished one of those swims where no matter what you did you couldn't raise a bite? If not, you must be the luckiest angler alive and probably don't need to read this. More than likely, though, you have experienced this frustrating problem – where bait changes, different hook sizes, line, floats, and even rod and reel meet with the same response – nowt! But there is one thing that you may very well not have tried.

The bait is known to pigeon fanciers as the 'pigeon pea'. Anglers prefer to call it the 'tare'- it is in fact a seed. Although it's a rather unlikely looking bait – a bit like a black pea in appearance – on the right day it can resurrect a dead swim.

The time and place

The great secret with tares is to pick the venue and time of year to suit the bait. Although carp, bream and chub certainly like tares, no species seems to get so thoroughly hooked on them as roach. Small roach have mouths that are roughly the same size as a large tare and have difficulty swallowing the bait. Roach above 4oz (113g)

▲ *You can buy tares in their uncooked form from fishing tackle and pet shops. They are bullet hard.*

▼ *Top Trent angler Dave Thomas with the kind of quality catch of roach that you might catch on tares – with a bit of luck!*

Cooking perfect tares

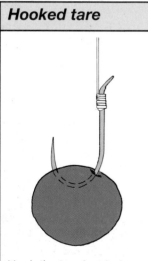

1. You can speed up the process of cooking tares quite considerably by soaking them overnight. Choose an old saucepan so that if anything goes wrong you won't get into so much trouble. Put about 1½ cups of tares in the pan, cover with water, bring to the boil and simmer.

2. It generally takes about 35 minutes to cook them. You can do them a little quicker by turning up the heat but they tend to boil over – making a nasty mess. When they are nearly cooked, pop a teaspoon of bicarbonate of soda in. This turns the tares an attractive purplish-black.

3. Take a couple of tares from the pan and squeeze them to see if they are ready. If they are soft enough, pour them into a sieve and wash in cold tap water. Tares keep well in the freezer so you could cook a few cups of tares in one go and freeze them for using later.

Hooked tare

Hook the tare just below the skin. Leave plenty of the hook exposed so that its hooking power is not impaired.

▶ **To see whether a tare is cooked properly, sqeeze it between finger and thumb. It should squash as you increase the pressure. A tare that does not squash is too hard.**

don't have this problem. As a result, the size of tare-caught roach tends to be pretty good.

Look, then, for a venue with a good head of roach above 4oz (113g). Rivers tend to be better than still waters but there are no hard and fast rules.

Why mid-July, August and early September should be the best time for this bait is not clear, but this is certainly when the best catches are taken. A prolonged spell of hot weather – when water levels are low – seems to be particularly good.

Tare tactics

If you are after roach, fish the tare on light tackle – 1-1½lb (0.45-0.68kg) b.s. line is about right. A hook made of wire that is too fine tends to make the bait slightly awkward to hook – cutting through the soft tare – and may well straighten if you hook a good roach. Go for a slightly thicker, fine wire hook in a size 18 or 16. Step the tackle up for bigger species.

Floatfishing works best for this bait. As a general rule the float should be as light as you can get away with. Often it is more effective to fish tares right under the rod tip with a light float than to cast farther with a bigger one – it is surprising how close roach will come.

This filling bait is best reserved mainly for the hook, using hempseed for the bulk of your loosefeed. Feed little and often with the hemp and just occasionally throw two or three tares in (every three or four casts, say – depending on how the fish are responding.)

It can take a while for tares to work, so be patient. Try another bait while you are waiting – giving the tare an occasional go – but whatever you do keep feeding. When the roach arrive bites can be very fast. But if the roach are really feeding you should be able to hit the bites in spite of their quickness. Get them going and you could be on for 20lb (9kg) or more.

Succulent sweetcorn

Any bait that catches the record British carp can't be bad. Sweet and juicy, the bait in question is sweetcorn – don't leave home without it, says Andy Orme.

Sweetcorn is a superb bait. It's relatively cheap, requires little preparation and you can use it on a wide range of waters, both running and still, for a variety of fish. Roach, bream, tench, carp, chub and barbel are especially fond of it. They home in on its bright yellow colour and sweet smell and find its equally sweet taste very much to their liking.

Brightest and best
Tinned corn is more effective than the frozen or dried corn that you can buy in bulk – it's a much brighter yellow and comes ready-soaked in sugary juice.

▼ *On hard-fished waters fish learn to associate yellow corn with danger. It can then pay to dye it different colours, such as red. You can even change its flavour by soaking it in one of the many concentrated flavourings available.*

Sticky fingers
Sweetcorn is ready to use straight from the tin and indeed it's a simple enough matter to open a tin and tip the contents into a bait box. The drawback is that on the bank your fingers, rod and reel soon get covered in sticky juice, which in summer also attracts gnats and midges.

The way round this is to drain off the juice (not down the sink, but into a container, to keep for mixing groundbait), then rinse the corn in a sieve under a cold tap before putting it in the bait box. Before putting on the lid, cover the box with clingfilm to seal in the moisture and flavour of the now non-stick corn.

There's no reason, however, why you can't store a spare tin of corn in your tackle box, in case you forget to take some or run

▼ *Tinned corn – convenience food for the shopper, but more than just convenience bait for the angler. Barbel, chub, roach, bream, tench and carp all love it.*

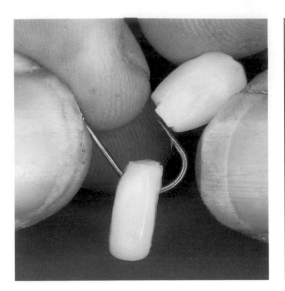

▲ *Two grains of corn fit snugly on a size 10 hook. For single corn, use a 14. For three or more grains, use an 8, 6 or 4. For carp and barbel you can use a hair rig to fish single or double corn on a big hook.*

▼ *Sweetcorn has seen the downfall of many a sweet-toothed specimen tench. Fish it under a float close to marginal weeds or at range with an open-end feeder.*

Tip Sweetcorn soup

Juice from a tin of corn adds flavour to groundbait but you can go further. All you need is access to a food processor.

Put equal amounts of water and tinned corn - juice and all – into the processor and liquidize. Take the resulting soup to the waterside in a vacuum flask (so it stays fresh) and use it instead of water to mix groundbait.

out one time. And all is not lost if you don't remember the tin opener – simply punch a hole in the tin with a large bank stick then shake out the contents. But be sure to take the tin home with you at the end of the day. Don't discard it at the waterside – any litter is unsightly, and the jagged edges of a rusting tin are a danger to birds and animals.

Catching with corn

Small baits such as maggots attract all sizes of fish. Sweetcorn is large by comparison and small fish find it difficult to get their mouths round even a single grain. It's

therefore a selective bait, very good for when you're looking to pick out the bigger fish in a swim.

Rivers Loosefeeding a few grains of corn every cast and trotting or legering one or more grains is an excellent way of catching roach, chub and barbel. It pays to vary the depth when trotting because you often find that chub take the corn in mid-water while barbel and roach usually want it near the bottom.

Still waters Laying-on (floatfishing a bait on the bottom) close-in over a bed of corn, especially alongside weed beds, can be deadly for roach, bream and tench. If the fish are farther out, use an open-end feeder: pack it with corn and plug it with ground-bait. There's nothing to stop you adding other baits such as hemp and casters to the groundbait, or trying cocktail hookbaits such as corn and breadflake.

Stalking Sweetcorn is a first class bait for stalking fish in clear, shallow water. Many a huge carp and chub has fallen for this method, but when feeding it's essential not to land the corn right on the noses of these wary fish.

Place it in their path or wait until they temporarily leave the swim. Being bright yellow, the grains shine like miniature underwater beacons, not only attracting the fish but making it easy for you to watch the bait being taken.

Beans and peas for carp and tench

Although often regarded as only a reasonably successful change bait, beans and peas take large numbers of carp and tench every year. Peter Mohan shows how to use them properly.

Pulses (all kinds of beans and peas) are excellent baits for carp, and also catch other species such as tench. They can be introduced to a water in quite small quantities yet they often produce immediate results.

Their success may be due partly to their similarity to the natural foods of carp. Peas or beans thrown in as free offerings lie about in small groups, much like freshwater snails, for example, and are of a similar size. Carp are therefore likely to look on them as food straight away.

Cooking beans

Preparation is essential – you should never use pulses as bait or free offerings when they are dry. Unsoaked, uncooked beans

▼ *A handful of runner beans to tempt any carp. Lying around on the bottom, a group of colourful beans like this is quite visible and soon attracts the carp.*

and peas absorb water and swell up inside the stomach of the unfortunate fish which eats them. At best, this causes discomfort to the fish, but at worst it can be fatal.

All pulses must be soaked in cold water for at least three to four hours and then cooked. After soaking, put them on to boil for three or four minutes, and then allow them to simmer for another five to ten minutes. Some beans can be harmful even to large animals like humans if not prepared thoroughly. Kidney beans in particular should be soaked overnight and then well cooked. Even so, try to avoid overcooking or boiling for too long as this removes some of the nutrients, making them less attractive to the fish or too soft for effective use as hookbait.

Feeding and using

As with any new bait, pre-baiting can increase the effectiveness of pulses. Carp

▼ *Haricot beans fished singly or doubly can be deadly when fishing for big carp. The secret is not to overfeed, as pulses can be very filling. Just leave a small handful of free offerings on the bottom to attract the attention of any cruising fish, and top up with the same amount every time you catch.*

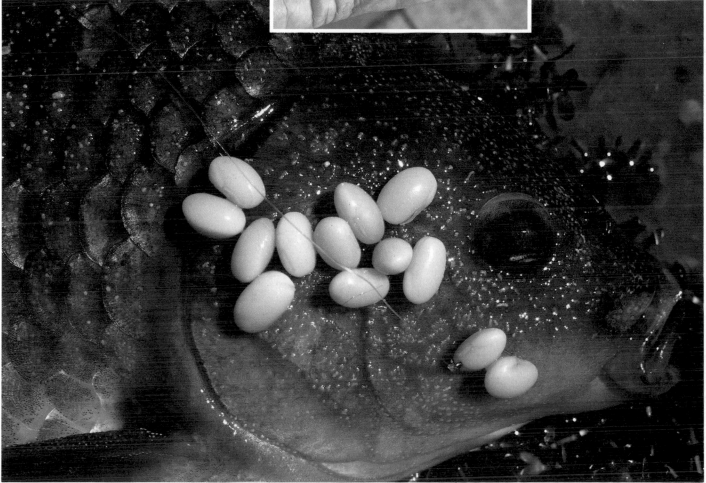

and tench sometimes need time to get used to the idea that a new object is edible. Often, however, the possible resemblance of pulses to natural food seems to ensure that fish take them from the start.

Very heavy pre-baiting, as with boilies on a new water, is not necessary, although you may need more on waters heavily stocked with other species. You'll find that on most waters, light pre-baiting is all that is necessary to switch the fish on to whichever pulse you want to use.

Beans to try include black-eye beans, tic beans, adzuki (aduki) beans, pinto beans, mung beans, lima beans, soya beans, coffee beans, butter beans, kidney beans and haricot beans. The larger ones – such as butter beans – are less successful as multiple, or particle baits. The carp seem to lose interest in them more quickly – perhaps because of their size.

Of the peas, chick peas are usually regarded as the best, and indeed they generally outfish all other pulses. Other peas to try include maple peas, gunga peas and dun peas. The smallest pulses, such as maple peas, are often successful with species other than carp and tench.

Bean shopping

Many tackle shops now sell beans and peas, particularly those which specialize in carp gear. They can also be bought in bulk from suppliers who advertise in the angling press. Other good sources include health food shops, delicatessens and food stores devoted to Asian foods, which often have a huge variety of pulses.

The advantage of pulses as baits, espe-

cially for carp, is that fish seem to take to them very quickly. On hard-fished waters where boilies and other large baits are mostly used, they are an excellent alternative. Their only real disadvantage is that it can be difficult to bait up with them at long range, even with a catapult. Chick peas, however, are quite hard and can be fired quite a distance.

If you are looking for a new bait to try for carp and other species, which doesn't require huge quantities of pre-baiting, try one of the pulses. They're comparatively cheap too!

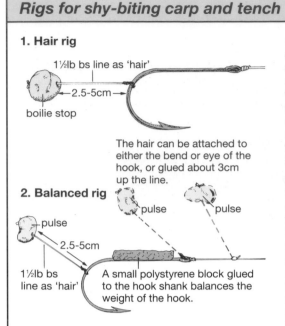

Rigs for shy-biting carp and tench

1. Hair rig

1½lb bs line as 'hair'

←— 2.5-5cm —→

boilie stop

The hair can be attached to either the bend or eye of the hook, or glued about 3cm up the line.

2. Balanced rig

pulse

pulse

pulse

2.5-5cm

1½lb bs line as 'hair'

A small polystyrene block glued to the hook shank balances the weight of the hook.

1. The standard rig for carp fishing with boilies can also be used with success for pulses. Mount the bean using a needle or simply tie it on. You can also fish multiple baits, using two hairs attached to different parts of the hook or line.

2. Since pulses are light, a frequently-caught fish may drop the bait because of the added weight of a hook, especially a large one. This is when a balanced rig is best. Glue a piece of polystyrene to the shank to balance the weight of the hook. A piece of cork on the hook eye has the same effect.

Tip Bean flavour

Only bait up with small numbers of pulses, and if the fish start to go off them, add flavour to the next batch while soaking, and a tablespoon of sugar during cooking. Maple syrup, paprika, oxtail soup and curry sauce work well, as do the commercial carp flavourings.

Hookbeans

On waters where a hair rig is unneccessary, mount beans as shown. Push the bait over the eye of the hook, which helps keep it on, but don't let the bean impede the hookpoint.

▶ *In the early summer when most tench are hungry, some big specimens can be caught on beans. This trio of four pounders (1.8kg) fell to legered chick pea.*

Basic boilies

**Boilies have helped transform carp fishing
from a specialist pursuit to the fastest growing branch
of coarse angling, says Peter Mohan.**

◀ *Boilies are the most popular bait for carp but can also catch big tench, bream, chub and barbel. Indeed, you can now buy mini-boilies, which are pea-sized to make it easier for these fish to take them.*

Twenty years ago carp fishing was the preserve of a dedicated few, and their successful baits were closely guarded secrets. Commercial carp baits as such didn't exist. Each carp angler had secret recipes for paste baits containing all sorts of weird and wonderful ingredients.

The trouble with paste baits was that while they caught carp, other, smaller fish could nibble away at them. To overcome this, carp anglers came up with the idea of binding their paste ingredients with raw egg, rolling the mixture into marble-sized balls, then boiling the balls in water for a few minutes to form a tough skin that would resist the attentions of nuisance fish. Thus was born the basic boilie.

Boilie power
By the early 1980s boilies fished on hair-rigs were proving so successful that people began to make and sell the bait commercially. For the first time, ordinary anglers could fish for carp with a bait and rig that gave them every chance of success. Ready-to-use, off-the-shelf boilies of every imaginable colour and flavour are now the most widely used bait in carp fishing.

On some heavily fished waters so many boilies are thrown in that they form the staple diet of the carp. In extreme cases

the amount of boilies thrown in is directly responsible for the carp steadily gaining weight from one season to the next.

On the minus side, boilies have been banned on some carp waters because so many have been thrown in that some lie uneaten on the bottom until they rot and contaminate the water.

Make or buy?
Dedicated carp anglers make their own boilies – a laborious task, but one that does let you make them cheaply and in

▼ *Together with the hair-rig, the development and commercial production of boilies in all sorts of colours and flavours has helped bring carp fishing within the reach of the ordinary coarse angler.*

Making floating boilies on the bankside

You can prepare floating boilies at home by cooking them in a microwave oven, or by grilling or baking them. But there's a quick and easy way at the bankside. Cut off

the top of the boilie with a sharp knife. Make a hole in the middle of the boilie with a drill bit (1). Put a small ball of polystyrene in the hole formed (2). Suitable polystyrene

balls are sold as bean-bag fillers. Stick the top of the boilie back on with a drop of instant glue (3). The result is a 'pop-up' – a bait that can outscore the ordinary boilie.

bulk. Moreover, you can experiment with new recipes, colours and flavours.

For the occasional carp angler, however, commercial boilies are more convenient and more than adequate. They are sold in sealed plastic packets. Unopened, they can be kept fresh for several months if stored in a cool place away from direct sunlight. Once the packet has been opened your best bet – if you want to save any boilies left over from a fishing trip – is to freeze them.

Boilie breakdown
The basic ingredients of boilies are egg, which binds everything together, and the bulk, which can be various mixtures of proteins, carbohydrates, fats, minerals and vitamins. The theory behind these bulk ingredients is that carp recognize their nutritional value. Whether this is

true is debatable. What is certain, though, is that it's the flavour of boilies – and to a lesser extent their colour – that entices carp to eat them in the first place.

Flavour seems to be more important than colour because boilies are usually fished on the bottom, where carp generally find food more by smell than sight. Strong meat, fish and fruit flavours are all proven carp-catchers, but to find out what works best in a particular water you have to ask around or use trial and error.

Using boilies
In waters where boilies are used a lot, the carp are used to eating them so you only need to throw in 20 or 30 free offerings around each hookbait. If boilies are not used very much on the water, or if you are trying to wean the carp on to a new flavour, you may need to throw in several hundred and wait longer to get results.

Each time you catch a carp, throw more boilies in – about 10 is usually enough unless you are fishing a heavily stocked, 'hungry' water, in which case it's worth putting in twice as many.

Boilies are best fished on a hair-rig rather than threaded on the hook. Partly this is because boilies are hard baits, but the main advantage of the hair-rig is that it increases the chance of a carp hooking itself. The carp sucks in the boilie and hook, feels the hook and tries to blow it out – and the point of the free hook catches in the carp's mouth.

To make it easier for carp to spot your boilie hookbait and suck it in, try a 'pop-up' – a floating boilie anchored over your bed of free offerings by shot on the hook-length. To make boilies float, cook in a microwave oven on full power for a few minutes, or gently grill or bake them.

▼ *When fishing at range you can use a boilie catapult to feed a swim. But for greater accuracy, especially at night, thread the boilies on to a piece of PVA string tied to the hook. The string dissolves, leaving the boilies around the hook.*

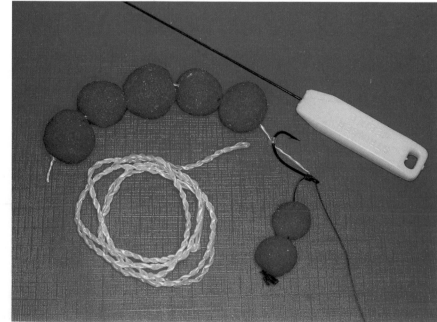

Making boilies – cooking for carp

With so many commercially-made boilies on the market, most of which contain excellent ingredients, why do many anglers still make their own? Peter Mohan (who's been making his own for years) answers the question.

For some anglers, a greater sense of satisfaction and achievement comes from catching a carp on baits they have made for themselves. Making your own isn't hard and you can create your own killer baits.

Dee-licious boilies!

Specific recipes vary, but ingredients are usually very similar. They all contain a binding agent and bulk matter. Many also contain colouring and flavouring. If you bulk-buy, your boilies should work out cheaper than the shop-bought variety.

Binding agents usually contain a high proportion of protein or starch. Sodium caseinate (a powder derived from milk) and eggs are excellent for this. Wheat gluten and wheat germ are also used.

Bulk ingredients make up the weight as well as adding nutrient value and sometimes a good basic flavour. For a fish-type bait, fish meal or crushed trout pellets are ideal. Other bulk ingredients include soya flour, peanut meal or meat and bone meal.

Liquid sweeteners are the basis for many sweet flavoured boilies, topped with whatever suits your taste (or the carp's!). You can make savoury boilies with liquidized squid or whatever takes your fancy. You can also use food dye to create baits in almost any colour.

Flavours are available commercially – and there are a lot of them – but many anglers use their own flavours to create a unique bait, giving them the edge at their favourite venue.

You can buy all the ingredients from the many firms which specialize in baits and bait materials. Many advertise in the angling and specialist carp fishing press.

Peter's method

For years Peter Mohan has been successfully catching carp on his home-made boilies. The method is easy and rarely goes wrong. He recommends you start with a simple recipe.

The dry ingredients are 85g (3oz) sodium caseinate, 85g (3oz) wheat germ, 57g (2oz) fish meal, 28g (1oz) soya flour and 28g (1oz) Equivite (a vitamin and mineral supplement). Weigh them out carefully and mix them together in a bowl. This mixture takes about four parts liquid to five parts dry ingredients by weight.

▼ *Boilies and hair rigs probably account for more specimen carp each year than all other baits and methods combined. This hair-rigged boilie is attached to the eye of the hook though many other positions can be effective.*

How to cook 'em

1. Mix the dry ingredients together, then beat three size two eggs in a bowl. Once familiar with the method, you can vary the ingredients.

2. Add the other liquid ingredients – the colouring, flavouring and the liquid sweetener. A syringe is a useful measure for this.

3. Gradually add the dry mixture to the liquid, stirring with a fork. You may have to keep adding more powder until you get a stiff paste.

4. Mix and knead the paste until it is slightly tacky and putty-like. The more you knead, the denser and faster-sinking your boilies will be.

5. Roll a portion into a sausage, and then cut it into evenly sized pieces. Roll these chunks between your palms into the typical ball shape.

6. Place the baits in a chip basket or ladle and submerge them in boiling water for 60-90 seconds. Boiling for longer produces harder baits.

⊗ Overkill

About 5-10ml of flavouring is enough and it is not a good idea to increase this – even if the bait doesn't seem to be working. Adding more flavour may put the fish off, rather than attracting them. It's much better to experiment with small amounts of different flavours until you find the ones which work for the fish you want to catch.

The liquid ingredients bind the powder into a paste. The main component is egg – full of protein for the hungry carp. Three size two eggs are about right for use with the dry ingredients above. Beat the eggs, then add any sweetener, flavouring and colouring and mix thoroughly.

Mix wet and dry ingredients and roll the paste into balls of whatever size you require. Boilies of 12-18mm (½-¾in) diameter are the most common. This recipe makes 100-120 boilies of this size – enough for one or two sessions. Remember that for other species such as tench and chub, smaller boilies often make excellent baits.

After cooking, allow the boilies to dry on a cloth. Turn them after a few minutes so they dry all over. You can use them after an hour, but the outer coat continues to harden with time. After four or five hours the skins are pretty hard and they harden even more overnight.

To make a few pop-ups for hookbait, take some finished boilies and cook them for a further three to four minutes in the microwave. If you don't have a microwave, grilling your boilies can also produce floaters, though this is less effective.

Any boilies you do not need straight away can be kept in the freezer for several weeks. You are now free to experiment with shapes, flavours and colours and to produce your own deadly (and secret) baits.

Tip What you knead

Test the finished baits to check that they sink. If they float, use some water instead of one of the eggs in the next batch. If you continue to get floaters by mistake, replace some of the light ingredients such as caseinates and milk powders with heavier ingredients such as ground rice, pasta, semolina or corn meal. Finally, the harder you knead the main lump of bait, the more air you force out of the mixture. This makes it denser and so helps it to sink.

Hard-boiled recipes

Peter Mohan has been dishing up the home cooking to carp for years. His advice is to follow the formula before you let rip and design your own unique boilie baits.

Tip Go heavy on the water

If your boilies seem too light, or if they don't sink well, add a little water in place of some of the eggs. You could also use heavier ingredients such as semolina, but this lowers the protein content.

▶ *There's no doubt about it – if you get the recipe just right, carp go for boilies in a big way.*

Milk recipe

1. 3oz casein (P)
2. 2oz wheatgerm (V/P/C)
3. 2oz dried milk powder (P/M/V/F/C)
4. 1oz wheat gluten (P/C)
5. 1oz yeast (P/M/V)
6. 1oz lactalbumin (P)

P=protein;
V=vitamin;
M=mineral;
C=carbohydrate;
F=fat

Mystery abounded in the 1970s when boilies were the new thing. There was a kind of boilie underworld dealing in secret recipes and under-the-counter exchanges of the latest baits – all very hush-hush!

Boilie boom

It's pretty well above board now. Boilies are established as a more consistently successful carp bait than pretty well anything else and are more popular than ever. There is a staggering range of boilies – in a huge number of colours and flavours – available from

bait suppliers and tackle shops around the country.

Many anglers, however, prefer to make their own rather than buy ready-made boilies in packets. Shop-bought boilies are expensive but buying the ingredients to make your own can cost a fair bit too. Getting together with some friends to buy ingredients in bulk is one way to keep the cost down. Home cooking is perhaps not as convenient as buying off the shelf, but it has certain advantages apart from cost.

Because you know the exact make-up of the bait, you can judge which recipes work best in the waters you fish, and alter the ingredients accordingly. By making only slight adjustments to the recipe you may well create a highly successful bait to beat anything out of a packet. Detailed fine tuning and in-depth experimentation can help to give you confidence in your own baits – and if you catch a specimen on your own creation, that's an extra buzz.

Making your own also gives you the chance to score with a secret weapon – once you've cooked up a killer bait, keep the secret recipe to yourself!

Domestic science

Boilies consist mainly of high protein ingredients (HP), but they also usually contain a balance of proteins, fats, vitamins, minerals and carbohydrates. They are often referred to as 'HNV' – high nutritive (nutritional) value baits – because they contain the concentrated elements which give the carp a balanced diet.

Perfumed principles When making your own boilies, aim for mixes which follow the HNV principle. Initially this means sticking to recommended recipes until you get a feel for the right sort of proportions and balance of food types needed.

In addition to using ingredients with a high protein, vitamin and mineral content, you need to put in others that give stickiness and bind the substances together – wheat gluten or flour for example. And don't forget the important taste and smell ingredients that can be the key to a successful bait.

Once you have grasped the principle of creating an effective boilie base, you can start to experiment with myriad flavours and tinker with proportions until you discover your own personal favourite combinations.

Walk first Before you start to improvise it's a good idea to get the boilie basics under your belt; make your first attempts from ingredients which have proved themselves as carp catchers. There is now a whole range of easily obtainable substances which are established ingredients for HNV baits.

Basic method

For a bait of the highest possible protein content, start with dry ingredients such as

► *Waste not – spare baits keep well in a freezer.*

Fishmeal recipe

1. 2oz sodium caseinate (P)
2. 2oz herring meal (P)
3. 2oz Casilan (P)
4. 1oz wheat gluten (P/C)
5. 1oz mineral/vit supplement (M/V)
6. 2oz soya flour (P/F/C)

Tip **Log logic**

Keep a record of the recipes you try out. By noting how effective each combination of ingredients is, you should be able to come up with improved blends, until you have a range of home-made boilies for all occasions.

► *Try adding bun spice flavour or liquid sweetener.*

Seed recipe

1. 2oz Casilan (P)
2. 4oz soya flour (P/F/C)
3. 2oz Robin Red (bird food/P/F/C)
4. 1½oz mineral/vitamin supplement (M/V)
5. ½oz ground almonds (P/F)
6. 20ml 'Spice' Sense Appeal (attractor)

Get stuck in

MIXING IT UP
1. Mix all the dry ingredients in a bowl.
2. Beat three eggs in another bowl, then thoroughly mix in any flavours or colours required – usually about 5-10ml per 10oz dry stuff.
3. Gradually add the dry ingredients to the liquid until you get a smooth paste. Don't add all the dry stuff in one go – a little at a time is best.
4. Knead the paste until it is stiff enough to cut into strips and roll into balls. Make sure you have pressed out all the air.
5. If the mix is too sticky, add more dry ingredients until you can roll balls of bait between your hands without too much sticking to your fingers.

COOK AND DRY
1. Roll the bait balls into the size required – anything from 6-25mm (¼in-1in) or more.
2. Bring a large saucepan of water to the boil.
3. Put 30-50 baits into a chip basket or metal sieve and lower it into the pan of boiling water – leave for 1-1½ minutes.
4. Take out the baits, and put them on a dry cloth, then repeat stage three with the rest of the baits until all are done.
5. After a few minutes carefully turn each bait over on the cloth so that they dry on the other side, then leave to cool. If you want the baits to be very hard leave them out for several hours or even all night.

casein (the main protein in milk), calcium caseinate or sodium caseinate. These, consisting of at least 90% milk-based protein, should not make up more than 50% of the bulk of your recipe. Most anglers use only about one third.

Make up the rest of the mix from carbohydrates, vitamins and minerals to give a balanced food product. Add a binding agent and any flavours or colourings to complete the ensemble.

Boilie recipes generally combine a selection of these dry ingredients with eggs which provide liquid. The eggs also put a skin on the surface of the bait after it is dipped in boiling water, making it hard.

The method shown here for preparing your different recipes gives you a bait that stays on the hook or hair, lasts in the water and is to some extent selective – attracting carp rather than irritating tiddlers.

Three of the best

Once you've mastered the basic method for making boilies you must decide on what exactly to put in the mix. The list is enormous and to some extent all recipes are

Tip **Acquired taste**

Ground-up trout pellets have a strong flavour, contain a lot of fish meal and can be a useful addition to your boilie recipe. You can buy them from fish farms, shops selling pond fish foods or bait suppliers. A coffee grinder is useful for crushing such materials into workable powders.

made by trial and error.

You can grind up or liquidize any edible substance and mix it in with eggs and other ingredients to make boilies, but over the years certain raw materials have emerged as consistently successful bait ingredients; they are now recognized as the most powerful options on the boilie artist's palette.

Some of these regulars are mentioned in the recipe suggestions included here, which are designed to cover three popular and proven boilie mixes – milk-based, fishmeal-based and seed-based. Many other suitable raw materials for HNV boilies are listed in bait suppliers' catalogues.

Tip **Nuff's enough**

Always make sure the eggs and other ingredients are fresh – only the best for the finicky carp.

Don't overdo it with flavourings as they tend to be very concentrated – too much may actually put fish off (5ml or one teaspoon of any flavour is usually ample for a standard batch).

Floating baits

Surface fishing is fascinating because you can see your quarry. If you are light of foot you can stalk them along the bank. But what baits tempt surface feeders?

It's a balmy day in mid summer. Only mad dogs and fishermen go out in such midday sun, but these are ideal conditions for surface-feeding fish. Creeping silently along the river bank you come across a swim where you can see a languid carp or a large chub. Farther out a sudden swirl on the surface reveals a feeding shoal of rudd.

It's no use thrashing the water with the usual maggots or boilies. These are just going to sink. The fun is in catching the fish on the surface – but to do this you need to have the right bait.

Bread crust has always been used as a surface bait. Provided it is fresh it should float well. You can use it in cubes of varying size, depending on the type of fish you want to catch. For large carp use a piece the size of a matchbox on a size 4 or 2 hook. Rudd or roach will take smaller pieces on size 12 or 10 hooks. Dace eat smaller pieces still.

Boilies have all the natural buoyancy of a brick – they won't float unless you make them. Two ways of coaxing these prime carp baits into floating are to fill them with polystyrene or to boil them further. To fill with polystyrene, cut off the top with a knife and make a hole in the middle of the boilie with a sharp instrument – a drill bit is ideal. Now put a polystyrene ball – of the sort you find in packaging or bean-bags – into the hole and seal the top back on using a little instant glue. It's an easy enough job that can be done at the waterside.

An even easier method, provided you have planned beforehand, is to microwave or boil your boilies for a few minutes. The only problem is the smell. If they are pre-flavoured, it is pretty intoxicating – a kitchen full of the aroma of tutti frutti or

Tip **Keep it up**

Determined to surface-fish a favourite bait even though it won't float? Baits such as bread flake can be suspended with a polystyrene ball.

▼ *Carp are frequently tempted by surface baits, particularly floating pet biscuit and bread crust. You can intercept carp on the surface because they have a regular 'patrol' route. Where you have seen a carp once it is likely to return.*

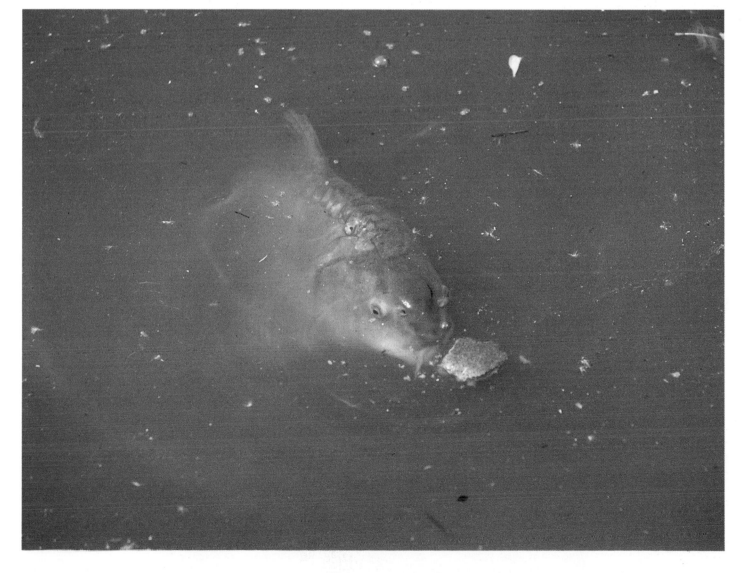

Floating ideas

▲ 1 and 2. Boilies – when microwaved or boiled – float well and are an irresistible carp bait.
3. Pet biscuits are good for chub and carp.
4. Sugar Puffs are effective but may need a controller for casting.
5. Marshmallow – fish these whole for carp on a size 2 hook.
6. Bread crust is good for carp, chub and rudd.
7. Nearly hatched casters are buoyant. At this stage they are called 'floaters'.

strawberry yoghurt is very whiffy!

A further choice is given by proprietary floating boilies. These are prepared exactly as normal bottom-fished boilies and simply baked for twice as long in the machines.

Casters are pupated maggots. They normally sink, but the ones that are nearly ready to hatch into flies are lighter in weight and known as 'floaters'. They are good for rudd and chub, will catch carp and can also account for dace – a species that won't take the larger baits.

Cereals such as Sugar Puffs can prove effective surface baits – soak them in water for 15 seconds and strain them off. They lack weight for casting so they might need the addition of a controller.

Floating bait mixes can be successful but the mixes are not available at all tackle shops. Add egg to the mixture, following the instructions on the packet, whisk and bake it well to make sure it floats. The arrival of floating boilies has hit this bait's popularity – though it is easy enough to prepare.

Marshmallows sound an unlikely food to be used as bait – but fished whole on a large hook for carp they have proved effective.

Pet food biscuit is one of the best of all floating baits. Cat and dog biscuits are as effective as floating bait mixes but at a considerably lower price. Chub and carp in particular enjoy it. Mixer biscuits with cut patterns are handy for attaching to your hook, while the rest can be either drilled or soaked for a while until they are soft enough to put a hook through. An additional alternative is to Superglue them to the hook. You can add flavourings while you soak them. (See Floater Fishing for Carp, on pages 185-8 , for an in-depth look at how to fish with such baits.)

Trout pellets were originally prepared as food for fish farms, but these high protein pellets were discovered by carp anglers and for several years were the *in* bait. Normally they are ground into paste but it is possible to drill them and fish them on the surface. Trout pellets can be bought in pet shops.

Floating maggots

Maggots are not normally thought of as surface baits. But fresh maggots placed in a small amount of water for 20 minutes absorb the water. They then float well and attract chub, rudd, dace and even carp.

It is quite easy to prepare them on the waterside in a spare bait container. Put a palmful of maggots in 6mm (¼in) of water and leave them to soak for a while.

Using your loaf – flake, mash and crust

It never goes out of fashion. It's cheap, clean, easy to prepare and catches all species of coarse fish, apart from predators. John Bailey tells you about bread.

B read's effectiveness as a bait is under-estimated and it's a pity it is not used as widely as it was 20 years ago. Bread interests roach, rudd, bream, barbel, chub, tench or carp – even if they have never seen the bait before. It has no off-season and is as eagerly accepted in the winter frosts as it is in the dog days of summer. What is more, it tends to attract a better stamp of fish.

What makes bread good?
To us, a slice of bread tastes and smells rather bland and this is probably why we invented the sandwich spread, but to fish it is just this clean, natural taste that is so enticing. Maybe colour has something to do with it too. Unless the fish has its head

buried in the mud, a white morsel lying on the bottom is likely to attract the attention of even the most heavily preoccupied tench or carp.

Our daily bread
Forget the baps, baguettes, cottage loaves and cobs. Humble, medium-sliced and unsliced loaves – fresh ones, mind – are the finest choice for bread baits. These two types of loaf are effectively half a dozen baits in one. Three of the simplest are flake, mash and crust.
Flake The advantage of flake is that it is light, fluffy, sinks slowly and rests on top of weed and mud rather than sinking into them.

Choice of hook size depends on bait size

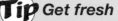

Tip **Get fresh**

When you're asking the head of your household for a few slices of bread for fish bait, make sure you don't get fobbed off with stale stuff. It is good enough to attract the fish but it won't stay on the hook long enough to catch them.

Always go for the freshest you can get. Keep it in a polythene bag so that it retains its moisture and keep it out of the sun – dry bread is good for making mash but useless for hook bait.

▼ *This fine tench fell to a big piece of flake fished hard on the bottom under a peacock quill – a method that has accounted for more tench than any other.*

▲ *Prebaiting with bread mash the night before you intend to fish is a good way of attracting tench and carp into a swim. Early morning feeders are caught quite close in, so don't throw your bait too far.*

which in turn depends on the species you expect to catch. Don't go too small – sizes 8-14 are about right for flake.

Simply pull a piece of bread from the middle of a slice – roughly round and 1-2.5cm (½-1in) in diameter. Push the hook through the middle and pinch the bread firmly around the hook's shank, leaving the bend and barb free. If the bread is fresh and the cast not too vigorous, flake stays hooked for at least 20 minutes.

A good place to try flake is a spot on a river, lake or canal where the ducks are regularly fed by the public. Big roach get used to mopping up pieces of bread which the ducks have missed and a piece of flake fished on the drop may get you a real beauty

(but make sure the ducks aren't around).

Mash Flake fished over a carpet of mashed bread is a good method for taking bream, tench and carp. Simply soak some bread thoroughly and mash it until the mix is firm enough to throw or catapult into the swim but sloppy enough to cloud the water.

Floating crust An uncut tin loaf provides one of the most effective surface baits for carp or rudd– floating crust. Use a fresh loaf – a dry crust cracks and comes off the hook.

Match the size of bait to the type of fish you expect to catch, and match size of hook to bait size. An 8lb (3.6kg) carp is quite capable of swallowing a piece of crust the size of a matchbox – a bait which easily hides a size 2 hook. A 1½lb (0.7kg) rudd has a comparatively small mouth, and a thumb-nail sized piece of crust on a 12 or 14 is perfect.

Flavourings

Often the subtlety of an unflavoured, uncoloured bait works perfectly but sometimes the fish prefer a souped-up bait.

Flavoured flake is excellent. You can use an atomizer containing liquid flavouring. Open the wrapper of a sliced loaf at both ends and spray with a few bursts from an atomizer. Reclose the wrapping, put the loaf in a polythene bag and store it in the freezer. On the bank the bread thaws and draws the flavour through the loaf. Liquid flavourings such as cream cheese, blue cheese and salmon are excellent but there are plenty more to experiment with.

▼ *A ragged piece of fresh flake pinched on to the shank of the hook is an attractive bait. White bread is the usual choice but brown can work just as well.*

▼ *A matchbox sized piece of crust, fished right on the edge of, or among, lilies is a traditional way of catching carp, but a scaled down version of the same method is excellent for specimen roach and rudd.*

▲ *You can let water into a hollow plastic bubble float to vary its casting weight, making it ideal when fishing floating crust.*

Better breadpaste

Versatile and easy to use, breadpaste probably caught more fish than any other bait during the first half of this century. Later it was eclipsed by newer – more fashionable – baits, but now it's time for a revival.

A large number of anglers first started fishing using breadpaste. It's ideal for the beginner – easy to obtain and use – and it doesn't squirm around in your hand. But don't fall into the trap of thinking it is just a beginners' bait. It's easy to prepare, simple to use and very attractive to fish such as roach.

A better bait
The best thing about breadpaste is its versatility. Few other baits appeal to such a variety of fish. It catches dace, gudgeon, rudd, roach, tench, carp, bream, barbel and chub.

It has several advantages over other forms of bread baits such as flake and crust. The size and texture can be altered depending on the type of fish you are hunting and the water conditions. It can be made firm for faster water, yet temptingly small and soft for fishing lakes and reservoirs. It is also easy to add colourings and flavourings to give further appeal.

Adding taste and colour
The step-by-step guide on page 112 shows the basic ingredients and how to make breadpaste. Use slightly stale bread, at least a couple of days – and up to a week – old. Some anglers use milk instead of water to add flavour when mixing the paste.

Colourings and flavourings have become something of an art form. Thanks to baits such as boilies, a whole variety of new flavourings and colours are available. Take your pick from exotic flavours such as salmon supreme and strawberry yoghurt. More traditional flavourings are cheese, ground hemp, aniseed, custard powder, honey and sugar. Some very unlikely ingredients have been used over the years, such as ground almonds, tinned pet food, Marmite and even beer!

Colours can vary widely. Many proprietary colourings are available, though you must not use aniline-based colourings such as Chrysoidine as they can cause cancer. Cochineal, a red cake colouring, is useful,

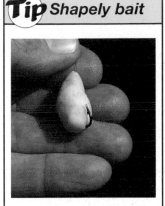
▼*This fine tench fell to breadpaste which seems to attract larger tench and roach in particular. This specimen's bright greenish yellow colour reveals it came from a clear lake.*

and saffron makes an effective yellow. Custard powder makes an interesting pale lemon – as well as adding flavour – and red Leicester cheese, which gives a good flavour, produces an orange colour. Bear in mind that you might want to keep back some untreated paste; it is frequently the simplest baits that are the most effective.

You can firm up the mixture by using flour – the amount depending on the texture you need. Store the paste in an airtight container or in the fridge or freezer if you are not fishing with it immediately.

Fishing with breadpaste

No special techniques need to be followed, but take care when casting that the bait does not fly off the hook as it travels or when it hits the water. Breadpaste is a little prone to parting company with the hook!

Use it firm for swift streams, and as a soft paste in slow or still water and when you only need to cast a short distance.

To make your breadpaste sink slowly – for example when fishing over weed – add a piece of crust to the bend of the hook. This slows down the bait and allows it to rest on top of the debris – rather than falling through out of the sight of most fish.

If you have flavoured the breadpaste it is a good idea to add the same flavouring to your groundbait so that the fish get a taste for kiwi-fruit – or whatever unlikely sounding flavour you are using.

Breadpaste postpones the decision of whether to fish for small dace or large carp until you actually get to the bank – as you can use it in a variety of sizes.

Colour scare

Anglers should be aware that there have been reports of an alleged connection between aniline-based colourings and cancer. Chrysoidine (orange), Auromine O and Rhodamine B were formerly popular colourings used in fishing to turn maggots bronze, and to colour breadpaste. If you still have them, don't use them. Food colourings are a safe alternative.

Preparing breadpaste

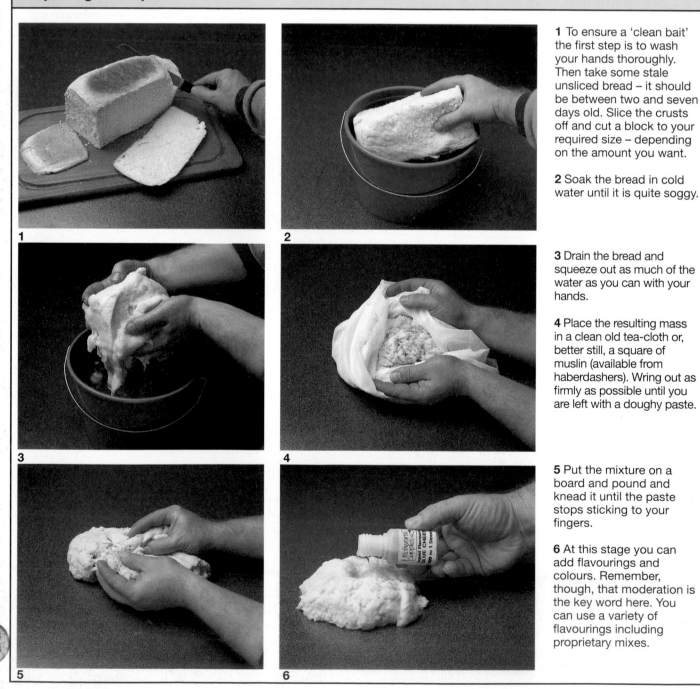

1 To ensure a 'clean bait' the first step is to wash your hands thoroughly. Then take some stale unsliced bread – it should be between two and seven days old. Slice the crusts off and cut a block to your required size – depending on the amount you want.

2 Soak the bread in cold water until it is quite soggy.

3 Drain the bread and squeeze out as much of the water as you can with your hands.

4 Place the resulting mass in a clean old tea-cloth or, better still, a square of muslin (available from haberdashers). Wring out as firmly as possible until you are left with a doughy paste.

5 Put the mixture on a board and pound and knead it until the paste stops sticking to your fingers.

6 At this stage you can add flavourings and colours. Remember, though, that moderation is the key word here. You can use a variety of flavourings including proprietary mixes.

Breadpunch – pellets that produce

Without doubt bread is a major weapon in the specimen hunter's armoury, but as punch it can catch fish of all sizes and at all venues for pleasure angler and matchman alike.

Breadpunch is simply a pellet of bread cut from a slice of fresh bread with a sharp-edged circular tool. This simple, clean bait is most commonly associated with roach fishing, but it is also deadly for small tench, crucians and carp.

Punch is often reckoned to work best on cold, clear canals. When bites seem impossible to come by, the punch seems to produce like magic.

Matchmen all over Britain know how effective it can be. In many areas, turning up without a round or two of bread is like arriving without your rods! Matches are also won with the punch on other types of venue – rivers and lakes as well as canals.

Choosing and using

Many anglers swear by their own favourite brand of bread, some of which are only available locally, though any bread can be used for punch. It should be as dense as possible with few air holes. Medium sliced is best (about 1cm/⅓in thick), but above all it must be fresh.

If the bread dries out, it is almost impossible to punch or to keep it on the hook. Before your trip, cut two or three slices into quarters, put them in an airtight plastic bag, and expel all the air. If you take out a quarter at a time, you always have fresh bread handy.

Casting any distance with a waggler and shipping a pole too quickly or jerkily can mean your hookbait comes off before it reaches the fish. To overcome this tendency, press or roll some of the bread with a rolling pin or jam jar, making it a bit denser and tougher.

To punch out a pellet, lay the slice on a clean, hard surface and push the breadpunch into the bread with a slight twisting motion. The pellet is now lodged in the head of the punch, ready for hooking.

▲▼ There are many types and makes of breadpunch available, and most are very good. What you need is a range of sizes with a sharp cutting edge and a slot for hooking the pellet. They are often sold in packs of different sizes or with a few interchangeable heads.

Tip Steaming punch

Only extremely fresh bread is suitable for punching. If your bread isn't fresh, try steaming it over a pan of boiling water. About 20-30 seconds for each side puts moisture back into slightly stale bread.

Hooking punch

To hook breadpunch simply pass the hookpoint through the slot (right) and pull the pellet out of the head of the punch (far right).

You can often use a larger hook with punch than with maggot – the bread swells in water to hide the hook and because it has a soft texture it won't impede the hook on the strike.

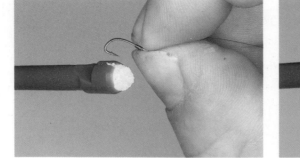
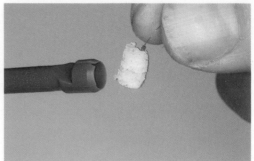

Feed and feeding

The two main types of feed used when fishing the punch are cloudbait (very fine groundbait) and liquidized bread.

Cloudbait must be as fine as possible, so sieve your shop-bought bag through a flour sieve. Mix it with water either very dry or very wet (sloppy). Sloppy groundbait forms a bigger cloud and is heavier, so you can throw it more accurately when it's windy.

Liquidized bread is best fed completely dry on still or slow flowing shallow waters. On deeper water you can dampen it with an atomizer or mix it with groundbait to help it sink more quickly.

There are no hard and fast rules for using either feed, but 'a thumbnail a chuck' is a good start. As with all baits and methods, you must experiment to find the most productive feeding pattern.

Remember that the particles of liquidized bread swell up in water, making it very easy to overfeed a shoal of shy roach on a cold day. Take it easy – you can always put more in if the fish are really feeding, but you can never take any out.

When fishing the punch, use a light fine wire hook so the hookbait doesn't fall through the water too quickly. And finally, whichever float rig you use, make sure it allows the hookbait to sink naturally through the bottom third of the water.

Tip Size matters

If bites dry up, change the punch size. This often gets the fish going again. If bigger fish move in, try your biggest punch or double punch (2 pellets).

▲ **To make liquidized bread, cut the crusts from a loaf and whizz it in a blender, one slice at a time, until it looks like this.**

▶ **Weighing a catch of small roach with the odd bonus hybrid. The punch can produce catches like this when nothing else works.**

Say 'cheese' for chub

Apart from being a popular filling for anglers' sandwiches, cheese is a good bait for fish. It takes all species except predators like pike and perch, but the fish that loves cheese most is chub, reckons Graham Marsden.

C heese is one of those baits that is often unfairly neglected. The advantage of cheese over other, more popular baits – such as maggots, for example – is that it tends to attract better quality fish. Although cheese is a fairly expensive food item, it is not an expensive bait – you don't need much for a day's fishing and a pound of Cheddar is cheaper than a pint of maggots. Cheddar, Gruyère, Camembert, Red Leicester, Stilton or Double Gloucester – there really are no bad cheeses when it comes to bait, but some are better than others.

Smelly cheeses make the best bait – so it's not suprising that Danish Blue and Stilton reign supreme. In winter, when rivers are in flood and the water is highly coloured, fish rely heavily on scent rather than sight. It is easy to imagine how cheesy smells trailing downstream from a legered bait can attract the attention of a 4lb (1.8kg) chub.

Firm cheeses such as Cheddar and Edam can be fished in cube form. Simply cut the cheese into cubes of a size to suit the hook size. A 6mm (¼in) cube sits nicely on a size 12 hook, a 12mm (½in) cube on size 10 and 8, and a 20mm (¾in) cube on size 6 and larger.

Crumbly cheeses such as Stilton and Danish Blue can be kneaded into paste form and then moulded around the hook.

Very soft cheeses are sold in tubs and tubes as sandwich spread. Mix them with powdered cheese – like Parmesan – or very fine groundbait to stiffen them up sufficiently for moulding.

Swine and cheese As an alternative to fishing plain cheese you can try a cocktail. Sit a cube of luncheon meat on the hook bend and then mould cheese around the shank. Both chub and barbel often respond to such a bait when neither bait on its own is enjoying a great deal of success.

Parmesan cheese is extremely smelly and when added to paste baits gives them a pungent aroma which the fish (and anybody else who might be standing in the vicinity) can't fail to notice.

Cheesy mixes It is always satisfying to catch fish on new baits – especially one you've discovered for yourself. If you are stuck for ideas then you might like to try Graham's potent, cheesy mix (see overleaf).

Cheesy tactics

If you are after specimen chub on a smallish,

▼ *Graham unhooks a 3lb (1.4kg) chub, taken on a legered cheese bait. Graham carries as little tackle as possible so that he can rove about searching for fish.*

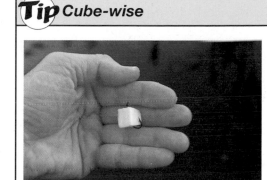

Tip **Cube-wise**

You can fish firm cheese in cube form but on hard-fished waters fish are often wise to this shape. Use your fingernails to rough up the corners of the bait, or try an unusual shape such as a pyramid.

Marsden's magic mix – it's good enough to eat

The ingredients are as follows: at least 4oz of Danish Blue, a bag of ground hempseed and a tub of grated Parmesan cheese. A microwave oven makes the job easier. You'll also need a microwave-proof bowl and a tablespoon.

Anglers are notorious for being messy. So for household harmony, keep a damp cloth at hand in case of spillages.

Put the cheese in the bowl and break it up with the spoon – this way it'll cook a bit quicker. Pop it in the microwave and give it about 30 seconds on full power. Be sure to take the spoon out of the bowl before putting it in the oven or else you'll get a firework display. If you've got it right the cheese should melt completely.

Stir in a tablespoon of ground hemp and a tablespoon of Parmesan. Hemp is a great attractor – chub, roach and barbel love it and it helps to bind the bait together so it stays on the hook. The Parmesan soups the bait up even more.

When the mix is cool put it in an air-tight tub. Don't refrigerate it, but allow it to mature – the smell can be foul.

Hair-rigged cheese baits

boilie-stop — cheese cube

silicone tube trapping hair to hook shank

'hair' – 1lb bs nylon 1.5 – 2.5cm long

You may have fished boilies on a hair rig on still waters but have you ever thought of fishing cheese on the hair in a river? It works perfectly and leaves the hook free to do the job for which it was intended – hooking the fish.

fast-flowing river – like Cheshire's River Dane, for example – then you can't beat the leger for rolling a bait into likely looking holes. Any of the usual rigs – sliding link leger or fixed paternoster – are perfectly suitable for this.

Work the bait Cheese attracts fish that are not already in the swim but you can improve your chances by taking your bait to the fish. Walk the banks quietly, keeping a sharp look out for likely spots where you can introduce your cheese.

In summer try dropping a cheese bait in the clear runs between streamer weed, in among the roots beneath trees and bushes, or in the fast water below weir pools. Sometimes you can tempt fish from right under the bank where the current has undercut the riverbank and formed a hollow where fish often like to hide.

In winter try the deeper pools and backwaters away from the full force of the flow. The bait really comes into its own at this time of the year. Even when there is snow on the ground and the line is frozen to the rod rings, you can still tempt fish on cheese. What better way to end a crisp December day's fishing than with a brace of 2lb (0.9kg) chub on cheese?

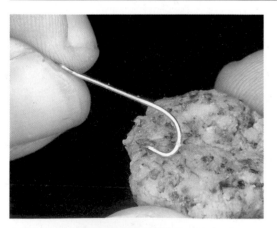

▲ *When Graham is using his special mix on the hook, he uses a salmon worming bait holder hook (such as the Mustad 92641). This has two little barbs on the shank which help to keep the bait on when casting and as it rolls around in the current.*

Tip Hard-to-swallow baits

Particularly in winter, cheese can go very hard on the hook when it's left in cold water for a long time. Don't worry about this putting the fish off – chub have very powerful pharyngeal (throat) teeth that can crush snails – but the hard bait can make hooking fish a problem.

Mould the bait around the shank of the hook but leave the point exposed. Then when you strike you won't pull the bait out of the fish's mouth.

Making the most of meat baits

Many species of fish go for luncheon meat and bangers. Meat baits make an excellent alternative to maggots and worms, yet – luncheon meat excepted – they have been neglected in recent years.

Chub, barbel and carp enjoy meat as much as we do. Even fish as different as dace and catfish will occasionally feast on it. Luncheon meat is the most popular of the meat baits and sausage meat is also effective. The very latest bait is stewing steak – in 1990 match fishermen on the Trent started winning consistently with it. It could be the boom bait of the nineties.

We have all heard tales of fishermen who, often out of desperation, have hoiked a piece of pork or beef from their sandwiches, attached it to a hook and caught a massive barbel. But, being honest, if cuts of beef, mutton and pork were at all consistent, we would be using them every day because they are far easier to obtain and use than maggots or worms.

Lovely luncheon meat

On rivers as far apart as the Hampshire Avon and the Yorkshire Ouse luncheon meat is both popular and successful.

▶ This handsome barbel, caught on the Hampshire Avon, was hooked using luncheon meat. Barbel are bottom feeders so legering with luncheon meat or sausage meat is an effective method of catching them.

Barbel, chub and carp all succumb to it.

Luncheon meat is available both in tins and fresh from the delicatessen. Both types have their devotees.

Getting fresh Fresh luncheon meat is easier to keep on the hook than the tinned variety. Buy it in a 1lb (0.45kg) block rather than sliced. Freeze half for the next time you go fishing. Cut the rest into cubes and store it in a polythene bag to prevent it drying out.

Cans can Any of the other well known brands of tinned luncheon meat are very handy bait. The cans are easy to carry and

▼ Magic ingredients for meatbaits include: stewing steak (1) – use in maggot size slivers; luncheon meat (2) cut into hook sized cubes – the cubes on the right were lightly fried for a few minutes.

Sausage meat and fine groundbait (3) mixed together make a good groundbait (4). For use as an effective hookbait, mix these two ingredients to a finer paste.

▲ *Chub sometimes take baits such as bacon and rind but they respond best to luncheon meat. A chub bite on luncheon meat can vary from the slightest of cautious twitches to a mighty thump.*

Tip **Adding a maggot**

The trouble with using tinned luncheon meat as a bait is that it tends to be slippery and very easily flies off the hook when casting.

One answer is to use a maggot or a piece of grass placed between the meat and the hookbend to hold it in place. A maggot may also make the bait a little more tempting if the fish aren't biting.

you can take home any unopened tins for another day's fishing.

Tinned luncheon meat is not as easy to keep on the hook because it has a higher water and jelly content. But many anglers prefer it to the fresh version because it has a higher fat content that – they believe – leaves an irresistible trail for barbel and chub.

Cut the meat into cubes – the size depends on the hook you are using. Most anglers believe that the point should just be showing. There's a simple way of keeping tinned luncheon meat on the hook; place a slip of grass between the luncheon meat square and the hook bend. If the grass is flat against the meat its central spine provides rigidity.

If you believe that fat is the key to a successful luncheon meat bait you can increase its fat content still further. Melt some fat or lard in a frying pan and drop in your pre-cut cubes. Turn the bait lightly in the fat and then remove it. When it cools it is enveloped in a thin film, which is attractive to fish and makes for a slightly firmer bait.

Can it! Some waters have banned cans altogether because at one time the banks of the rivers and lakes were littered with cans. Clubs were threatened with the loss of their waters and a number of anglers were banned. If you *are* allowed to use them, make sure you take your tins home with you.

Sizzling sausages

Sausage meat has nearly the same attraction for chub and barbel as luncheon meat. For carp it seems less successful, though in still waters they do try it.

Chewable chipolatas Modern small sausages are easy baits to use because their plastic skins hold them firmly on the hook. However, the plastic skins kill the essential meaty smell and trail of the sausage, and

perhaps spoil the bait for the fish. Continental style spiced sausages can be effective, especially around houseboats where fish have developed a taste for them from scraps.

Banger boom The good old fashioned banger is relatively popular as a bait. Fried and cut into sections it can be fished on every sized hook from a no.10 to a no.2. If you boil the sausages they become softer and less likely to float unexpectedly to the surface. Bangers are particularly successful when legering – the sausage can cover the hook point completely.

Sausage meat This is a successful bait whether raw or cooked. As with luncheon meat, frying a 'patty' in lard for five minutes gives the meat a stiffer texture and increases fat content.

Used raw it is very successful when mixed with a little flour or, better still, fine groundbait. It forms a kind of paste that attracts chub and barbel and can be moulded on the hook.

While you are fishing give the fish a taster of your hookbait by feeding the river with fine loose sausage meat. A cheaper method is to make a groundbait of bread and sausage meat.

High steaks

Stewing steak was the discovery of 1990. A number of high catches have been recorded with it. The secret is to mince it up very fine and fish with small – maggot-sized – pieces on the hook. On the occasions when you would normally use maggots, switching to stewing steak may help you to catch a much bigger stamp of fish.

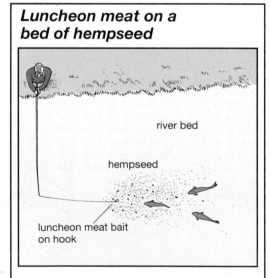

Luncheon meat on a bed of hempseed

It's cheaper to groundbait using hempseed rather than meat. Lay a bed of hempseed about 5ft (1.5m) in length for chub and barbel and introduce your hookbait of luncheon meat on to it. The fish are attracted to the swim by the hempseed and discover the tasty lump of luncheon meat, standing out from the hempseed, in the centre – with obvious consequences.

Plugs for pike

Pike plugs come in a bewildering array of colours, shapes and sizes. Where one doesn't work, another one might.

Pike plugs are artificial lures, usually made of plastic, wood or metal, that 'swim' or wobble upright through the water – unlike spoons and spinners which spin or wobble about an axis. They are usually single-piece but some are jointed to give them a more pronounced wobble.

Most plugs are designed to mimic sick or injured fish. Some are vividly coloured, vaguely fish-like shapes not designed to look like anything in particular but just to provoke an instinctive strike. Others are realistic imitations of frogs or mice.

Plug particulars

Try to buy a complete range of plugs, each for a specific job, rather than just collect them at random.

Colour You need some silver plugs to imitate such fish as roach, dace and skimmer bream; some with stripey patterns, to mimic perch and small jack pike (pike being cannibalistic); and some in really garish colours such as bright red and yellow. Even plain black plugs have their days. Finally, trout-patterned plugs are worth trying in waters holding trout – a favourite food of pike.

Size Pike do take large plugs, but as a rule 5-10cm (2-4in) ones work best.

Action Most plugs are *shallow-diving* floaters; they have sharply angled vanes on their heads which, on retrieve, cause them to dive a few inches or feet.

Deep-diving floaters have low-angled vanes which make them dive very steeply when you retrieve them.

Some floating plugs have adjustable vanes, allowing you to vary the diving depth from one cast to the next.

Finally, there are *sinkers*, which sink when first cast in, rising higher in the water the faster you retrieve them.

▼ *A huge variety of pike plugs is available, and collecting them can be a hobby in itself. Choose a basic range of different colours, sizes and actions to cover every eventuality.*

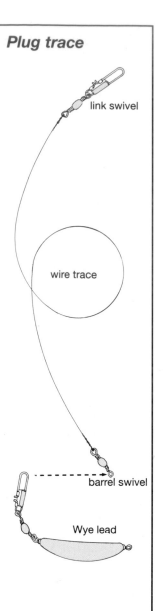

Plug trace

link swivel

wire trace

barrel swivel

Wye lead

▲ *This jointed plug is designed to look like a baby pike. The metal vane on its head can easily be adjusted to vary the diving depth.*

▲ *This unjointed plug has a sharply angled vane for shallow diving. The bold colours provoke pike to attack it instinctively.*

Which, when and where

Generally speaking, plugs work best in summer and autumn, when pike and prey are most active. Unfortunately there is no way of predicting which will work on any particular day. Many anglers believe trial and error is the only way to find out, but certain guidelines apply.

On hot, sunny days, pike often lie up near the surface in weedy, shallow water and may be tempted with a slowly retrieved shallow-diving floater.

When you can see pike feeding on fry in the shallows, try fast-retrieving a small, silver shallow-diving floater.

On cooler autumn days, when pike are likely to be in slightly deeper water, try a sinker or deep-diving floater.

But never just 'plug away' if you aren't catching. Keep changing plug colour, size and type, and keep varying the rate and depth of retrieve, until you discover what's best on the day.

Plug traces

Always use a 30-45cm (12-18in) wire trace when pike fishing because pike can bite through any nylon line, however thick. If you want to cast a small, light plug a long way, attach a Wye lead at the top of the trace to provide the extra casting weight.

▼ *A shallow-diving floater worked slowly and enticingly through the shallow margins proved the downfall of this fine double-figure pike.*

A trace should have a link swivel so you can quickly and easily change plug.

Spinners and spoons

Pike expert Barrie Rickards takes us into the colourful world of spinners and spoons – including that new wonder-lure, the buzzer.

Luring them on...

Two Norwich spoons in pike and mackerel colours. Though spoons don't look realistic fish find their action tantalizing.

Lures are artificial baits used for catching predatory fish such as pike, perch and chub which mistake them for smaller fish. There are three main types: the plug, which quite closely resembles a small fish and normally floats (described on pages 119-20), the spinner and the spoon.

A spinner has a blade which rotates around a fixed bar axis, while a spoon – as its name suggests – is a piece of metal shaped like a spoon. This does not usually spin, but wobbles as it is retrieved.

The spoon

There are essentially three different types of spoon; the Norwich spoon, the Vincent and the Toby.

The Norwich spoon is the basic version. It has an egg-shaped outline and has been popular for many years. It comes in various colours and with numerous names. Copper versions are popular. When they are wound in gently their slow wobble and colour resemble an injured rudd.

The Vincent looks similar to the Norwich spoon, but has a more elongated shape. It tends to give a slow, shallow wobble.

The Toby is convex in shape and is also more elongated in its outline than the Norwich spoon. It is excellent for distance casting and depth.

Spoons vary widely in colour, size and weight. However, the great variety of spoons, whatever their commercial brandname, fall into the above categories – even though they may have subtle variations in action.

This is a classic spoon, a silver Vincent. It has an elongated shape. The Vincent's action makes it particularly effective for trolling

The spinner

The three basic kinds of spinner are artificial minnows, buzzers and barspoons, also called blade spinners. Again, there are numerous variations and brandnames for them, but the basic three patterns remain the same.

Barspoons Don't be confused by the name – barspoons are really spinners! They have a wire axis, around which spins an egg-shaped blade which is attached at one end. Some of the smaller types are superb for trout, perch and chub, and they all work well with pike and with sea fish. They

A typical spinner, confusingly called a barspoon. This effective spinner is well known by its tradename – Vibro.

◀ *This is the buzzer, a fairly new and very effective spinner. Though it looks like nothing on earth its action and appearance provoke fish to attack almost instinctively.*

▲ *Quill minnows (bottom right) and Devon minnows (top left and top right) are the 'missing link' between imitation fish (plugs) and ordinary spinners (bottom left).*

vibrate noticeably when retrieved, and can be drawn back very slowly.

There are a number of variations on the barspoon. The kidney spoon has a kidney-shaped blade. The Colorado spoon has wings and a blade at both ends.

Minnows are made of wood, plastic, metal or quill, and are very like a small fish. They are driven by two side vanes, and adorned with tiny treble hooks. Unlike the barspoon, minnows are pure imitation and are very useful for game fishing.

The buzzer, also known as the spinnertail, is a relative newcomer, and has become the most successful of all lures. It is a 'Y'-shaped bar of wire with a fluttering spoon on one arm and a hook, weight and colourful skirt on the other. There is no way that this could ever be mistaken for an imitation of any kind of animal.

Such has been the success of buzzers that they are now probably the most successful of all lures. It must be something in their movement and appearance that causes pike to strike instinctively. Fish them deep or 'buzz' them along the surface. Whatever other lures you buy, get some half-ounce (14g) buzzers. When lure fishing, begin with a buzzer and then try the rest.

▶ *This pike was caught on a barspoon spinner. Pike grab spinners because of hunger, territorial aggression or sheer cussedness!*

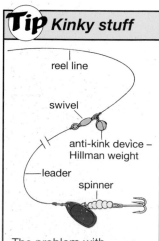

Tip **Kinky stuff**

reel line

swivel

anti-kink device – Hillman weight

leader

spinner

The problem with spinners is that they can kink the line. It's solved by using an anti-kink device such as this Hillman lead.

Deadbaits

Many anglers believe livebaiting is no longer acceptable. You're just as likely to catch by deadbaiting – and it can account for bigger, better specimens.

▲ *Snap-tackle: at the end of a wire trace are two treble hooks (size 8 for pike), set a small distance apart. Push your bait firmly on to the hooks.*

▼ *Deadbaits such as this roach are too tempting for a hungry pike to leave alone.*

There are several species of fish whose main diet is other fish – dead or alive. Pike, zander, perch, eels and catfish all take legered deadbaits without a qualm.

It is a very effective way of catching **big** fish. The older and bigger a pike becomes, the less it wants to start chasing off after fast, healthy prey. It gives up 'fast-food' in favour of slow, wounded fish. If your deadbait is in view – either on the bottom, suspended or twitched to resemble a stricken fish – the pike and its fellow predators will go into action.

Differing deadbaits

Predatory fish take all types of available deadbaits. The following are the more popular baits.

Freshwater fish Bleak and bream are fished whole. Dace are a bait that will take perch, as well as the larger predators. Eels, fished in segments wherever they are naturally present, make good bait.

Minnows form a large part of the diet of predatory fish. As well as catching the usual species, they are an excellent bait for perch and even the occasional chub. They can be preserved in salt – which may well boost their taste and desirability.

Rainbow trout, if you have the money, are a good bait for pike. Another very successful fish is the roach – they're quite colourful, and therefore very visible. They form a large natural part of a predator's diet and are arguably the best of the freshwater fish.

Sea fish Herring, either used whole or cut

Paternostered deadbait

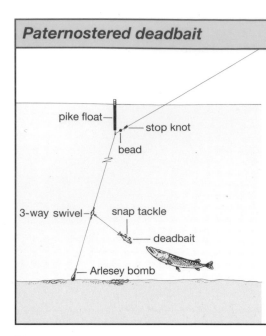

pike float
stop knot
bead
3-way swivel
snap tackle
deadbait
Arlesey bomb

One way of keeping small deadbaits such as roach or sprats visible above the river bed is to suspend them on a paternoster rig. The fish appears to swim slowly.

Use a swivel leading to an Arlesey bomb on one length and a wire trace with a snap-tackle rig on the other. The rig will suspend the fish invitingly – and hold it still.

▲ A small herring on a classic snap-tackle rig. Pike bite through line so the snap-tackle must be attached to a wire trace.

▼ Well-known pike angler Ken Whitehead attaches a sprat to a snap-tackle rig. Ken believes in taking the deadbait to the fish, rather than hoping the pike finds his hook, so he likes to move his bait fairly often.

in half, are a very popular bait. Though not normally part of a pike's staple diet, they are smelly and oily and can be detected from quite a distance. Bigger herring – cut in half – release more juices, which increases the pike's chances of locating them by following the potent smell trail.

Tip Hooked on pike

Anglers who have the welfare of the pike at heart prefer a rig with one treble hook and one single hook. This way deep-hooked pike are not caught on two sets of hooks – so improving their chances of survival.

Mackerel are another highly successful bait for pike. Fished whole, mackerel are more successful in certain waters than herring. They are good for long-range casting because they are firm and so stay on the hook easily. An advantage of casting with half a mackerel is that it is extremely aerodynamic in shape and slips through the air.

Smelt and sprat are both useful baits – sprats have the advantage of being easy to obtain from fishmongers. One last alternative is squid. Chopped into strips they make excellent bait for catfish.

Using deadbaits

Deadbaits are attached to the line by snap-tackle rigs and are frequently legered. As an alternative, you can sink-and-draw to make the bait imitate a sick fish swimming in an erratic way. Cast the bait in the water and raise the rod top – drawing the bait up through the water. Then lower the rod, reeling in a small amount of line. The bait will sink – wobbling towards the bottom. Keep repeating this sequence, re-casting and retrieving along the bank until you find a fish. You can cover lots of water this way.

CHAPTER THREE

KNOW YOUR FISH

The pike: a streamlined predator

The pike is Britain's largest native predatory freshwater fish. Its size has made this fish the target of many anglers hoping for the catch of a lifetime.

Record pike

● The official British rod-caught record stands at 45lb 6oz (20.58kg) for a fish caught by Gareth Edwards from Llandegfedd Reservoir in South Wales in 1990.

● Off the record, perhaps the largest pike caught on rod and line in the British Isles is a fish taken by John Garvin from Lough Conn, Republic of Ireland, in 1920. It weighed some 53lb (24kg) and is supposed to have regurgitated a 10lb (4.5kg) salmon when landed.

Fast, efficient and streamlined, the pike cannot be mistaken for any other fish. Most of its characteristics are adaptations to its predatory lifestyle. Camouflage colouring, eyesight, body form and fin arrangement all contribute to the pike's success as a hunter.

Hunting habits

With their camouflage and short-lived bursts of speed, pike prefer to ambush their prey rather than chase it. They lurk, hidden in the weeds, waiting for the quick sprint – followed by feeding.

The jaw is extremely flexible, allowing large meals to be swallowed whole; small (jack) pike will often demonstrate this by gobbling up their siblings. Prey is usually taken from the side and then manoeuvred round to be swallowed head first.

When water conditions prevent the pike's highly developed eyesight from being

Distribution

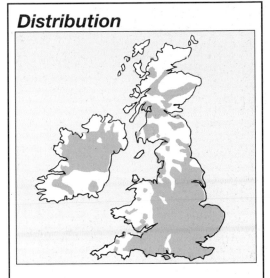

Pike are widespread throughout Britain and Europe in lowland rivers and lakes. They do not thrive in either highland waters, which tend to be acidic and poor in nutrients, or in fast-flowing spate rivers.

Vital statistics

Scientific name: *Esox lucius*
Maximum weight: 70lb (32kg)
Maximum length: 4ft 2in (1.27m)
Average weight caught: 7-8lb (3.2–3.6kg)
Life-span: 18-25 years.

The green and yellow body markings help disguise the pike as a harmless patch of weed.

Note the eyes set well forward in the head. This provides a degree of binocular vision which helps pike judge distances accurately.

All the dorsal and anal fins are grouped near the tail giving the pike tremendous power to launch itself after prey.

The mouth contains many sharp teeth giving prey little chance of escape.

20cm (8in) roach

Top ten pike waters

Neville Fickling, pike specialist, suggests . . .

● **River Thurne, Norfolk**: three 40lb (18kg) plus pike make this one of Britain's best waters for big pike.

● **River Bure, Norfolk**: many 20lb (9kg) pike.

● **Abberton Reservoir, Essex**: huge water with pike to over 30lb (14kg).

● **Weirwood Reservoir, Sussex**: prolific trout and coarse fish water with many 20lb (9kg) plus pike.

● **Ardingly Reservoir, Sussex**: top class coarse water with pike over 30lb (14kg).

● **Llandegfedd Reservoir, South Wales**: home of the British record of 45lb 6oz (20.58kg) and other 40lb (18kg) plus pike.

● **Broadlands Lake, Hampshire**: popular day ticket pike water.

● **Blithfield Reservoir, Staffordshire**: trout water with pike to over 35lb (16kg).

● **Loch Awe, Scotland**: lots of escaped rainbow trout have made this a big pike water.

● **Loch Lomond, Scotland**: huge Scottish loch with many large pike to 35lb (16kg).

effective, it can fall back on its efficient sense of smell. It also has a highly sophisticated tracking system rather like radar.

Favourite food is fish of between a tenth to a fifth of the pike's body weight, but it can swallow much larger ones, as well as small mammals, frogs and water birds. However, pike usually eat only about two and a half times their own body weight in a year.

Key feeding seasons are dictated mainly by the breeding cycle and water temperature. Sixty per cent of a mature pike's yearly food intake is consumed in the two months following spawning (round about March and April). Females also feed heavily in October when their ovaries are beginning to develop, and there is a smaller peak in feeding just before spawning in January and February. Little is eaten over the summer months as pike tend to be lethargic at higher water temperatures. This means fishing is often poor in summer.

Life-cycle

Much of the year pike spend in the deeper water, usually between 3-10m (10-33ft), but in spring, from March onwards, they move into the shallows to spawn. Females usually carry up to 20,000 eggs per pound of body weight, so large specimens may be carrying more than 500,000 eggs each spring. The female pike is much the larger of the sexes weighing up to 20lb (9kg) or more; males rarely top 12lb (5.5kg).

After spawning, the pike feeds heavily to regain its strength. The usual victims are other fish, such as perch and roach, using the shallows to spawn. Very young pike eat water fleas and other tiny aquatic life but after only a few weeks they move on to members of their own species and other fry.

▲ *Large pike should be returned to the water carefully as they play a vital role in preserving the balance of species in a fishery.*

Monsters

● The Endrick Pike (1934) was found dead near the River Endrick, a tributary of Loch Lomond. The size of its head indicates it could have weighed about 70lb (32kg).

● John Murray (1774) captured a fish reputedly weighing 72lb (33kg) in Loch Ken, Scotland.

TYPICAL PIKE WATER: a combination of lake, river and fen drain

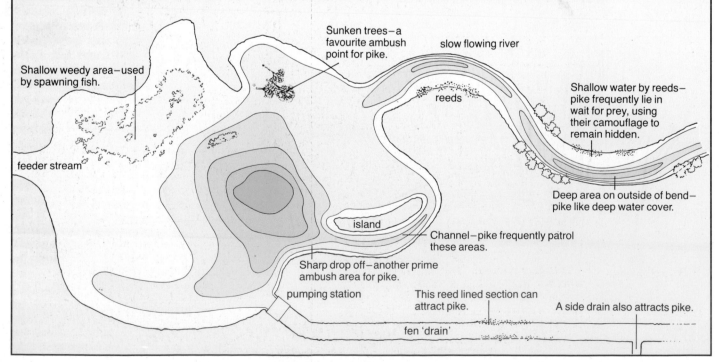

Sunken trees—a favourite ambush point for pike.

slow flowing river

Shallow weedy area—used by spawning fish.

reeds

Shallow water by reeds—pike frequently lie in wait for prey, using their camouflage to remain hidden.

feeder stream

island

Deep area on outside of bend—pike like deep water cover.

Channel—pike frequently patrol these areas.

Sharp drop off—another prime ambush area for pike.

pumping station

This reed lined section can attract pike.

A side drain also attracts pike.

fen 'drain'

The hardy roach

Its tolerance of moderate pollution and low levels of dissolved oxygen has helped the roach thrive. It is now one of the most abundant lowland fish in England.

Record roach

● The British rod-caught record roach weighed 4lb 3oz (1.899kg). It was taken from the Dorset Stour by Ray Clarke in October 1990. The 4lb (1.8kg) barrier was broken in the mid 1970s.

● The specimen weight for a roach is 2lb (0.9kg). Anything over 3lb (1.4kg) is rare and well worth a celebration.

The inexperienced may be forgiven for failing to distinguish the roach from the rudd. Judging from the numbers of hybrids between the two species, the fish themselves find identification difficult. Both have large scales and greenish backs but the flanks of the roach are silvery whereas the rudd has a golden sheen. Roach-bream crosses are also quite common, as are hybrids with chub and bleak.

Follow the feeding

Fry and very young roach feed on plankton but as they grow they include algae and invertebrates such as snails and insect larvae, especially bloodworms, in their diet. Large specimens, particularly roach-bream

Distribution

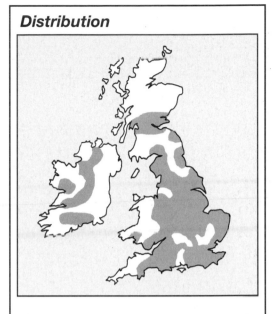

Widespread throughout England, the roach is not as common in either Wales or Scotland where the rivers tend to be too fast and the water too acidic. The roach is not native to Ireland but has spread rapidly from the waters where it was first introduced.

Vital statistics
Scientific name: *Rutilus rutilus*
Maximum weight: 4½lb (2kg)
Average weight: 4-6oz (110-170g)
Maximum length: 14in (36cm)
Life-span: 10-15 years

The front edge of the dorsal fin is in line with the base of the ventral fin. In rudd, the front edge of the dorsal is behind the base of the ventral.

The white lumps or tubercles on the head of the male are common to all members of the carp family during the spawning period.

The upper lip protrudes slightly, the sign of a bottom feeder.

Note the red eyes and the red-orange fins.

The lateral line has between 42 and 45 scales.

hybrids, can become cannibals and feed mainly on fry. Roach do most of their feeding on the bottom, though at times they feed in midwater and even come up to take insects that have fallen on the water surface.

Life-cycle

Roach are widespread throughout England but are much less common in Wales, Scotland and Ireland. They prefer slow-moving rivers and still waters but are also found in faster flowing rivers that are reasonably deep. They do not do well in fast, shallow streams. They are a fairly tolerant species and can even be found in quite barren or polluted waters.

In some waters roach are not subject to much predation and this can lead to overcrowding, with large numbers of small roach up to about 4oz (113g). Stunting can also occur in acid waters that are poor in nutrients. In reservoirs, gravel pits and chalk streams which are nutrient rich and where pike, perch and trout tend to reduce numbers, the roach are far fewer but larger. It is at waters like these that specimen and record roach can be caught. On average it takes about nine or ten years for roach to reach full size though this does depend on the availability of food.

Spawning takes place in the shallows between April and June, the yellowish eggs sticking to plants and stones. Roach are prolific, averaging 20,000 eggs per 1lb (0.45kg) of body weight – another reason they are so widespread. With a mild spring, spawning takes place early and a greater number of the fry survive. Usually, though, this simply means that there is more food available for the predators.

▲ *A 2½lb (1.1kg) fish in beautiful condition. You must take care when unhooking and returning roach to the water as they are rather fragile. Make sure your hands are wet or you will damage the fish's scales.*

In common with many other members of the carp family, male roach often develop grey-white warty lumps on the head (and occasionally the body) before spawning. These are known as tubercles and are about the size of a pinhead. Males can only be easily distinguished from females when these lumps are present.

Top ten roach waters

Neville Fickling, angler and specimen hunter for almost 30 years, recommends these venues for quality roach.
● **Tring Reservoir, near Aylesbury, Bucks** Famous for fish around 3lb (1.4kg).
● **Hampshire Avon** Contains specimens over 3½lb (1.6kg).
● **Stanford Reservoir, Northants** Very good winter fishing with fish of up to 2½lb (1.1kg).
● **River Wensum, Norfolk** Not as good as in the 70s and early 80s, but still producing fish to 2lb (0.9kg) in its middle reaches with good nets of lesser fish in Norwich.
● **Great Ouse cut-off relief channel, Norfolk** Best around Hilgay Bridge area for good quality fish of 1-2lb (0.45-0.9kg).
● **River Nar, Norfolk** Noted for its roach of 1-2lb (0.45-0.9kg).
● **River Hull, North Humberside** In the Hempholme area the roach are of a good size, around 1-2lb (0.45-0.9kg).
● **Grafham Water, Cambs** A trout fishery which cannot be fished using usual coarse fishing methods. Huge roach of over 4lb (1.8kg) have been found dead here, though, so dedicated record breakers may like to try for them with the fly.
● **South Cerney gravel pit, Wilts** Some of the pits yield specimens of over 2lb (0.9kg).
● **River Trent at Dunham, Notts** Excellent winter sport with fish of 1-2lb (0.45-0.9kg).

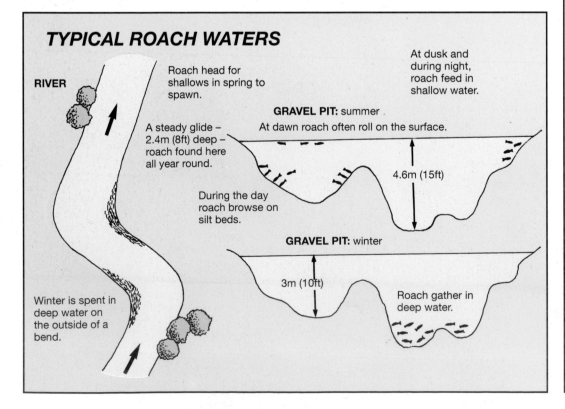

TYPICAL ROACH WATERS

RIVER

Roach head for shallows in spring to spawn.

A steady glide – 2.4m (8ft) deep – roach found here all year round.

During the day roach browse on silt beds.

Winter is spent in deep water on the outside of a bend.

At dusk and during night, roach feed in shallow water.

GRAVEL PIT: summer
At dawn roach often roll on the surface.

4.6m (15ft)

GRAVEL PIT: winter

3m (10ft)

Roach gather in deep water.

Perch: striped hunter in the weeds

Difficult to mistake for any other British fish, this stripey predator will attack almost anything small enough when young. Those that live to grow large become far more cautious.

Distribution

The areas without perch are generally upland – very few waters lost their entire populations during the 1960s-70s plague. However, big perch are still not as common as they were before the disease.

Perch plague

In the 60s and 70s an ulcer disease decimated the perch population in Britain. On waters where tests were carried out it was estimated that up to 99% of the perch had died, with only a very few immature fish left.

Even though the disease appears to have died down, its effects are still being felt. In many waters, which previously held large specimens, there are now numbers of stunted perch. With the sudden death of all the big perch which had kept the numbers of juveniles down, far more young have survived. This leads to greater competition for the available food, so they all remain small.

The perch is a handsome fish, with striking looks well suited to its predatory life. Its flanks are an olive-green with six or seven black stripes, camouflaging it among weeds and reeds. The tail is rather small, so it is not a high speed swimmer, but it can cruise fairly fast for long periods.

Follow the feeding

Perch are hunters, preying on other species. Fry feed on water fleas and other tiny crustacea but they soon graduate to insect larvae such as bloodworms. If small enough fish are available, perch switch to a mainly fish diet when they weigh about 4oz (113g). Perch that have made this transition grow very rapidly. Where there is no prey of this type, perch remain stunted, weighing only 4oz (113g) at about seven years old.

Young perch hunt in schools, lying in wait among water plants, until small fish such as bleak or roach stray too close. The school then sets off in pursuit, harrying the quarry until it is too tired to swim further. Perch catch their prey by biting the tail repeatedly from behind and below to restrict swimming. Characteristically the capture and swallowing of the perch's prey

Vital statistics
Scientific name: *Perca fluviatilis*
Maximum weight: 7lb (3.2kg)
Average weight: 6-8oz (170-228g)
Maximum length: 20in (50cm)
Life-span: 13 years

The first dorsal fin is separate from the second and has 14-15 spines. It can be raised to frighten predators and rivals.

Note the distinctive black spot at the back of the first dorsal fin.

The second dorsal fin has 1 or 2 spines and 13-14 soft rays.

The large mouth contains only small teeth

There is a strong spine on the gill cover.

The lower fins, and often the lower part of the tail, are red.

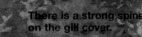
20cm (8in) roach

▲ Specimens as large as this 3lb 6oz (1.5kg) beauty are well worth recording on film, though there are tales of fish last century which reached 7lb (3.9kg). One day British waters may again produce such monsters.

is always tail first.

Perch usually eat small fish with a 1-2lb (0.45-0.9kg) specimen typically taking prey of about 1-2oz (28-57g). Odd though it might seem, perch seem particularly fond of catching and eating the fry or smaller members of their own species.

Life in school

Perch prefer slow-moving or still waters with a good head of small prey species. Good visibility is essential for their style of hunting and so they do best in clear water. They can also survive in relatively fast-flowing rivers if there is not too much suspended silt making the water cloudy. Perch are not found either in high, rocky streams or in acid lakes.

When young, perch form schools consisting of one age group but as they grow older they become more solitary. This is not because the older fish lose the instinct to form schools but is due to the shrinking of each school of perch as fish die and are eaten.

Breeding

Male perch can be sexually mature at only 6-12 months old even though they are usually no more than 5-8cm (2-3in) long whereas females are seldom ready to mate until they are three years old. The females usually grow to a larger overall size than the males.

Spawning occurs between March and June when the female lays up to 300,000 eggs in lacy strands over weeds, twigs, stones or any other solid object in the shallows. The eggs begin to hatch out about a week after they are fertilized.

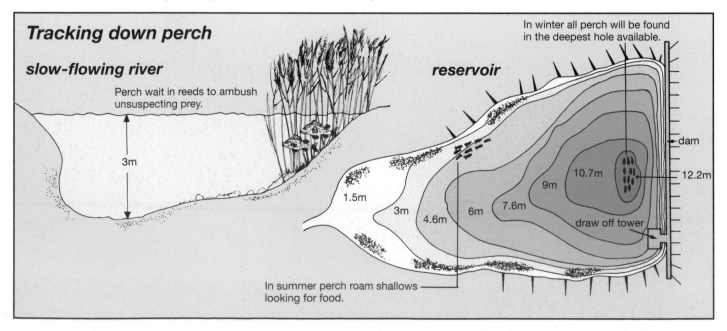

Tracking down perch

slow-flowing river

Perch wait in reeds to ambush unsuspecting prey.

3m

In summer perch roam shallows looking for food.

reservoir

In winter all perch will be found in the deepest hole available.

1.5m
3m
4.6m
6m
7.6m
9m
10.7m
12.2m

dam

draw off tower

Wels – the ugly freshwater giant

This odd-looking immigrant to British waters is called a catfish because of its whiskers – which are, in fact, feelers packed with taste buds.

Record wels

● The British rod-caught record wels is a 43lb 8oz (19.73kg) fish caught from Wilstone Reservoir, Tring in 1970 by R J Bray.
● Though fish up to 70lb (31.8kg) have been netted at Woburn when draining the 'Shoulder of Mutton' lake, few wels over 30lb (13.6kg) have been caught in Britain. One of this size is a very large fish. Any wels over 20lb (9kg) is regarded as a specimen.

The wels catfish – also called the catfish wels, catfish or wels – cannot be mistaken for any other fish in British waters (except the burbot which is probably now extinct in Britain). It has a long tapering body, a large head and dull, mottled skin. Colours vary, but generally it has a dark grey back with pale brown flanks and a whitish belly.

Follow the feeding

Wels are predatory fish and, like most predators, spend their early life feeding on invertebrates. As they grow, they start to feed mainly on fish. They are noted as nocturnal predators, though many have been caught in daylight.

As with all species of catfish (which is

Distribution

There are only a few waters stocked with wels, so their exact locations are marked.

only a term for fish, both freshwater and marine, which have 'whiskery' features), wels are mostly active near the bottom, so other bottom dwellers such as tench are a particular favourite, as are the larger freshwater shellfish. They also sometimes feed higher in the water, coming to the surface to take wildfowl and – according to myth – the

Vital statistics

Scientific name: *Silurus glanis*
Maximum weight: (Britain) 75lb (34kg)
  (E. Europe) 700lb (318kg)
Average weight: 10lb (4.5kg)
Maximum length: (Britain) 6½ft (2m)
  (E. Europe) 16½ft (5m)
Life-span: 30 years

The dorsal fin is very small.

The body is slimy and scaleless.

The anal fin is long – half the total body length – and joins with the tail.

The large mouth is filled with small teeth.

There are six feelers in all – four short ones on the lower jaw and two longer ones, like a moustache, on the upper.

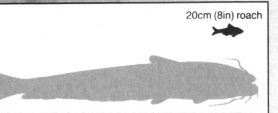

20cm (8in) roach

occasional dog and even sheep. Wels have huge jaws, so there is no problem about being able to gulp down a small hound in one mouthful.

These catfish were introduced to Britain relatively recently – the late 19th century – and so have not reached anything like their maximum size. They are also adapted to warmer weather than is usual in Britain, so it is highly unlikely that British wels will ever grow large enough to worry pets or livestock.

A nesting fish

Wels do best in still waters and large, slow-flowing rivers. In Britain they are confined to a few reservoirs, lakes, gravel pits and canals in the South East and Midlands but they are slowly spreading as a result of both legal and illegal stocking.

The wels is one of the rare freshwater fish which forms a crude nest for the protection of its eggs. The male hollows out a small depression in the bottom and often partly lines it with vegetation. Spawning takes place when the water temperature is high enough – about 19°C (66°F) – usually between May and July in a warm summer. The female sheds a sticky pile of up to half a million eggs into the nest. These are

▲ *Kevin Maddocks proudly shows off a 72lb (32.7kg) monster from the River Ebro in Spain. Though night fishing is best, this 'cat' came during the day, and fought for a full 40 minutes on 22lb (10kg) main line.*

guarded by the male until after they hatch.

Obviously the vast majority of the fry must die during the first few months – probably over winter – otherwise any water would quickly become overrun.

After about three weeks the eggs hatch and the male loses interest in his offspring, except perhaps as a tasty snack. The young fish take between three and five years to mature, at which point they can weigh anything from 2-10lb (0.9-4.5kg). In England, wels reach weights of around 20-30lb (9-13.6kg) in ten to fifteen years. At this weight they usually stop growing even though they can live for much longer than this. It seems British waters are too cold, or perhaps the prey species too small, to encourage growth to the huge proportions of Eastern European fish.

Introducing the wels

This species of catfish is native to Eastern Europe and the South West USSR. Populations have been established in much of continental Europe as well as Britain.

They were first successfully introduced to England at Woburn Abbey in 1880, though there had been an unsuccessful attempt some 15 years earlier. Most British wels are descended from this original stock.

Their range was extended considerably in the 1960s, with many people illegally stocking waters. Now the Ministry of Agriculture, Fisheries and Food must be consulted before any further introductions are made and their rules state that these fish may only be stocked in completely enclosed still waters.

Top wels waters

The best waters for wels in Britain are:
● **Claydon Lake, Beds** The most famous wels water in Britain. Though only small it regularly produces wels up to 34lb (15.4kg).
● **Tiddenfoot Lake, Leighton Buzzard, Beds** A very popular fishery where many anglers have caught their first wels. Fish up to 20lb (9kg).
● **Rackley Hills, Leighton Buzzard, Beds** This holds a small number of wels but it has produced fish of up to 34lb (15.4kg).
● **Woburn Park, Beds** The original home of these catfish but fishing is restricted.
● **Woburn Sands Pit, Beds** Contains fish up to 28lb (12.7kg).
● **Jones Pit, Heath and Reach, Leighton Buzzard, Beds** There are fish to 20lb (9kg).
● **Withy Pool, near Hitchin, Beds** A private water open to anglers – some wels.
● **Marsworth Reservoir, Tring, Herts** This has produced some small wels but there are supposed to be larger ones too.

European waters include:
● **Carp Fishers Abroad,** Metz, North East France.
● **Lake Cassein,** Var, France.
● **River Ebro,** Zaragoza, Spain.
● **Schnackensee fishery,** Gunzenhausen, Germany.
● **Rivers Regen, Rott and Nabb,** North Bavaria, Germany.

TRACKING DOWN WELS

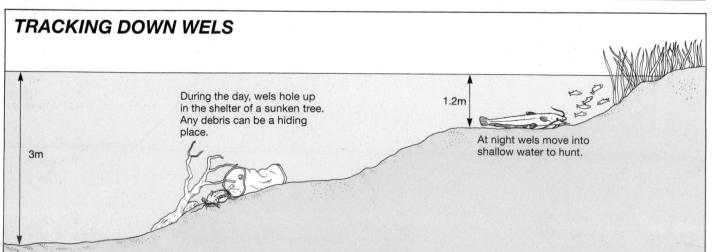

During the day, wels hole up in the shelter of a sunken tree. Any debris can be a hiding place.

3m

1.2m

At night wels move into shallow water to hunt.

The barbel: fast-water fighter

Barbel are one of the most exciting sport fish a coarse angler can try to catch as they never give up in the fight.

Record barbel

● The British rod-caught record is for a 14lb 6oz (6.52kg) fish captured by Aylmer Tryon in 1934 at the Royalty Fishery, Hampshire.
● Salmon fishermen have landed larger barbel in Britain up to 16lb 1oz (7.3kg) but these have been foul-hooked during the coarse close season.
● A specimen barbel weighs 7lb (3.2kg) and the magic weight is 10lb (4.5kg) which few anglers ever achieve without real dedication.

Barbel are slim and streamlined – a sure sign that they are mainly river fish. Their colours are typical of the carp family they belong to, with green or brown backs, golden-bronze flanks and pale bellies, though in clear water they can be a much darker brown-black.

Feeling for food

These fish are well adapted for bottom feeding in fast-flowing rivers. Their long, pointed heads with underslung mouths are ideal for digging around in the gravel over which they prefer to live. Their barbels – the distinctive feelers after which they are named – are extremely sensitive to touch and taste and so are very useful in scouring the bottom in search of insect larvae and other tasty morsels.

Favourite foods are worms and insect larvae, crustaceans such as crayfish and shrimps, and molluscs including snails and freshwater mussels. Barbel also eat small fish, especially those living on the bottom of

Distribution

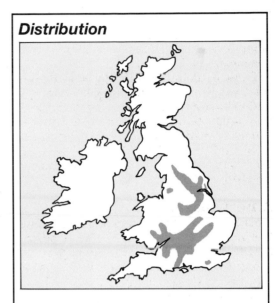

Originally found only in some British rivers flowing into the North Sea, the barbel's popularity as a sport fish has led to it being stocked in many other suitable rivers. The barbel in two of the most famous barbel rivers – the Hampshire Avon and the Severn – are the result of stocking. There has been no successful stocking of rivers in Ireland or Scotland.

the river, such as loach and bullheads. Hard foods present no difficulty as barbel, like all members of the carp family, have powerful crushing teeth in their throats.

In winter, when the water is colder, barbel feed with less enthusiasm. But in the floodwater conditions common in winter

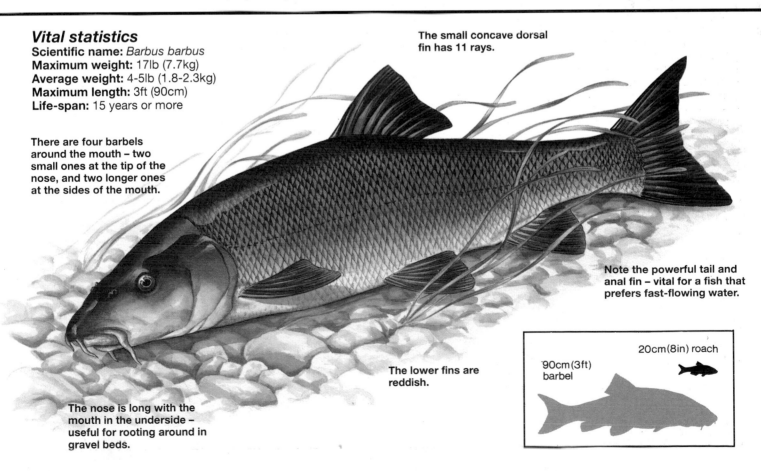

Vital statistics
Scientific name: *Barbus barbus*
Maximum weight: 17lb (7.7kg)
Average weight: 4-5lb (1.8-2.3kg)
Maximum length: 3ft (90cm)
Life-span: 15 years or more

There are four barbels around the mouth – two small ones at the tip of the nose, and two longer ones at the sides of the mouth.

The small concave dorsal fin has 11 rays.

Note the powerful tail and anal fin – vital for a fish that prefers fast-flowing water.

The lower fins are reddish.

The nose is long with the mouth in the underside – useful for rooting around in gravel beds.

20cm(8in) roach

90cm(3ft) barbel

► *This 10lb 12oz (4.9kg) barbel in beautiful condition was taken from the Hampshire Avon. It fell to fried luncheon meat fished over a bed of hemp. Fish as large as this tend to forage in small groups rather than in the big shoals of their smaller cousins, so this is worth watching out for if you want to try stalking for a specimen fish.*

Top ten barbel waters

The following rivers hold large heads of good sized barbel.
● **River Derwent, Yorkshire** Home to some very big barbel weighing up to 12lb (5.4kg).
● **River Ure, Yorkshire** Large numbers of barbel of 4-8lb (1.8-3.6kg). Further downstream at Dunsforth (some regard this as being on the River Ouse) there are bigger barbel to 10lb (4.5kg).
● **River Severn, Atcham, Shropshire** Well known for barbel reaching double figures.
● **River Trent, East Stoke, near Newark, Notts.** Numerous barbel between 3-5lb (1.4-2.3kg) and some larger ones.
● **River Wensum, Norfolk** Home of a few very large barbel up to 13lb (5.9kg).
● **River Ouse, Buckingham, Buckinghamshire** Contains a head of big barbel.
● **Hampshire Avon** One of the most famous barbel rivers – fast flowing, with many barbel up to 13lb (5.9kg).
● **River Stour, Wessex** The big barbel river with fish up to 14lb (6.4kg).
● **Bristol Avon, Avon** A good number of barbel to over 10lb (4.5kg) are caught here.
● **River Thames** This is particularly good upstream of Oxford and in its tributaries – the Lea, Lodden, Kennet and Wey.

Water levels

In the 1960s and 70s, water was drained from much of the land and many of the rivers in South East England to make it suitable for arable farming. This reduced both the water tables and the levels of the rivers. Such water abstraction causes many rivers to silt up and can ruin the barbel's favourite gravel beds.

Drainage also results in loss of weed and bankside cover. These problems have made life difficult for many fish, but especially for the barbel which has suffered in some waters and has even been lost to stretches of others.

and early spring, barbel can become highly active, feasting on the prey animals washed into the river.

Gravel-loving fish

Although stillwater populations of barbel exist, they are far more common in rivers, especially where the flow is fast enough to prevent silt being deposited. This means they are usually found over a clean gravel bottom where they like to spawn and feed. They also prefer water with a high oxygen content so you can often find them in the outfalls of weirs.

Barbel spawn between May and July, when they make their way upstream in large shoals to gravel beds in shallow water. Once there, the female makes a redd (a depression in the gravel for the spawn), where the sticky eggs are fertilized. After spawning, the exhausted fish rest up in still water under the banks until they have regained their strength.

Young barbel appear dappled and are covered with numerous dark spots and blotches. It is easy to mistake one of these for a large gudgeon, though gudgeon have only two barbels. They reach maturity after about four to five years, when they are anything from 25-75cm (10-30in) long. A 50cm (20in) barbel weighs about 5lb (2.3kg).

In common with many other coarse fish, specimens from the Continent are usually bigger and can reach 20lb (9kg). The warmer weather provides longer periods of rich feeding in the summer.

Tracking down barbel

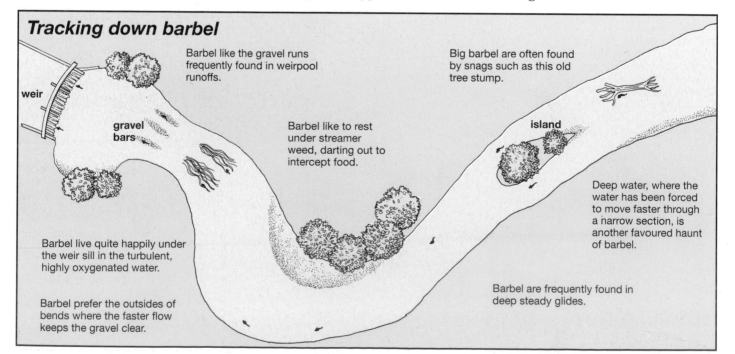

Barbel like the gravel runs frequently found in weirpool runoffs.

Big barbel are often found by snags such as this old tree stump.

weir

gravel bars

Barbel like to rest under streamer weed, darting out to intercept food.

island

Deep water, where the water has been forced to move faster through a narrow section, is another favoured haunt of barbel.

Barbel live quite happily under the weir sill in the turbulent, highly oxygenated water.

Barbel prefer the outsides of bends where the faster flow keeps the gravel clear.

Barbel are frequently found in deep steady glides.

Mud-loving tench

An inhabitant of shallow ponds and lakes, the hardy tench is one of the main reasons for summer angling.

Record tench

● The British tench record stands at 14lb 3oz (6.435kg). It was captured at Wraysbury, Middlesex in 1987 by P. Gooriah.
● Until the 1970s, the specimen weight for tench was about 5lb (2.3kg) and a tench of 7lb (3.2kg) was the fish of a lifetime, but now hundreds of this size are caught in a season. This may be due to advanced methods or, more likely, the amount of free food (in the form of boilies and groundbait) thrown into the waters. Whatever the reason, the specimen weight is now 7lb (3.2kg).

There is something very satisfying about the appearance of the deep-bodied tench. It is a member of the carp family and can vary in colour from almost black through green to pale yellow. The most usual colouring is a deep olive green back and flanks, with a paler belly. There is also an ornamental golden variety which sometimes has black patches on its back and sides.

Follow the feeding

Tench feed almost exclusively on the bottom – finding their food by rooting around in the mud. As they do this they often release strings of fine bubbles. These come from pockets of marsh gas (mainly methane) disturbed by the fish as they feed in the mud. The gas filters through the tench's mouth and gills, and the fine gill rakers produce characteristic pinhead bubbles.

Tench eat all the small prey animals found on the bottom but are especially fond of bloodworms, jokers and other insect lar-

vae. They also eat larger items such as worms, snails, mussels and even some small fish. They feed mainly at dawn and dusk, but sometimes continue through the night. In winter they hardly feed at all, lying inactive on the mud for long periods.

Distribution

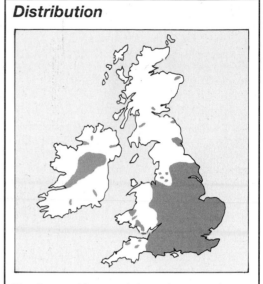

Tench are widespread throughout south-east England but are less common in Scotland and Wales. They are found throughout Ireland but are most common in the centre, along the course of the River Shannon.

Vital statistics

Scientific name: *Tinca tinca*
Maximum weight: 15-16lb (6.8-7.3kg)
Average weight: 3lb (1.4kg)
Maximum length: 24-26in (60-66cm)
Life-span: 20 years

The 'wrist' of the tail is extemely thick.

The tail is very slightly concave.

Males have longer pelvic fins than females and this can be used to tell the sexes apart. On males the fins reach back as far as the anal vent.

All the fins are large and rounded.

Tench are covered in tiny scales which are well embedded in the skin and covered with a thick layer of slime.

The small eyes have red irises.

The upper lip is larger than the lower – a help to the bottom-feeding tench.

There are two tiny barbels at the corners of the mouth.

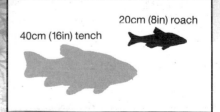

40cm (16in) tench   20cm (8in) roach

Increasing numbers of large tench are being caught in Britain and this may in part be due to the quantity of high protein baits (boilies) thrown into waters every year. Tench, like carp, eat them readily and may put on weight as a result.

Lazy stillwater fish

Though some tench are found in quite fast-flowing rivers such as the Trent, they thrive best in rich still waters, sluggish rivers and canals. You won't find them in very fast water or poor upland lakes, but they are highly tolerant of low levels of dissolved oxygen, and so do well in shallow ponds which have low water levels, or even become stagnant, in summer.

Tench won't spawn unless the water has remained at 18°C (64°F) or above for at least two weeks. They therefore spawn later than most other British coarse fish – between May and August. Each pair takes several weeks to spawn, leaving many clusters of pale green eggs stuck to the stems of water plants. Large females carry

▲ *A fine (male and female) pair of tench. Tench often forage in their breeding pairs and are caught together. The female is the one held slightly higher, with a rounder (roe-filled) belly and shorter pelvic fins.*

The doctor fish

Tench slime was thought to have magical medical properties – other fish would deliberately rub against them and be cured of all ills!

In the middle ages tench slime was believed to cure headaches, toothaches, jaundice and many other illnesses.

People also believed that pike would not eat tench, perhaps because of their mythical powers. Those anglers who have felt the frustration of losing tench at the net to pike know this just isn't true.

as many as 750,000 eggs.

The eggs hatch out in four or five days but the larvae remain stuck to the plants by their heads until the yolk sac attached to their bellies is used up. Then the fry must forage for food. The young fish live in the weeds and are very rarely seen or caught, though obviously large numbers of them die in the first year, probably during the winter.

Growth is very slow at first – they only reach 20-30cm (8-12in) after three years, and spawn for the first time after at least four. In ideal conditions, they reach about 5-6lb (2.3-2.7kg) after ten years and can live up to twice that age.

Top tench waters

These waters contain either big specimen tench or good quantities of middle-sized fish.
● **Lough Ree, Westmeath, Rep. Ireland** Huge water on the Shannon with many tench.
● **Burton Stather Brickpond, South Humberside** Many fish of 3-5lb (1.4-2.3kg).
● **Taverham Mills Lakes, Norfolk** Plenty of 3-5lb (1.4-2.3kg) fish.
● **Sywell Reservoir, Northamptonshire** This 100 acre water yields many 7lb (3.2kg) fish and some 8-9 pounders (3.6-4.1kg).
● **Wilstone Reservoir, Tring, Hertfordshire** Few fish but they reach over 12lb (5.4kg)!
●**Blenheim Lakes, Oxfordshire** Lots of good sized fish.
● **T.C. Pits, Oxfordshire** Used to produce fish over 8lb (3.6kg) and there are still some big specimens.
● **Bradley's Lake, South Cerney, Gloucestershire** Fabulous (and large) gravel pit for quality tench.
● **Johnson's Lakes, Kent** Big fish up to 10lb (4.5kg).
● **Yately Lakes, Leisure Sport, Hampshire** These waters hold many big fish.

TRACKING DOWN TENCH

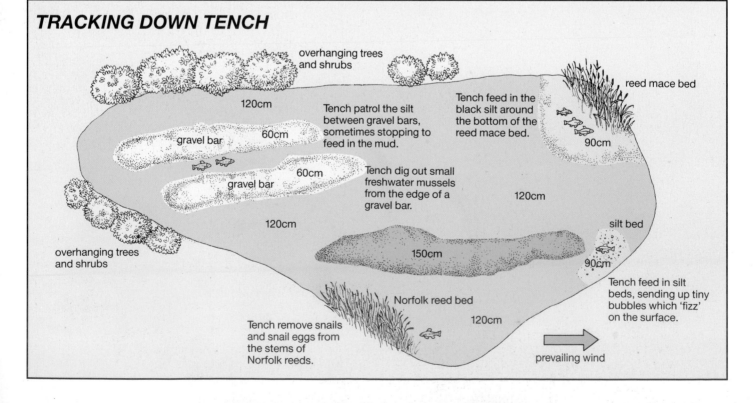

overhanging trees and shrubs

reed mace bed

120cm

gravel bar

60cm

Tench patrol the silt between gravel bars, sometimes stopping to feed in the mud.

Tench feed in the black silt around the bottom of the reed mace bed.

90cm

60cm

gravel bar

Tench dig out small freshwater mussels from the edge of a gravel bar.

120cm

120cm

silt bed

150cm

overhanging trees and shrubs

90cm

Tench feed in silt beds, sending up tiny bubbles which 'fizz' on the surface.

Norfolk reed bed

120cm

Tench remove snails and snail eggs from the stems of Norfolk reeds.

prevailing wind

The greedy chub

The chub, found mainly in England, has a large mouth to accommodate its voracious appetite, and pound for pound it's one of the best fighting fish you'll hook.

Record chub

● The record British fish weighed 8lb 4oz (3.74kg) and was caught by G F Smith on the Royalty Fishery, River Avon, Hampshire in 1913. The fish was deleted from the record list, but now it has been reinstated after members of the National Association of Specialist Anglers located the cased fish and the facts behind its capture.

● An 18lb (8.2kg) chub has been caught and recorded on the Continent. The warmer waters help some species grow large.

In many ways chub look like dace at first glance. Both have black tails and grey or green backs. Chub, however, usually have brassy coloured flanks, orange anal fins and big mouths, and they grow much larger than dace. Their dorsal fins are convex (arched) while those of the dace are slightly indented (concave).

Feeding characteristics

Small chub of 3in (7.5cm) or so eat large invertebrates, worms and fry (recently hatched spawn). Chub are omnivorous; that is, they eat fish, insects and vegetable matter (such as silkweed, berries and bread). In fact, if an elderberry tree is overhanging a river bank, for example, chub often gorge themselves with ripe berries. Fish of over 3lb (1.4kg) may eat small bullheads, minnows, roach and dace. They don't have teeth in their mouth; their mighty pharyngeal teeth,

located at the base of the throat, can crush just about any food item. This includes crayfish which, despite their hard shell, are quickly demolished.

Habitat

Running water is the best place to look for chub – especially in any steady-flowing low-

Distribution

Chub are found throughout England but they don't thrive in the clear, cold rivers of Scotland and are rare in Ireland.

Vital statistics

Scientific name: *Leuciscus cephalus*
Maximum weight: (Britain) 8-9lb (3.6-4.1kg)
Maximum length: 22-23in (56-59cm)
Average weight: 2 3lb (0.9 1.4kg)
Life-span: 10-12 years

Rising from the shelter of weeds, chub often eat insects on the surface of the water.

Chub have large mouths for their size.

Chub can be distinguished from the dace by their convex dorsal and anal fins.

Its fins are rounded.

The flanks are brassy, and the anal and pelvic fins are orange.

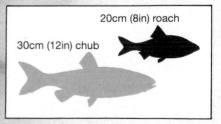

20cm (8in) roach

30cm (12in) chub

land or middle reach of river. They don't thrive in upland waters, which are more suited to trout, salmon and grayling. Chub are a retiring fish, and they rely much on the shelter of overhanging trees, rafts of debris, underwater weeds and undercut banks – cover is an essential part of their habitat.

During the afternoon, however, chub often sun themselves. You can see them on clear, windless summer days, but be careful when approaching them, for they spook easily. They may also spook if you try to cast directly above them. Casting a yard or so upstream and in front of the fish often does the trick.

Because chub are adaptable, they can also survive in still waters; it's here where they grow fat as barrels. Crystal-clear gravel pits contain many large specimens. On shallow

Top ten chub waters

Neville Fickling suggests...
● **Hardwick Gravel Pit, Oxfordshire** Some huge chub, perhaps over 8lb (3.6kg).
● **River Stour, Dorset** A famous chub river with many 4-7lb (1.8-3.2kg) fish.
● **River Avon, Hampshire** This is another famous chub river.
● **Chesterfield Canal, Retford, Notts.** Matchwater with 3lb (1.4kg) fish.
● **River Welland (Lincs.)** Many fish.
● **River Trent** (tidal) Home of many big chub up to 7lb (3.2kg).
● **Manor Farm Fishery, South Muskham, Notts.** Many 4-5lb (1.8-2.3kg) chub.
● **River Derwent, Borrowash, Derbyshire** An excellent water with big stocks of chub, the matchman's dream.
● **River Wensum, Norfolk** Along with big barbel and roach, the Wensum upstream of Norwich offers good chub fishing.
● **River Derwent, Yorkshire** Many 4-5lb (1.8-2.3kg) chub.

gravel bars between 30-90cm (1-3ft) deep you can find them basking in the sun.

Life cycle
Chub usually spawn between April and June, depending on the temperature of the water. The adults swim upstream to shallow gravelly runs and breed only in flowing water. Each female can shed up to 100,000 eggs over gravel, weeds or debris on the river bed. After eight to ten days the eggs hatch. The fry feed in shoals on microscopic organisms (plankton). As they grow, they remain in shoals. Even the mature fish group together. Only the very large fish become solitary.

▲ *Taken from a small, slow-moving river, this excellent chub weighed 4lb 9oz (2.1kg). Trotting maggots is one of the most popular means of catching chub in rivers.*

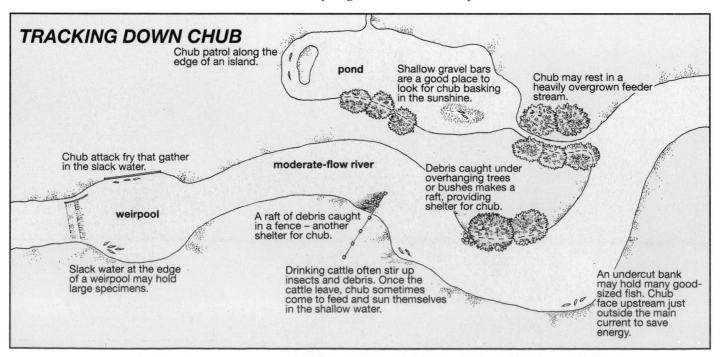

TRACKING DOWN CHUB

Chub patrol along the edge of an island.

pond

Shallow gravel bars are a good place to look for chub basking in the sunshine.

Chub may rest in a heavily overgrown feeder stream.

Chub attack fry that gather in the slack water.

moderate-flow river

Debris caught under overhanging trees or bushes makes a raft, providing shelter for chub.

weirpool

A raft of debris caught in a fence – another shelter for chub.

Slack water at the edge of a weirpool may hold large specimens.

Drinking cattle often stir up insects and debris. Once the cattle leave, chub sometimes come to feed and sun themselves in the shallow water.

An undercut bank may hold many good-sized fish. Chub face upstream just outside the main current to save energy.

The crafty carp

The carp, once stocked as a food fish, grows large, fights hard and can tax the ingenuity of even the best anglers.

The name carp covers a variety of species including the common, crucian and grass carp. The carp most frequently found throughout Britain is the common. But just to make things more confusing, there are three cultivated varieties of common carp – leather, mirror and 'common' – in addition to yet another, the wild type.

Most carp have broad, deep bodies and brown backs. Their flanks range from the deep brown and yellow of most leathers to the golden sheen of wildies.

Follow the feeding

Carp fry feed on plankton and water fleas, but adult carp, with their sensitive feelers (barbels) and vacuum-like mouths, are best suited to bottom feeding. They spend most of their time rooting around in the mud at the bottom of lakes and rivers. Nothing that lives on or in the mud is safe from the digging of carp – including snails, crayfish,

Distribution

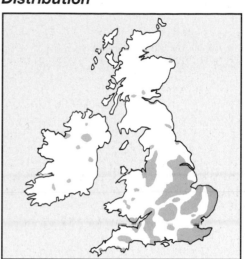

Carp have been introduced to many lakes, rivers and ponds throughout England and Wales during the last 50 years. They are not as common in Scotland and Ireland.

bloodworms, mussels and shrimps. However, as any angler can tell you, carp also feed in mid-water and come up to the surface for floating food.

Though not strictly predators, large carp have on occasion been known to eat other fish. They have extremely sensitive taste

Vital statistics

Scientific name: *Cyprinus carpio*
Maximum weight: (Britain) 45-55lb (21-25kg)
(Continent) 100lb (45kg)
Average weight: 10lb (4.5kg)
Maximum length: (Britain) 35in (89cm)
Life-span: 40 years or more

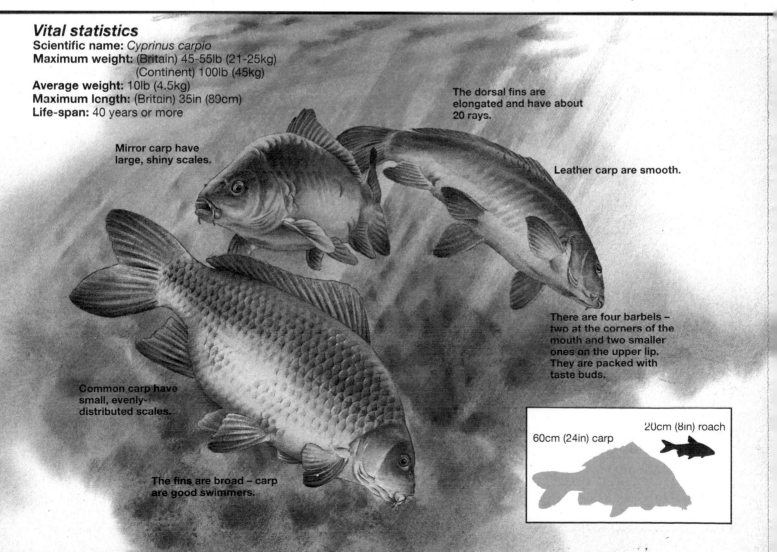

The dorsal fins are elongated and have about 20 rays.

Mirror carp have large, shiny scales.

Leather carp are smooth.

There are four barbels – two at the corners of the mouth and two smaller ones on the upper lip. They are packed with taste buds.

Common carp have small, evenly-distributed scales.

The fins are broad – carp are good swimmers.

60cm (24in) carp   20cm (8in) roach

▲ *These two 18lb (8.1kg) common carp were taken on a small lake. Good-sized specimens in Britain, fish of this size are usual on the Continent.*

and smell receptors and can distinguish one sort of shellfish from another. This is what enables them to avoid baits on which they have been caught before. They can be spooked easily, so be careful – and quiet – when approaching shallow waters.

Temperature also affects feeding. If the water is colder than 14°C (57°F), carp feed less readily. However, canny anglers have proved that carp can still be persuaded to feed even in winter. Well-aerated water – the shallows and the surface during windy weather – also encourages feeding.

Life-cycle

The preferred habitat of carp is still water – a mature lake, rich in plant life and nutrients, is ideal. Nevertheless, they are extremely adaptable fish and are common in lowland reservoirs, many lowland rivers with a slow to moderate rate of flow and even some fast-flowing chalk streams. River-dwelling carp are slimmer and more athletic-looking than their stillwater cousins.

Spawning, like feeding, depends upon temperature. Carp only spawn when the

water temperature is between 18-20°C (64-68°F), usually in late May and early June, as you would expect with a fish introduced from the warmer climes of the Continent. Very often the young carp do not have enough time to build up reserves of fat before winter sets in, and so die. This prevents them from taking over many waters. However, carp are so long-lived, surviving for 40 years or more, that even the few which do reach adulthood ensure the survival of the species.

When the water is warm enough, each female lays over one million eggs among the weeds in the shallows. The eggs, small, sticky and yellowish, hatch in three to eight days, again depending on temperature. The larvae live off their yolk sacs for a few days. After that, they begin to feed on tiny water organisms.

Growth is rapid where the water is warm and rich in food. They can reach 2lb (0.9kg) in a year and continue to grow at that rate indefinitely, but many of the waters in Britain are too cold to encourage maximum size.

Top ten carp waters

The following are ten of the best known waters for large-sized carp.
● **Redmire Pool, Hereford and Worcester** Produced last two British records.
● **Savay Lake, Denham, Bucks**. Many 20-30lb (9-13.6kg) carp in this season and day ticket water.
● **Yateley Complex, Surrey** Fish over 40lb (18kg).
● **Darenth, Dartford, Kent** A leisure water with carp up to 38lb (17.2kg).
● **Waveney Valley Lakes, Suffolk** Fish up to 30lb (13.6kg).

● **Withy Pool, Bedfordshire** Many carp to 35lb (15.9kg).
● **River Trent, Notts.** This stretch regularly produces 20lb (9kg) fish.
● **Brooklands Lake, Dartford, Kent** Excellent day ticket lake with fish up to 20lb (9.1kg).
● **Manor Farm Fishery, South Muskham, Notts**. Many 20lb (9kg) mirrors and commons.
● **Tilery Lake, North Humberside** This Hull and District water is the most famous northern carp water.

TRACKING DOWN CARP

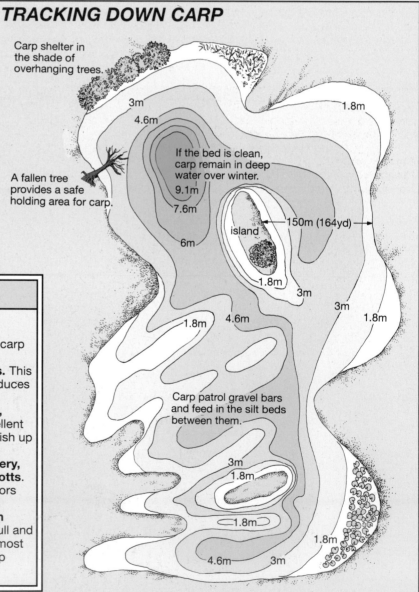

Carp shelter in the shade of overhanging trees.

A fallen tree provides a safe holding area for carp.

If the bed is clean, carp remain in deep water over winter.

150m (164yd)

island

Carp patrol gravel bars and feed in the silt beds between them.

3m
1.8m
4.6m
9.1m
7.6m
6m
1.8m
3m
4.6m
1.8m
3m
1.8m
3m
1.8m
1.8m
4.6m
3m

Bream – 'dustbin lids' of the bottom

Bream, a sought-after matchman's fish, live in shoals and can grow fairly large. Catch one, and you're likely to hook a few more.

Distribution

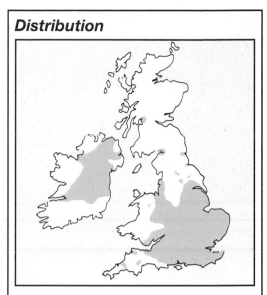

Common bream are found in most parts of England – except in the Pennines – and in central Ireland and southern Wales. They're also found in a few waters in Scotland.

Tip: Common or silver bream?

● Small common bream, called skimmers, are often confused with silver bream, a different species altogether. One way to tell the difference is to look at the eyes – common bream have much smaller eyes than silver bream.
● Another difference is that common bream have about 25-27 rays on their anal fin, whereas silver bream have about 19-21.

Common bream are one of the larger members of the carp family found in British freshwaters. They have deep, narrow bodies (hence the anglers' name 'dustbin lids') and can swim with ease through weedy or reedy shallow water. Their long, dark dorsal fins are set well back near their blackish, deeply forked tails. Bream have small, underslung mouths which can project forwards while they root on muddy lake or river bottoms in search of food. Another distinctive feature is their covering of thick slime.

Young bream, called skimmers, are silver. As they mature, they turn a dark, golden-olive colour. Fully mature bream have dark backs and greenish-bronze flanks with white undersides. Some bream with disorders of the nervous system appear two-toned – one half of their body is darker than the other half.

Bottom rooters

Skimmers begin feeding on algae and plankton and then graduate to water fleas. Adult fish eat whatever food is available –

Vital statistics

Scientific name: *Abramis brama*
Maximum size: (Britain) 16lb (7.2kg)
(Europe) 18lb (8.2kg)
Average weight: 3-4lb (1.4-1.8kg)
Average size: 14-16in (35-40cm)
Life-span: 15-20 years

The colour of mature bream varies considerably depending on the water – from a golden-bronze to a greenish-black.

Bream form shoals as a defence against predatory fish such as pike.

The dark dorsal fin is set well back near the tail.

Their deep, narrow bodies are well suited to shallow waters.

The dark tail is deeply forked.

The small underslung mouth is specially adapted for rooting out insect larvae, vegetable matter and small crustaceans on the bottoms of rivers and still waters.

Bream feed with their mouths pointing downward, and their bodies rising almost vertically upwards.

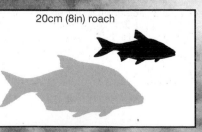

20cm (8in) roach

▲ *Summer is an excellent time to fish for large bream, as these fine specimens suggest.*

Top ten bream waters

● **River Welland, Lincs.** This excellent river produces big catches of 3-7lb (1.4-3.2kg) bream.
● **Tring Reservoir, Hertfordshire** A long history of producing many 10lb (4.5kg) fish.
● **Castle Loch, Lochmaben, Scotland** One of the few top class bream waters in Scotland – many 5-7lb (2.3-3.2kg) bream.
● **Hickling Broad, Norfolk** Mainly boat fishing at night. Total weights of fish over 100lb (45.5kg) have been recorded in one night's fishing.
● **River Trent, Holme Marsh, Weirfield, Nottinghamshire** Packed with many 3-5lb (1.4-2.3kg) bream.
● **River Witham, Lincs.** Pleasure and match anglers enjoy catches of 20-40lb (9.1-18.1kg) of fish.
● **Queenford Lagoon (Oxfordshire)** A famous water which produces large fish – up to 10-15lb (4.5-6.8kg).
● **T.C. Pit, Oxford** Regularly produces many bream between 10-15lb (4.5-6.8kg).
● **Attenborough Gravel Pits, Nottinghamshire** Series of gravel pits with large shoals of 4-5lb (1.8-2.3kg) bream.

The key to large bream populations is the diversity and quantity of food available. Waters rich in silt and plant life are an excellent source of food and cover. They usually contain great numbers of insects and snails – an important food source for skimmers. Some heavily fished waters may also sustain large populations of bream, for many anglers use vast amounts of groundbait and loosefeed, providing food for the fish on a regular basis throughout the fishing season.

including a wide range of plant material, insect larvae, minnows and bottom-dwelling invertebrates. Larger, older bream sometimes feed at night on fry and small minnows. Members of the shoal frequently roll on the surface of the water as a prelude to feeding. A variety of baits will tempt bream – corn, worms, boilies, maggots and bread – provided you fish them directly on the bottom.

Habitat

Bream are a shoal fish – the 'cattle' of the underwater world. A shoal of bream, for example, can comprise hundreds of individual fish between 3-4lb (1.4-1.8kg). One possible reason for grouping together is that it serves as a defence against predators. It appears that there's safety in numbers.

Bream are thought of as stillwater fish. They are attracted to shallow, reedy bays to feed and bask in the sun. They are, however, more adaptable than many anglers think – they can thrive in moderate to fast-flowing rivers, sheltering just outside the main current under tree roots, in deep pools or near undercut banks.

Life-cycle

Spawning usually occurs at the end of May or early June – when the water temperature reaches 14-17°C (57-63°F). The males establish territories and develop hard, spawning tubercles on their heads and bodies. It is thought that the males swim alongside the females and buffet them, brushing the tubercles against the flanks of the females. This is a signal to the females to lay their sticky eggs, masses of which are deposited on weeds, reeds, underwater tree roots or debris on the bottoms of rivers or lakes.

Each female lays as many as 300,000 to 400,000 eggs which hatch in three to twelve days, depending on the water temperature. Warmer water may help the eggs hatch faster than colder water. Only a small fraction of the fry that hatch will survive.

During the first year, the fry reach 3-5in (7.5-12.5cm) in length. Overall, growth is slow. It takes five to six years for a fish to reach 2lb (0.9kg), and ten years for one to reach 5-7lb (2.3-3.2kg).

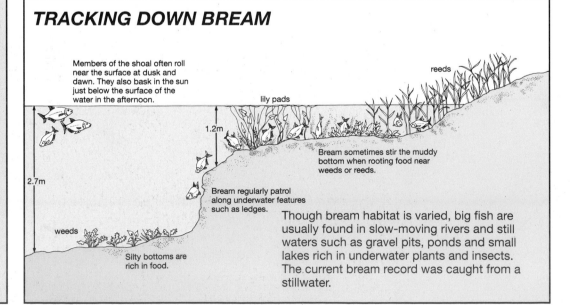

TRACKING DOWN BREAM

Members of the shoal often roll near the surface at dusk and dawn. They also bask in the sun just below the surface of the water in the afternoon.

reeds

lily pads

1.2m

2.7m

Bream sometimes stir the muddy bottom when rooting food near weeds or reeds.

Bream regularly patrol along underwater features such as ledges.

weeds

Silty bottoms are rich in food.

Though bream habitat is varied, big fish are usually found in slow-moving rivers and still waters such as gravel pits, ponds and small lakes rich in underwater plants and insects. The current bream record was caught from a stillwater.

The zander – sharp-eyed predator

Since it was introduced to the Great Ouse Relief Channel in 1963, the zander has done well, spreading into many waters in England.

Record zander

● R. Meadows caught the largest British zander in a Cambridgeshire stillwater in March 1988; the fish weighed 18lb 8oz (8.4kg).
● A previous record, which lasted for many years, was the 17lb 4oz (7.82kg) zander caught by D. Litton in October 1977 from the Great Ouse Relief Channel.
● Germany holds the European record zander. E. Karmann caught the fish in 1964; it weighed an incredible 28lb 11oz (13kg).

Beautifully coloured with golden (and sometimes silver) flanks and a green-black back, the zander – a streamlined predator – is a member of the perch family. It has dark bars along its back, and like most freshwater fish it has a white underside and two dorsal fins. The front fin, which the fish can raise at will, is spiny.

A particular feature of the fish is its large eyes, adapted especially for seeing prey in coloured water or at night. A zander has 'glassy' eyes because there is a layer of pigment (called the tapetum lucidum) in the retina which helps it absorb light.

Its mouth, filled with sharp, fang-like teeth, is large and easily capable of devouring the small fish which are the zander's main prey.

Distribution

Since 1963 zander populations have increased steadily throughout Norfolk, Suffolk, Bedfordshire, Surrey, Lincolnshire and Gloucestershire.

A foreign fish

The zander is not a native of the British Isles. It came originally from eastern Europe but is now widespread in Germany, Holland and France. In 1878 the ninth Duke of Bedford introduced 23 zander from Germany to the Woburn Abbey lakes. They

A zander can raise its front dorsal fin – this is especially useful when the fish is young because it serves as a form of defence.

Vital statistics
Scientific name: *Stizostedion lucioperca*
Maximum weight: 35lb (15.9kg)
Average weight: 3lb (1.4kg)
Maximum length: 40in (1m)
Life-span: 20 years

Other species struggle to see at night or in murky-coloured water, but the zander's excellent vision gives it a distinct advantage.

With its large eyes and sharp, fang-like teeth which are curved inward to help grip its prey, the zander is a highly effective hunter.

Zander often hunt in packs, harrying small fish, grabbing them tail-first and then eating them.

The zander is a member of the perch family and has golden flanks with a green-black back – though their colours vary from water to water.

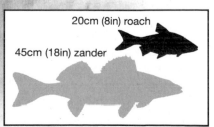
20cm (8in) roach
45cm (18in) zander

◄ *John Watson displays a specimen zander (weighing 12lb/5.4kg) taken from a fen drain in Norfolk. Most zander are caught at dusk and at night with either live or dead baits.*

remained localized until 1963 – when 97 were released into the Great Ouse Relief Channel in Norfolk. Since then they have spread all over eastern England, moving into many fens, rivers and lakes.

A survivor

It goes without saying that the zander, a shoaling fish, is highly adaptable. It thrives in large, slow-flowing fen drains and rivers. But it doesn't seem to do well in fast-flowing, clear rivers or in shallow waters where the oxygen content is low. Coloured waters and even tidal river stretches (where the salinity is high) produce many zander. In stillwaters you can find it during the day near drop-offs or holes because it avoids intense light.

Hunting habits

What makes zander exceptionally efficient hunters is that they sometimes gather in a pack to feed on small fish (usually at dawn, dusk and during the night). The zander chase after the fish, grabbing them from behind (often by the tail) and swallowing them.

Because other species cannot see as well in murky water or at night, the zander have a clear advantage. They feed on worms and leeches as well as small fish such as roach.

The spread of zander from 1968 coincided with the disappearance of small fish from many Norfolk rivers and drains. The zander received the blame. Many anglers believe, however, that industrial dumping and fertilizer run-offs were the main reasons for the decline.

Life-cycle

Zander usually spawn between April and June. A group gathers over stones or gravel, and the mature females dig a hollow in the gravel, lay about one to two million eggs and then guard them until they hatch. The males also protect the fry.

After hatching, the larvae live off their yolk sacs, reaching about ¼in (6mm) long after about a week. When the yolk sac is used up, the young eat plankton and insect larvae. Zander begin feeding on other fish at the age of three months – or when they are about 4in (10cm) long.

Top ten venues for zander

● **Great Ouse Relief and Cut Off Channels, Norfolk** The place where it all began in 1963.
● **Sixteen Foot Drain, Cambs.** Plenty of zander including many over 10lb (4.5kg).
● **Coombe Abbey Lake, Coventry, W. Midlands** An 80 acre stillwater with fish up to 14lb (6.4kg).
● **Old Bury Hill Lake, Dorking, Surrey** Home of fish up to 16lb (7.3kg).
● **Stewartby Brickpit, Bedfordshire** Plenty of small zander.
● **River Delph, Cambs.** More than 20 miles (32km) of good fishing.
● **Roswell Pits, Ely, Cambs.** Lots of average-sized zander.
● **River Severn, Tewkesbury, Glos.** Many 8-10lb (3.6-4.5kg) fish.
● **Great Ouse, Norfolk/Cambs.** This deep river holds many zander.
● **River Nene, Peterborough, Cambs.** Plenty of fish of all sizes.

TRACKING DOWN ZANDER

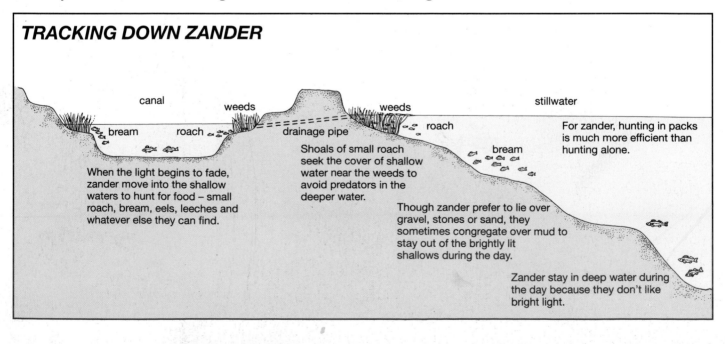

canal | weeds | weeds | stillwater

bream | roach | drainage pipe | roach | bream

For zander, hunting in packs is much more efficient than hunting alone.

When the light begins to fade, zander move into the shallow waters to hunt for food – small roach, bream, eels, leeches and whatever else they can find.

Shoals of small roach seek the cover of shallow water near the weeds to avoid predators in the deeper water.

Though zander prefer to lie over gravel, stones or sand, they sometimes congregate over mud to stay out of the brightly lit shallows during the day.

Zander stay in deep water during the day because they don't like bright light.

The golden rudd

Popular among anglers because it takes bait so readily, the red-finned rudd is often regarded as Britain's most colourful freshwater fish.

Record rudd

● The British rod-caught record – a long-standing one – is held by the Rev E.C. Alston who caught a 4lb 8oz (2.04kg) rudd in Thetford, Norfolk in 1933.

● The 4lb 10oz (2.097kg) specimen caught at Pitsford Reservoir, Northamptonshire on 28 September 1986 by D. Webb was a hybrid.

● The rudd record for the Republic of Ireland is a 3lb 1oz (1.389kg) fish from Kilglas Lake, Co. Roscommon. It was caught by A.E. Biddlecombe on 27 June 1959.

Easy to confuse at first glance with its close relative the roach, the rudd can be recognized by its red fins (brighter on the underside), deep bronze-gold flanks and a distinctive steeply angled, protruding lower lip. (The roach, less vividly coloured, has silvery flanks, dull orange fins and a receding lower lip.)

Another identifying feature in the rudd is that the beginning of its dorsal fin is set well behind the front of the pelvic fins – in roach the dorsal fin is directly above the base of the pelvic fins. The rudd also has a sharp ridge, or keel, between the pelvic and anal fins.

Rudd and roach hybridize freely and there is great confusion about its identity when a hybrid is caught. One way of checking a hybrid is to look at the lips – the roach/rudd hybrid often has equal lips, neither protruding nor receding.

Distribution

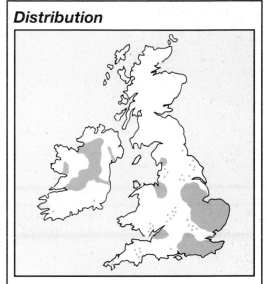

The rudd is common in stillwaters throughout southern England and in Ireland, but is rare in northern England. It is hardly ever found in Scotland or Wales.

Positive identification is only important when the catch may qualify for a new record. In this case the fish may have to be killed so that experts can examine its pharyngeal (throat) teeth. Rudd have two rows of throat teeth, while roach have only one row. Hybrids, intermediate between the

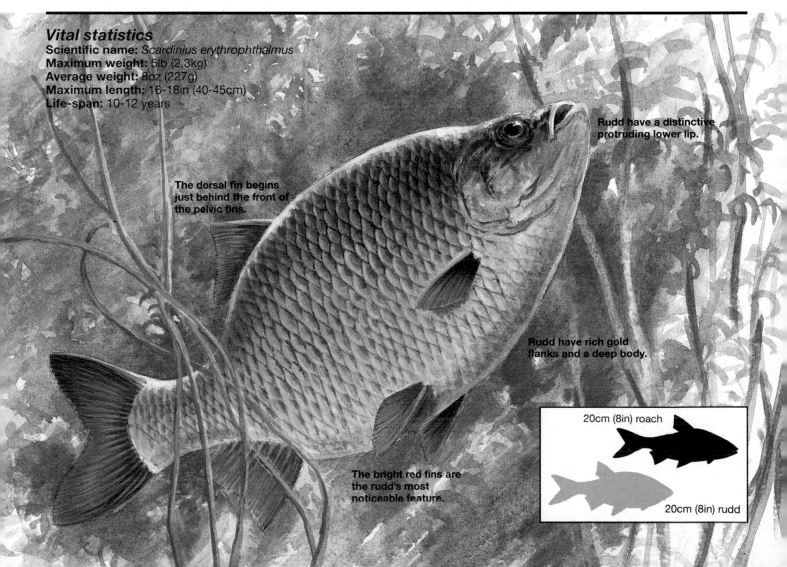

Vital statistics
Scientific name: *Scardinius erythrophthalmus*
Maximum weight: 5lb (2,3kg)
Average weight: 8oz (227g)
Maximum length: 16-18in (40-45cm)
Life-span: 10-12 years

Rudd have a distinctive protruding lower lip.

The dorsal fin begins just behind the front of the pelvic fins.

Rudd have rich gold flanks and a deep body.

The bright red fins are the rudd's most noticeable feature.

20cm (8in) roach

20cm (8in) rudd

▲ *A beautiful specimen rudd, its golden scales glowing with health. This one fell to a red maggot/sweetcorn cocktail, but floating baits, such as bread crust, can be equally successful for rudd.*

Top hotspots for rudd

Rudd populations are declining in many waters because of competition from other fish species – notably roach.
● **Swithland Reservoir, Leicestershire** Some of the biggest rudd in Britain, many over 4lb (1.8kg).
● **Horsey Mere, Norfolk** Large numbers of rudd – the shallow, reed-lined water suits them.
● **Slapton Ley, Devon** A big head of rudd.
● **Old Bedford Drain, Cambridgeshire** Rudd thrive in this crystal-clear, lily-covered drain.
● **Ivy Lake, Chichester, West Sussex** This water has produced many rudd of 2lb (0.9kg) or more.
● **Hollowell Reservoir, Northamptonshire** A water which may have some good rudd, but many of those caught have turned out to be roach/rudd hybrids.
● **Lough Ree, Galway, Republic of Ireland** Still produces big rudd in spite of the invasion by roach.

two, have only a partial second row.

The rudd's body is deep and a large well-fed specimen can be very broad across the shoulders. It is mainly a fish of still waters, with few populations thriving in rivers. It prefers reed or tree-lined waters where it can feed on fallen insects using its well-adapted mouth. The Norfolk Broads are ideal rudd habitat, but gravel pits, ponds, canals and lakes also have good populations.

Only nutrient-rich waters support large numbers of rudd. For some reason they tend to overpopulate suitable waters, resulting in thousands of stunted fish.

Follow the feeding

Because of the shape of the mouth – with the protruding lower lip – rudd feed more on the surface than roach. In warm weather they lie in shoals just under the surface, feeding on insects of all kinds. Rudd also take a variety of crustaceans and snails from the bottom, and a limited amount of plant matter – foraging about among weeds and reeds in the margins and middle depths of the water.

Large specimens occasionally take fish fry, while the young – like most members of the carp family – feed on animal plankton.

Rudd are known to come readily to a variety of baits – sweetcorn, maggots, bread and so on – but shoals take fright very easily, bolting away at the slightest disturbance. Because the fish scare so quickly they are tricky to approach and it can sometimes be quite difficult to catch more than one or two from a large shoal.

Summer spawning

Rudd spawn at the end of May or early June, each female shedding anything from 90,000 to 200,000 tiny transparent yellow eggs which stick on to weeds and reed stems. The young, which hatch after six to eight days, are no larger than the head of a pin and spend the first part of their life sheltering in shoals in the water margins.

As the fry grow larger, they move out into deeper water and begin to feed on insects – both adults and larvae. They are fairly slow-growing and in some waters can take up to four years to reach maturity.

Unfortunately, the rudd is declining in many waters perhaps because of competition from other fish – roach in particular. About fifty years ago roach were rare in Ireland, where they are not native. But in recent years the populations of introduced roach have pushed the rudd into the background in many places. The situation is similar in quite a few waters in England.

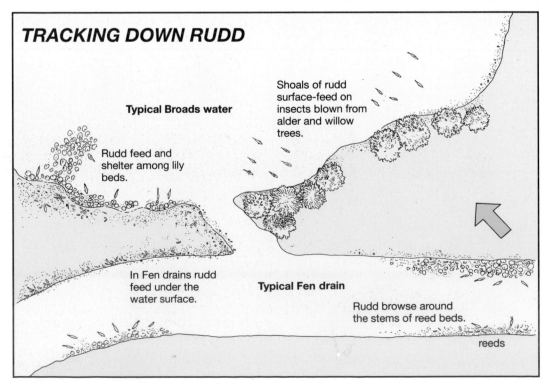

TRACKING DOWN RUDD

Typical Broads water

Shoals of rudd surface-feed on insects blown from alder and willow trees.

Rudd feed and shelter among lily beds.

In Fen drains rudd feed under the water surface.

Typical Fen drain

Rudd browse around the stems of reed beds.

reeds

The enigmatic eel

Although the eel, lurking in the depths of canals, rivers and oceans, has an elusive life-style, there are plenty to be caught.

No-one should have any difficulty recognizing the wriggling, snake-like common eel – also known as the freshwater eel. It has a long, slimy, sinuous body and a large mouth with a protruding lower jaw containing numerous small teeth. Its fins have become modified, the dorsal and anal fins forming a continuous line around the tail. Only the small pectoral fins bear any similarity to those of 'normal' fish.

Although its colouring changes with maturity, the eel is generally black or brown on the upper surface, with yellow or silver sides and a white underbelly.

Adult eels vary greatly in size. The female is larger than the male, reaching lengths of up to 1m (40in) – the male only grows to half this size. Slow-growing, they live for up to twelve years before reaching sexual maturity and being ready for migration (though a few may never migrate as they get trapped in their freshwater home.)

Record eels

● The British rod-caught record is an 11lb 2oz (5.046kg) eel captured by S. Terry in 1978 at Kingfisher Lake near Ringwood, Hampshire.
● The Welsh record is held by B. Phillips who caught a 6lb 5oz (2.95kg) eel from Trawsfynedd Lake, Gwynedd in 1978.

▶ *After its long journey from the Sargasso Sea, across the Atlantic to Europe, the transparent young elvers darken in colour as they wriggle their way into many lowland rivers and streams.*

Distribution

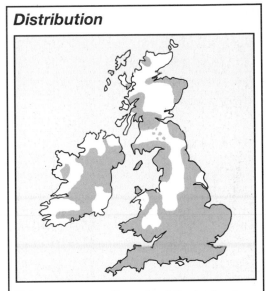

Eels are common throughout the lowland rivers and lakes of Britain and Ireland. They are also found as far north as Scandinavia and south to the Mediterranean.

Note how the dorsal and anal fins are continuous around the tail.

Vital statistics
Scientific name: *Anguilla anguilla*
Maximum weight: 15-20lb (6.8-9kg)
Maximum length: 1m (40in)
Average weight: 8-12oz (227-340g)
Life-span: Up to 25 years (average 14-16 years)

On the conger eel the dorsal fin starts above the level of the pectoral fins – on the common eel the dorsal fin begins lower down the back.

The nose is long with a protruding lower jaw - good for scooping up food from the bottom of gravel pits and lakes.

The body is covered in minute scales which are embedded so deeply in the skin that you cannot see them.

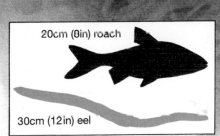

20cm (8in) roach

30cm (12in) eel

To many anglers they are a nuisance, tangling up the line as they try to wriggle free and covering everything in slime – but to the faithful few they provide an exciting challenge.

Follow the feeding

A nocturnal predator and scavenger, the eel uses its strong sense of smell and good eyesight to hunt prey. It is not a fussy eater, feeding mainly on fish, freshwater shrimps and snails. In gravel pits and rivers, eels rooting around on the bottom often cause damage to the spawning grounds of other fish.

Life-cycle

The most fascinating feature of this 'snake' is its strange life-cyle. The adult eel changes while in freshwater, turning from yellow to silver with the onset of sexual maturity. The head becomes more pointed as the eel ceases to feed – the fish stores up plenty of fat to sustain it on its long migration – and its eyes become larger, ready to adapt to life in the ocean.

The eel is now ready for migration, a journey which can last up to three years. Some of its passage may be overland. It survives out of water longer than most fish by closing its small gills and keeping them supplied with water held in a large gill cavity (seen as swellings on either side of its head).

The destination is the Sargasso Sea in the Atlantic, near Bermuda. Although spawning eels have never been captured – this is what makes the eel's life-cycle so mysterious – young larvae have been found in the plankton in this area. It is thought that the eel spawns in very deep water (up to 400m/1300ft deep). After spawning the eel dies.

When the young eel hatches it is carried by the Gulf Stream (North Atlantic Drift) until it reaches Europe's shores. During this journey it is transformed from a leaf-shaped larva to a tiny elver or glass eel – so called because its body is transparent. Darkening in colour as it makes its way upstream, the elver wriggles its way into many European waters.

Eel passes

Although extremely athletic, elvers often have problems gaining access to a water. Their task is made easier by man-made eel passes consisting of bunches of twigs covered in wire mesh which assist their journey over locks, dams and weirs. The River Severn is famous for its eel runs, and many elvers are trapped there each year to supply eel farms.

It is much better to start fishing for big eels in rivers, such as the Severn, than in lakes, where they are more difficult to catch.

▲ *Here is a fine catch of freshwater eels, enticed on to the angler's hook by lobworms. Eels hunt by smell, so the longer the bait is in the water the more likely they are to find it.*

Top eel waters

Listed here are some of the top waters for eels in Britain.

● **Abberton Reservoir, Essex** A good water for medium-sized eels.
● **Ardingly Reservoir, Sussex** Plenty of eels of 1-4lb (0.45-1.8kg) from this day ticket water.
● **Cheddar Reservoir, Somerset** Eels up to 5lb (2.3kg) from this concrete bowl.
● **River Delph, Norfolk/ Cambs** Eels of all sizes here.
● **Gailey Reservoir, near Cannock, West Midlands** Eels to 6lb (2.7kg) from this water.
● **River Idle, Notts** Possibly the most prolific eel river in Britain, though few large fish.
● **Slapton Ley, Devon** A good stock of medium-sized eels.
● **Weirwood Reservoir, Sussex** Produces very few eels, but those that have been caught have been very big – up to 8lb (3.6kg).

TRACKING DOWN EELS

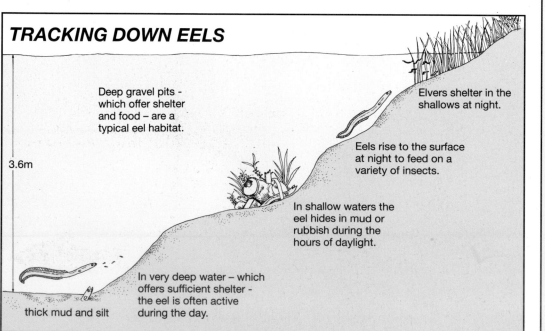

Deep gravel pits - which offer shelter and food - are a typical eel habitat.

Elvers shelter in the shallows at night.

Eels rise to the surface at night to feed on a variety of insects.

In shallow waters the eel hides in mud or rubbish during the hours of daylight.

3.6m

In very deep water – which offers sufficient shelter - the eel is often active during the day.

thick mud and silt

Darting dace

You need quick reactions and a rapid strike to catch these small, silvery fish. Dace often feed on floating insects, so in order to get a decent meal they must be as quick as lightning, otherwise potential prey is lost downstream.

Records: three of the best

● The British record has stood since 1960; it is held by J.L. Gasson for a 1lb 4oz 4dms (574g) dace, caught from the Little Ouse, Thetford, Norfolk.
● The Irish record is held by John T. Henry for a 1lb 2oz (510g) fish caught from the Blackwater River, Co. Cork, in 1966.
● T. Weaver holds the Welsh record for a 1lb (0.45kg) dace caught from Pochin Pond, West Glamorgan, in 1976.

With their silver colouring and similar river habitat, dace can sometimes be mistaken for roach or chub. However, you can distinguish dace from roach by their yellow, not red, eyes and slimmer bodies. Dace are generally smaller than both roach and chub and their dorsal and anal fins have concave edges (convex in the chub).

Dace (also called darts) are silver with a grey or dull green back. Larger specimens take on a brassy colour and the pelvic and anal fins may be tinged pink. Their slim bodies enable them to swim for prolonged periods in the main current of the river.

Life in the fast lane

Dace favour clear, fast-flowing rivers and streams, usually with a gravelly bottom. They live very successfully in trout domi-

nated waters, or large coarse fishing rivers such as the Thames. Once in a while they turn up in still waters as a result of becoming trapped when a river is dammed to form a reservoir. They live in large shoals to give themselves some protection from preda-

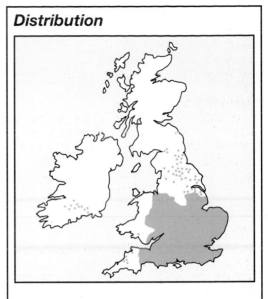

Distribution

Dace are found throughout England, but are less common in Wales, the West Country and the north. They are absent in Scotland and only found in the Blackwater in Ireland.

Both the dorsal and anal fins are concave at the edge.

Dace have narrow, pointed heads.

Dace have silver flanks and undersides, and grey or olive-green backs.

Vital statistics
Scientific name: *Leuciscus leuciscus*
Maximum weight: 1lb 4oz (630g)
Average weight: 4oz (112g)
Maximum length: 12in (30cm)
Life-span: 10-12 years

Their small, even mouths enable them to feed easily on both the bottom and the surface.

Yellow eyes distinguish dace from roach, which have red eyes.

The slender bodies of dace enable them to swim for prolonged periods in fast water.

The anal and pelvic fins are tinged with pink.

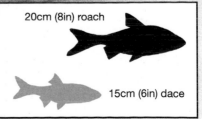

20cm (8in) roach

15cm (6in) dace

◀ *This dace was taken from the River Kennet, Berkshire, using stick float tactics. Maggots are the best bait for dace, but casters are also good. You can also catch dace on a small fly such as the black gnat, though you need to strike very quickly.*

tors. Older, larger fish tend to live in smaller groups.

Although dace are common throughout southern and eastern England, they are found only in localized spots in the north and Wales. Dace are not native to Ireland, but a small population was accidentally introduced to the River Blackwater, Co. Cork. No dace are found in Scotland.

Follow the feeding

With both top and bottom jaws projecting equally, dace feed well on both the bottom and the surface. They mostly eat invertebrates, intercepting drifting animals in mid water or taking floating insects from the surface. They are always on the lookout for food and readily take lures designed to catch game fish. They eat water shrimps, slaters, mayfly larvae, small snails and also a considerable amount of algae.

Getting in early

Dace breed earlier in the year than most coarse fish, so they are unlikely to form hybrids with other species such as chub and roach. In February and March shoals of dace gather in the riffles to spawn. Just before spawning the male's scales become very rough and bony tubercles develop on its head. The female's scales remain smooth.

The female lays up to 28,000 pale orange eggs among plants and stones – these hatch after 25 days. Dace grow fairly rapidly at first, and adult fish are mature after two years. Females live longer and grow larger than the males – so any dace you catch weighing more than 1lb (0.45kg) is most likely to be female and at least ten years old.

Top waters for dace

● **River Trent – throughout** Huge populations of dace to 8oz (224g), especially in the tidal reaches around Dunham, Notts.
● **Little Ouse – throughout** The river near Thetford, Norfolk is noted for its large dace.
● **River Ouse, Yorkshire** Dace to 14oz (392g).
● **River Kennet, Berkshire** Plenty of large dace from this venue.
● **River Blackwater, Co. Cork, Eire** The only river in Ireland with dace.
● **River Nar, Norfolk** Excellent dace in the 8-10oz (224-280g) class.
● **River Derwent, Derbyshire** Some fine dace in this trout river.
● **River Usk, Gwent, Wales** Big bags of dace produced in matches.
● **River Thames – throughout** The lower and tidal reaches are best.

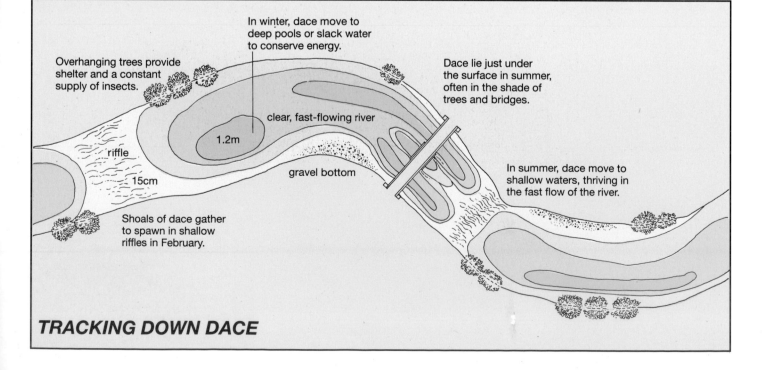

In winter, dace move to deep pools or slack water to conserve energy.

Overhanging trees provide shelter and a constant supply of insects.

Dace lie just under the surface in summer, often in the shade of trees and bridges.

clear, fast-flowing river

1.2m

riffle

15cm

gravel bottom

In summer, dace move to shallow waters, thriving in the fast flow of the river.

Shoals of dace gather to spawn in shallow riffles in February.

TRACKING DOWN DACE

CHAPTER FOUR

A SPECIALIST
APPROACH

Legering still waters for specimens

The leger is one of the deadliest methods for trapping really big fish. A simple approach on a good water scores for the thoughtful angler, says Nigel Witham of the Perchfishers.

⊗ Margins for error

Don't cast over the fish – they're often closer than you think if you haven't scared them by blundering around the bank. Start close in and work outwards if that doesn't succeed, covering the likely spots methodically.

▼ *The author, Nigel Witham, lands a good roach at Haversham Lake in Linear Fisheries, Milton Keynes. It took lobworm legered in a deep hole in the lake bed about 40m (44yd) out from the bank.*

To many anglers there is nothing that quite beats the sight of a perfectly set float disappearing beneath the ripple. But perhaps these anglers have yet to experience the thrill as a bobbin twitches to life and creeps towards the rod butt.

And maybe they've never felt that missed heartbeat as their quivertip pulls round to the surge of a good fish. These are just some of the joys of legering, the first choice technique of most big fish anglers.

Over the last 30 years or so, legering in its many forms has developed greatly, becoming infinitely more sophisticated. Indeed, legering has progressed so much that you can now buy almost as many bits of tackle for it as you can for float fishing.

There are non-toxic weights in many shapes and sizes, beads of all descriptions, feeders, swing, spring and quivertips, rods lined up in racks and books full of varying opinions on the subject. It's no wonder that the novice can become confused. So let's look at a basic approach that will help you put a few better-sized fish on the bank.

Choose your water

Firstly, you can't catch a fish that isn't there, so you must fish the right sorts of waters. But where do you look? Local and national press reports and tackle shops are good sources of information. Tackle shops also sell permits for day ticket waters and some have contacts with local clubs and associations.

Some types of water are more likely to yield a monster to the right approach than others. For example, your chances of a 2lb (0.9kg) roach are much better in a big reservoir than in your local farm pond.

Estate lakes are well established lakes which form the backbone of traditional still-water fishing. They are called estate lakes because it was the fashion in the 18th and 19th centuries for wealthy landowners to dam streams and excavate lakes on their estates – and a good thing too!

This type of water contains some species to good size although others, such as roach, rudd and sometimes bream and crucians, become stunted and rarely grow to specimen proportions. Tench are also common and often reach good weights, with carp, perch, pike and other species very likely to be present.

Gravel pits are another common type of

big fish water. Whole books have been written about angling on pits; they are a complicated subject. In many pits the fish can grow very large, sometimes with record potential. In fact most stillwater records are pit fish.

Gravel pits are often difficult waters when it comes to fish finding. They are comparatively new, most having been dug since World War II. This means that they are rarely silted, sometimes have sparse weed growth and the species present can vary widely.

Reservoirs are also worthwhile. They come in a huge variety of shapes and sizes ranging from giant dammed valleys covering several thousands of acres to small concrete bowls but they can contain some very big fish.

Choosing your swim is your first task once you've found a good water. Nowadays it is common to cast long distances, but never cast farther than you need. In most estate

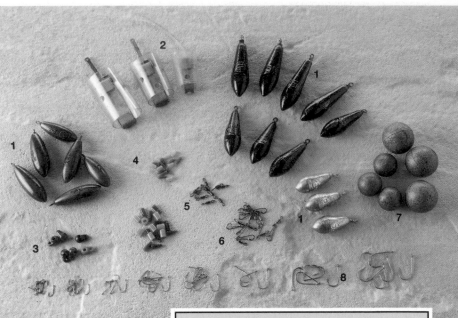

Leger kit for all sorts of specimens

For carp and big tench, especially in weedy waters, you need (left) a 2¼lb (1kg) TC carp rod of about 12ft (3.65m), coupled with a fixed-spool reel that holds around 250m (275yd) of 12lb (5.4kg) line.

For smaller species and less snaggy waters, (right) a 1¼lb (0.6kg) TC fast taper leger rod coupled with a fixed-spool reel with a capacity of 350m (375yd) of 6lb (2.7kg) line, is about right.

You also need spare spools filled with lines of various breaking strains to cope with different conditions and fish.

Your end gear

Terminal tackle is simple. You need a selection of swivel bombs (1) from ¼-2oz (7-56g), a few open-end swimfeeders (2), leger beads (3), leger stops (4), swivels (5), link swivels (6), a selection of poly balls (7) or rig foam for buoyant legers and hooks (8) in sizes 4-16.

lakes the fish are likely to be near the edge.

In addition, long range fishing can cause difficulty with bite detection and undertow – you often need special equipment, such as weighted bobbins, to combat drag on the line. So don't worry if you can't cast far. You may catch more than those who can!

Look for areas of cover such as weed and all sorts of snags. Plumb carefully for abrupt depth changes and drop-offs and put your baits at various depths on these features. Try to fish facing the direction of the prevailing wind. It is said that food collects on the windward bank and it's certainly a good place to start looking for the fish.

▲ *Bryan Culley fishes the feeder for big rudd and tench. He's using a sweetcorn and maggot cocktail on the hook, fished over a bed of crumb, corn and maggot.*

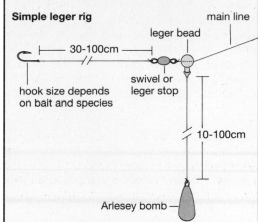

Nigel's stillwater leger rigs

Simple leger rig

main line

leger bead

30-100cm

swivel or
leger stop

hook size depends
on bait and species

10-100cm

Arlesey bomb

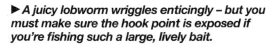
▲ *This bite detection set-up looks complicated but it's pretty simple. Monkey climbers give visual indication of runs and drop-backs, while electronic buzzers alert the angler with an audible alarm.*

The simple leger rig is often the best for exploring a new water or where there are few complications. You may need to vary the lengths or change rig if you have trouble with finicky bites or with excessive weed.

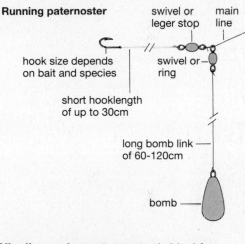

Running paternoster

swivel or
leger stop

main
line

hook size depends
on bait and species

swivel or
ring

short hooklength
of up to 30cm

long bomb link
of 60-120cm

bomb

Nigel's running paternoster is ideal for small baits and smaller species as it is more sensitive than the running leger. The essential feature is that the bomb link is longer that the hooklength.

Tip: How long a hooklength?

If you keep getting bites which never really develop, try a longer hooklength. This tends to give fish greater confidence. On the other hand, if you deep hook a fish, make the hooklength shorter and more sensitive, and remember to strike sooner.

Tackling essentials

Always use tackle that's strong enough to land your fish – don't be afraid to try heavy gear in weedy or snaggy water when you're after big fish. You're going to need heavier, carp-type gear and up to 12lb (5.4kg) line for big carp and tench in weedy water whereas light Avon-type leger gear with 4lb (1.8kg) line is perfect for big perch in a snag-free swim.

Lighter tackle and smaller baits can produce some good roach, rudd or bream. Other species may surprise you. Perch can show up at any time and the big ones are not as rare as you might think.

Fish 'n' rigs

What should you try to catch? If your water is an estate lake, it may well be quite silted. Tench and carp don't mind a bit of mud – in fact there's little they like more than a good root around. But roach, rudd, bream and perch prefer a cleaner lake bed.

Soft mud or weed rig

main line

leger bead

hooklength of
up to 120cm

swivel or
leger stop

hook size depends
on bait and species

poly ball or
rig foam

length of old line
equal to the depth of
weed, silt or mud

bomb

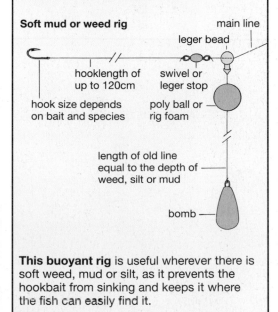

This buoyant rig is useful wherever there is soft weed, mud or silt, as it prevents the hookbait from sinking and keeps it where the fish can easily find it.

▶ *A juicy lobworm wriggles enticingly – but you must make sure the hook point is exposed if you're fishing such a large, lively bait.*

▲ *Sweetcorn, maggot and worm are three fine baits for legering in still waters. Maggot is excellent in many cocktails, and other good things to put on your hook include breadflake, boilies and particle baits.*

▲ *Baiting up at distance, as here, means you need to use groundbait to provide the weight and bulk. At close range, loosefeed is often better. Some species, such as bream, seem to prefer groundbait in the summer.*

Don't over-complicate things. Start with a simple leger rig and lobworm as bait. There is nothing quite as good as lobworm for helping you discover what species your lake contains. They all love them! If you find you're getting bites you can't hit, only then is it time to change your rig, or try varying hooklengths and bomb links.

If worm doesn't work or catches nothing but small eels, try breadflake or paste, sweetcorn, luncheon meat or boilies. Unless there aren't many small fish in the water, avoid maggots on the hook or you'll be plagued by twitches. Where there are still-water chub, try a deadbait quietly legered in the margins after dark.

The larger the bait, the more time the fish needs before you strike and the more freedom of movement you should build into your set-up. With a small bait like maggot or a single grain of corn, a swingtip or quivertip is best for spotting bites.

If you're using larger baits, a simple bobbin, such as a squeezy bottle top hung over the line at the rod butt, is usually better as they generally allow the fish more time to run. They work well with electronic bite indicators in many cases.

Groundbait lightly at first, or better still, loosefeed with samples of your hookbait, and perhaps some maggots or hemp as well. Only put in lots of feed when you're sure it's needed. You can afford to be more liberal with your free samples if you spot decent tench or carp rolling over your feed, or if you're getting plenty of bites.

A feeder can be a good idea. But don't try it in very shallow water as the splash can scare the fish. Make sure you cast accurately to the same spot each time.

With this basic approach and these few variations, you're well on your way to some highly productive stillwater fishing – and some excellent fish!

◄ *John Wilson displays the fruits of an intelligent approach to stillwater legering – a fine fat summer slab.*

The all-round roach

You can catch roach on the waggler, stickfloat, slider, swingtip, quivertip and all sorts of other methods from all kinds of waters – perhaps that's why they're so popular.

▲ *Plenty of waters hold two-pounders like this beautiful specimen – getting them out is another matter. But with light tackle, a quiet bankside manner and lots of patience you just might succeed.*

Softly, softly

Most big roach are very sensitive to vibrations and a heavy-footed angler clumping around the banks soon frightens them away. If you are to give yourself a chance of catching that magical two-pounder (0.9kg) you must tread lightly.

▼ *Few of our ponds, lakes, canals and rivers are without roach, but in spite of being found in most places these shy, handsome fish are a challenge – especially to young anglers.*

Think back to your first ever fish. The chances are that if it wasn't a perch then it was a roach – the species that has started a great many youngsters on the road to a lifetime's angling.

Small roach are much easier to catch than their bigger brethren, but they are fast biters and provide young anglers with a challenge that helps develop their skills. Really big roach are notoriously shy and most anglers never manage to capture one above the magical 2lb (0.9kg) barrier.

Roach respond to a variety of tactics and you'll find them in all types of waters from fairly fast flowing rivers to land drains, canals, lakes and small ponds.

Roach tackle

One of the more delicate, small-mouthed members of the carp family, the roach responds best to gossamer tackle.

Lines The trick is to strike the right balance between fishing light enough to get bites and heavy enough not to lose fish. In snag-free water, line of 1lb (0.45kg), b.s. is not too fine. If it is weedy and you are expecting roach above 1lb (0.45kg) then scale up slightly – 1½-1¾lb (0.68-0.79kg) b.s is about right. It is only necessary to go above 2lb (0.9kg) b.s if there is a chance of other species such as carp and tench, for example.

Hooks Roach are very particular about a bait behaving naturally, so avoid clumsy, heavy wire, eyed hooks. Go for a fine wire, spade end hook. (If you can't tie them your-

Hook size to bait size for roach	
Hook size	**Bait**
20	single maggot,
18	single maggot, single caster, hemp
16	double maggot, double caster, hemp, tares, bread paste
14	bread paste, bread flake
12	bread flake, sweetcorn

self then buy some quality hooks ready tied to a well known brand of line.)

Use the table above to match the size of hook to bait size.

Floats You don't necessarily have to use a light float for roach fishing – you can catch them on 2SSG wagglers. But the important thing is to dot the float well down so the fish feel the least resistance.

Leger indicators On some days quivertips tend to encourage fast bites from roach and in recent years there has been a trend back to swingtipping for them. A swingtip with a soft rubber allows bites to develop, making them easier to hit.

Favourite baits

Roach are not particular about what they eat but there are some good traditional baits.

Bread fished as flake, paste or punch is good for sorting out the better fish. Floating crust is normally associated with carp but small pieces fished in the margins are excellent for really big roach.

Casters Next time you are in the tackle shop and thinking of buying a pint of maggots for a session after the roach, try a pint of casters instead. Roach just love big, crunchy, golden casters and they tend to bring a better stamp of fish than maggots.

Hempseed has a pleasant nutty aroma which the roach find irresistible. Regular loose feeding of a few grains at a time often gets the fish queueing to intercept them on the drop. Fish a single grain on a size 18 or 16 hook. Push the bend of the hook into the seed slit – don't worry about the seed dropping off, it rarely does. The quality of big, hemp-caught roach has to be seen to be believed – the deep-bodied, brassy-scaled fish look almost like another species altogether. Hemp can produce very fast bites but if the fish are really turned on you should be able to hit them.

Tares are seeds sold originally in pet shops as pigeon food. They are now stocked by

▶ Roach are caught all the year round but the crisp, clear days of late autumn are traditionally the best. This is when big roach are fighting fit, with slightly brassy scales, deep creamy bellies and crimson fins.

most tackle shops. Boiled until soft enough to hook (but not split), tares make an excellent hookbait for roach when fished with loose-fed hemp. Hemp and tares work best during the summer and autumn. Compared to more conventional baits – maggots, for example – they look a bit unlikely and you need confidence to use them but once you've had a good catch you'll look for every opportunity to use them again.

Sweetcorn is a bait which the fish need to get used to but once you've got the roach turned on to it you can expect some big catches. Unlike hemp and tares it has the advantage of being a less selective hookbait, so you may get a suprise tench, carp or big bream among your roach.

Swims and tactics

There really is no such thing as a 'roach swim' or 'roach tactics' – that's the beauty of the all-round roach.

On rivers, medium flowing and even fast flowing swims yield roach to stick float and waggler tactics. A good catch of roach taken on the stick is a fair indication that you are on the way to mastering this method.

Still water roach can be taken on the drop with a waggler or on deep waters with a sliding float. A long pole can help you achieve perfect presentation – and it is useful for fishing the far bank of canals. Leger tactics often produce fish in the winter when the float has failed.

▲ Casters are an excellent alternative to maggots. They work well when loose-fed with hemp and tend to attract the bigger roach.

Catching big river roach

Roach wizard John Bailey has a very simple approach for big river redfins – he legers a nice fluffy piece of flake. The hard part is finding the fish...

By tradition, any roach of 2lb (0.9kg) or more is a specimen. This weight remains a kind of magical national target, reinforced by the angling press, but from many British rivers it isn't a realistic one.

At the top of the scale there are rivers like the Hampshire Avon, Wensum and Dorset Stour, where a 2lb (0.9kg) roach is a good one – but they have to be over 2½lb (1.1kg), at least, to be considered 'big'.

From most other rivers, however, a 2lb (0.9kg) roach really is the fish of a lifetime, so don't destroy yourself chasing 'super-roach' if they simply don't exist in the rivers you fish. Roach of 1¼-1¾lb (0.57-0.79kg) are very big ones anywhere and monsters from most rivers.

Big roach in residence

Choice of swim is vital. Look for one with slightly greater than usual depth. In water averaging 1.2m (4ft) deep, 1.5m (5ft) will do. If the river is generally 2.4m (8ft) deep, then look for a 3m (10ft) hole. Big roach just love such depressions, probably because they act as food traps.

Water speed is important too. Look for a

▲ *Roach don't have to weigh 2lb (0.9kg) or more to be classified 'big', says John Bailey. Any roach over 1lb (0.45kg) is a good specimen from most rivers in Britain.*

◄ *John Bailey legers for roach on his beloved River Wensum in Norfolk. Big roach tend to like a still bait.*

Tip Titbits

"When looking for roach in a swim you have regularly prebaited with mashed bread, watch the water surface closely," advises John Bailey. "Sometimes foraging roach dislodge small bits of bread which float back up to the top."

slightly slower area, close to the main flow. It doesn't have to be still, but big roach definitely favour the slacks just off the current – provided the bed of the river is reasonably clean. They will not tolerate too much rubbish or mud, preferring harder sand, gravel or chalk.

Overhanging trees play their part as well. Many of the best river swims for big roach slide under alders and willows, possibly because their branches keep a little light out of the water and provide some shelter from cold winds.

Marginal reed beds are also important; big roach like to forage around the roots for beetles, snails and shrimps.

Not all these features guarantee the presence of big roach and you will have to show some 'fish awareness'. Try to get down to the river at dawn, the best time to see big roach rolling. Observe the swim very, very carefully, for big roach often send up tiny strings of bubbles as they forage.

Winter warmers

The prime months for big river roach are from about the beginning of October to the end of the season. The very best conditions

at this time of the year are when air temperatures in the day are around 7-12°C (45-54°F), with a westerly wind bringing cloud and light rain. Conversely, the worst winter conditions are an easterly wind, clear skies, overnight frosts and daytime air temperatures below freezing.

But whatever the weather, don't despair – big roach always feed at some time. Generally, they feed best at dusk, or even in

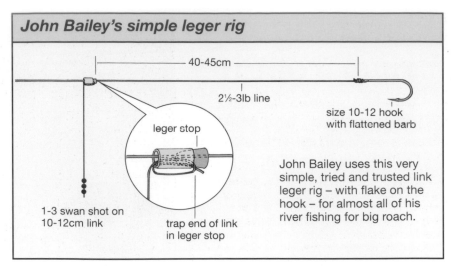

John Bailey's simple leger rig

40-45cm

2½-3lb line

size 10-12 hook
with flattened barb

leger stop

1-3 swan shot on
10-12cm link

trap end of link
in leger stop

John Bailey uses this very simple, tried and trusted link leger rig – with flake on the hook – for almost all of his river fishing for big roach.

Flake faith

John Bailey's absolute belief in breadflake for big river roach is easy to understand when you consider that this bait has caught him more than 300 two-pounders (0.9kg)!

Caring for your catch

A big roach is a wonderful sight... at least it should be. The unfortunate fish shown above has no top lip – the result of careless unhooking by a thoughtless angler.

This is why John Bailey recommends flattening the barb on your hook with pliers – roach have such delicate mouths that it is all too easy to damage them when trying to remove a barbed hook.

A fat specimen winter roach in almost perfect condition (right). Such fish might be caught many times over the years. Only when they are handled with tender, loving care by their captors do they stay in good condition. Bad handling not only spoils the good looks of a fish; scale, fin or mouth damage can make it susceptible to disease and might even stunt its growth.

A classic encounter

John Bailey well remembers his first 'super-roach' and the feeling of absolute awe it inspired in him...

"I had reached the River Wensum in the late afternoon and by the time I had settled into my favourite swim, fed in some pieces of bread and set up the tackle, the January dusk was falling.

"I was on a slight bend where the flow steadied and eddied a little. In front of me was a thick bed of died-back sedge and above was an alder tree. The water was tinged with colour but not chocolate – I could see about 12-15 inches into it.

"A piece of legered breadflake followed the free offerings about three or four yards from the the rod tip. As the current was so slow I decided to use a bobbin indicator at the butt.

"My first two casts lasted 20-25 minutes each – longer, and the bread is probably off – and at last, after about 15 minutes of the third cast, the bobbin twitched. It hung still for ten seconds, then shot up!

"The battle that followed was dour and undramatic – the fish was anything but! It weighed a massive 2lb 13oz (1.27kg), and although it carried old scars of disease and heron attack, to me it was the most beautiful creature in the world."

the late afternoon if the weather is mild. Strangely, the worse the conditions, the later they tend to come on the feed. Often this is between 8:00pm and midnight – if you can stand the cold.

Dawn is another excellent time to catch big roach. This is especially true in summer, but first light can also be a good time to fish through the autumn and winter, particularly if the night hasn't been too cold and

▲ *Prebait your chosen swim with mashed bread to wean big roach on to the bait, advises John Bailey. But mind not to overfeed them!*

▼ *Expert river angler Andy Orme with a magnificent winter river roach. Always take a camera with you to record your catch.*

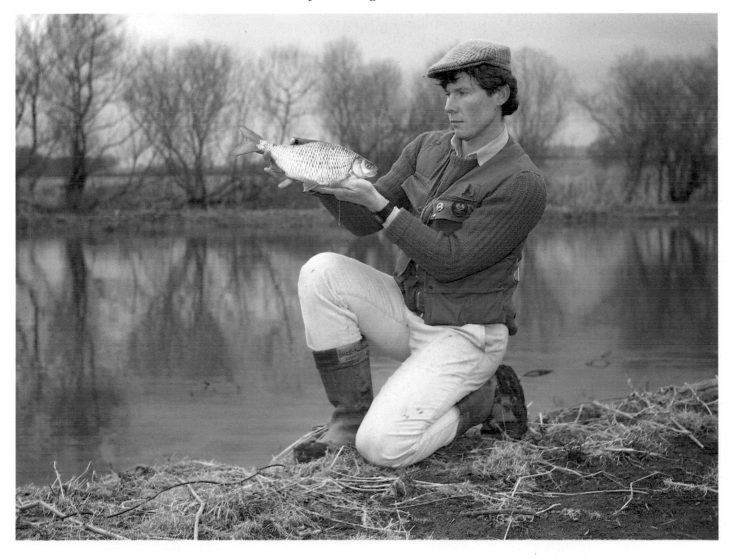

▼ *John Wilson gently returns a specimen roach to the water, fit to live on and fight another day – and provide other anglers with the chance to catch what many regard as the most special of all coarse fish.*

the wind is slight.

Of course, big roach can sometimes be caught in full daylight, but generally they strongly favour the protection of the low light levels of dawn and dusk.

River in trim

For your best chance of a big roach, the river should be neither too clear nor too coloured – a slight tinge so you can see 30-60cm (1-2ft) into the water is perfect.

Think bread

Make no mistake, bread is THE bait for big roach. Other baits do work, of course, but nowhere near as well or as selectively.

Prebait your chosen swim or swims with mashed bread as often as you can – at least once a week and ideally every day. Once bread starts appearing in a swim, big roach begin expecting it and stop there in their wanderings to look for it.

How much bread you put in a swim – either when prebaiting or actually fishing –

is crucial. You must put enough in to tempt them but not so much that it fills them up. Weather and river conditions dictate this decision. As a guide, in cold, clear water a big roach might eat half a slice of bread, while in mild weather when there's a touch of colour in the water it might eat a whole one. Given that most shoals of big roach number only three to six fish, the mathematics are easily worked out.

Big roach tactics

The best way to catch big roach is to leger a piece of breadflake firmly on the bottom. Float fishing does work occasionally, but most of the time big roach prefer to pick food up off the river bed at their leisure.

A simple 1-3 swan shot link – depending on the flow – with 2½-3lb (1.1-1.4kg) – line straight through to a size 8-12 hook is all you need. A white quivertip in a torch beam is easily seen, though a butt bobbin is excellent in slow water. Bites are generally confident and hard to miss.

Catching the mighty red-eye

Jim Gibbinson has been fishing for specimen tench for over 15 years with a variety of tackle and tactics. Here he passes on some of what he's discovered.

In the last 20 years or so there has been something of a revolution in tench fishing – the average and maximum size of tench has shot up. Until quite recently, a 5lb (2.3kg) tench would have been considered a specimen. Nowadays, in the 1990s, even a seven-pounder (3.2kg) is not that unusual.

No-one can be absolutely sure why this has happened, but it may be partly due to increasing water weed in British waters.

Rivers, lakes, ponds, pits and reservoirs certainly have become much weedier, possibly because farmers have been using more artificial fertilizers to bump up the yield of their land.

Much of this fertilizer is washed into rivers and still waters where it encourages strong water plant growth. More plants mean more insects and a richer supply of the tench's natural food.

With more big tench around there has never been a better time to get to grips with a specimen. Unfortunately, the increase in weed means that these big fish are harder to get out of the water. There are few places left where it is possible to fish light lines and expect to land that huge tench.

All this means you need to take some fairly hefty tackle to many big tench waters. However, try to remain flexible in your approach so you can take advantage of any less weedy waters by fishing with lighter tackle. That way you'll enjoy your tenching more and get better results.

◄ *As waters have got weedier, so tackle has had to get heavier to cope with pulling big tench out of the weeds. Here the author poses with the end result.*

▲▼ *You need heavy tackle (like that above), fixed-lead rigs and particles or 16mm (⅝ in) boilies to have a realistic chance of landing a specimen tench from most waters.*

Fixed-lead rig

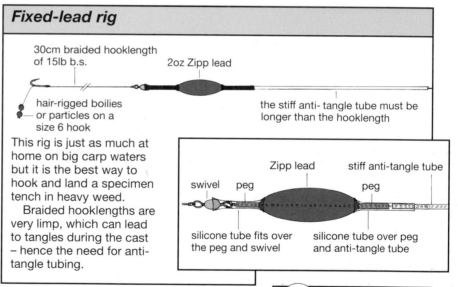

30cm braided hooklength of 15lb b.s.

2oz Zipp lead

hair-rigged boilies or particles on a size 6 hook

the stiff anti- tangle tube must be longer than the hooklength

swivel   peg

Zipp lead   stiff anti-tangle tube

peg

silicone tube fits over the peg and swivel

silicone tube over peg and anti-tangle tube

This rig is just as much at home on big carp waters but it is the best way to hook and land a specimen tench in heavy weed.

Braided hooklengths are very limp, which can lead to tangles during the cast – hence the need for anti-tangle tubing.

Tackling the weed

Many tench waters become heavily weeded, aquatic jungles in the summer and you must use appropriate gear. You need a 2¼lb (1kg) TC carp rod, coupled with about 200m (220yd) of 12lb (5.4kg) line on a sturdy fixed-spool reel.

Terminal tackle is a size 6 forged hook on a 15lb (6.8kg) braided hooklength. Fixed-lead, anti-tangle rigs are most effective in heavy weed. There's no getting away from it – you need carp tackle to get a big tench out of a weedy water.

Standard carp baits – boilies and particles – work best with carp gear. Tench seem particularly fond of fruity, creamy flavours such as Maple Creme and Strawberry Jam.

If you make your own baits, use a milk protein or bird seed base with these flavours. Tench also readily take fish flavoured boilies based on a fish meal mix.

The best of the particles are sweetcorn, black-eye beans, chick peas and maple peas. Fish both particles and boilies on a 2.5cm (1in) hair. Fish 16mm (⅝ in) boilies singly, but use particles and small boilies in tandem or as a trio on the hair.

An electronic bite indicator with monkey climber or swinging drop-off arm gives an accurate audible and visual signal of runs and drop-back bites. While not the most sensitive form of bite detection, if your rig and bait presentation are right you will only get sailaway bites.

Tip Times and places

The shallows are a good bet early in the season with lots of fish on the spawning grounds. Later many move into water up to 6m (20ft) deep.

Don't ignore the margins – you are just as likely to catch close in as at long range.

Don't fish the night and pack up at breakfast time. In pits the best time is often between 7am and noon with night time the worst.

A bit of subtlety

Where weed hasn't quite reached the horrendous proportions of the watery jungle, it's possible to be a little less brutish in approach.

Tackle can be lighter with 1¾lb (0.8kg) TC rods, 8lb (3.6kg) main line and a forged size 8 or 10 hook. A simple running leger with a ½-¾oz (14-21g) bomb works well with this particular set-up.

With an extending hooklength the leger becomes a fairly sophisticated rig. Devised by Ken Townley for carp fishing, it works equally well for tench in allowing the fish to take line without feeling resistance. This produces very confident takes.

Use the rig with a slack, drooping line. This gives a taking fish some low-resistance line and makes sure that the last few feet of line lie flat on the bottom – reducing line bites. Where drag caused by the wind or floating debris makes this impossible, use a small back-lead to avoid those liners.

Particle baits work well with this rig, as do mini-boilies. The best size for these is about 10mm (⅜in) across. Use them singly or, more commonly, in twos or threes.

▲ Feed 2-3 pouches of hookbait samples. At short range loosefeed with hemp and casters but farther out use groundbait as a carrier.

Crumbs before tench

Jim Gibbinson makes his own groundbait:
6 measures (by volume) of fresh white crumb
2 measures of layer's mash hen food
1 measure of roughly ground roast barley
1 measure of fish meal or finely ground trout pellets

▼ Where weed allows, use 1¾lb (0.8kg) TC rods and a running leger. It's an enjoyable and effective way to take big tench.

Concertina rig

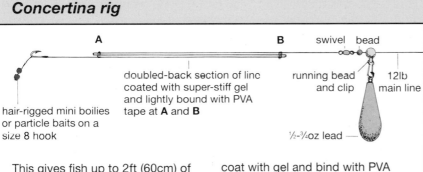

A B swivel bead

doubled-back section of line coated with super-stiff gel and lightly bound with PVA tape at **A** and **B**

running bead and clip

12lb main line

hair-rigged mini boilies or particle baits on a size 8 hook

½-¾oz lead

This gives fish up to 2ft (60cm) of line without resistance. Fold 2-3ft (60-90cm) of Dacron into a Z-bend, coat with gel and bind with PVA tape. The gel and tape dissolve in water, leaving a folded hooklength.

Ultra-light

On a very few lightly weeded venues you can still fish very light – 1¼lb (0.6kg) TC rods, 4lb (1.8kg) line, fine-wire size 12 hooks and a feeder. Where this is possible, it is without doubt the most effective way to catch numbers of big fish.

A hooklength of at least 3ft (90cm) on a

Rotary feeder rig

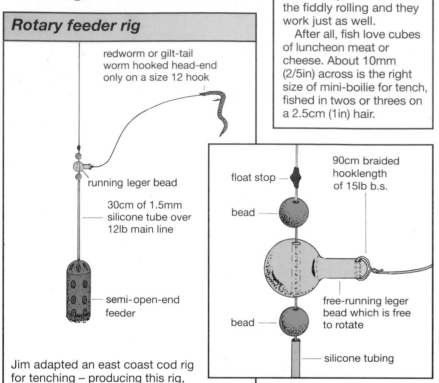

redworm or gilt-tail worm hooked head-end only on a size 12 hook

running leger bead

30cm of 1.5mm silicone tube over 12lb main line

semi-open-end feeder

float stop

bead

bead

90cm braided hooklength of 15lb b.s.

free-running leger bead which is free to rotate

silicone tubing

Jim adapted an east coast cod rig for tenching – producing this rig, though carp anglers now commonly use variations on it. The feeder is filled with maggots and plugged with groundbait.

Tip A cubist approach

If you want to make your own mini-boilies, you'll find it easier to make cubes instead of the usual round shape. It avoids all the fiddly rolling and they work just as well.

After all, fish love cubes of luncheon meat or cheese. About 10mm (2/5in) across is the right size of mini-boilie for tench, fished in twos or threes on a 2.5cm (1in) hair.

helicopter (rotary) rig works best. However, tench sometimes take delicately presented baits with such confidence that they become deep-hooked unless you use a shorter hooklength. With anti-tangle tubing above the feeder, this rig is as near tangle-free as a paternoster can be.

Feeding is easy – catapult two or three tangerine-sized balls of groundbait into the swim and cast your ready-loaded feeder rig into the centre of the spreading rings. Don't feed again until you've had a couple of runs or you'll put the big tench off.

The best bait for this type of tenching is a gilt-tail worm which looks like a redworm with a bright yellow tail. Look for them in the muck heap on a pig farm. You won't find many, but you will find lots of redworms which are a close second best.

Concentrate your efforts on the edges of the heap, where it's fairly cool. Near the middle of a muck heap it's too hot for redworms and gilt-tails – all you find are brandlings and these are greatly inferior as a tench bait.

If you do know of a virtually weed-free water that holds big tench – give light feeder tactics a try. The fishing is an absolute joy and well worth all that grovelling in pig heaps.

▼ *At waters without much weed you can land tench like this on light feeder gear. Give it a go and don't fish heavier than you need.*

Techniques for big perch

The Perchfishers is a club devoted entirely to the capture of specimen perch. Secretary Stewart Allum tells you about some of the techniques he uses for catching these beautiful fish.

In the seventies and eighties, perch virtually disappeared from many of our waters because of disease. Now stocks are recovering and the bold, stripy predator is enjoying a comeback throughout the British Isles.

Time and place

Perch are aggressive and you can catch them on a wide variety of methods. Indeed, where small perch are numerous they can be a positive nuisance to the angler seeking bigger game. However, by carefully selecting the right waters, methods and time of the year, it is possible to locate larger specimens selectively.

Even tiny ponds hold very large perch – provided there is plenty of food for them. They are a fast-growing species and an abundance of tiny roach, rudd or gudgeon is just the sort of diet they thrive on. So if you don't live near one of the famous perch waters, don't despair – there is probably a neglected farm pond or derelict canal nearby which could contain that elusive three pounder (1.4kg).

Autumn is the best time to seek big perch. This is when they shoal up in large numbers in the deeper areas of lakes and gravel pits before migrating to the very deepest water for the winter. At this time of the year they are hungry and extremely

▲▼ Perch (above) rely on cover such as weed beds, sunken piles or tree roots at the edge of pools and rivers, from which they dart out and ambush their prey. In summer you can sometimes hear them as they chase fry around marginal weed close to the surface. (They produce a sharp click as their jaws snap shut.)

Here Nigel Witham of The Perchfishers strikes into a good fish (below). Fishing for big perch is no longer a hit or miss affair.

Simple waggler rig

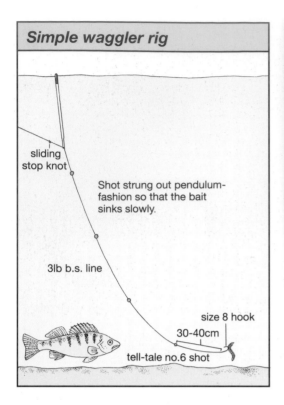

sliding
stop knot

Shot strung out pendulum-
fashion so that the bait
sinks slowly.

3lb b.s. line

size 8 hook

30-40cm

tell-tale no.6 shot

► *This fish fell to a spinner tied directly to the line but it is best to use a trace – you never know when a pike might strike.*

aggressive and there is avid competition among shoals for any available food.

Baits and methods

In recent years – largely due to the formation of clubs such as The Perchfishers – techniques have become more refined. Traditional perch baits – such as worms, livebaits, deadbaits and spinners – are used together with state-of-the-art tackle and methods (usually associated with other species) so that big perch are now caught more by design than chance.

Worm and feeder Lobworms are a reliable winter bait and a great favourite with perch everywhere. You can floatfish or leger with them. On large, deep waters – such as gravel pits – where the fish are harder to find, try attracting the fish to your bait. One way is to leger a lob and use

▼ *A typical winter perch swim on the Berkshire Kennet – the trouble is that it looks pikey too! If you are livebaiting and think there may be pike about, then use a braided hooklength.*

Swimfeeder and worm rig

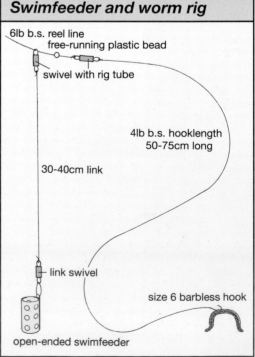

6lb b.s. reel line
free-running plastic bead

swivel with rig tube

4lb b.s. hooklength
50-75cm long

30-40cm link

link swivel

size 6 barbless hook

open-ended swimfeeder

Paternoster rig

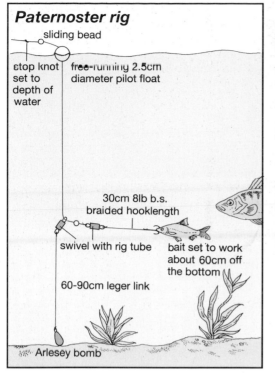

sliding bead

stop knot set to depth of water

free-running 2.5cm diameter pilot float

30cm 8lb b.s. braided hooklength

swivel with rig tube

bait set to work about 60cm off the bottom

60-90cm leger link

Arlesey bomb

Air-injected bait rig

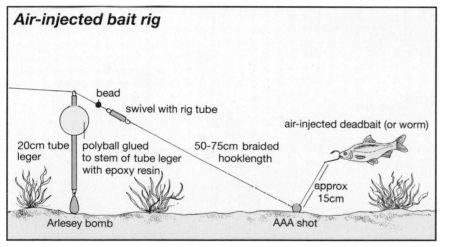

bead

swivel with rig tube

air-injected deadbait (or worm)

20cm tube leger

polyball glued to stem of tube leger with epoxy resin

50-75cm braided hooklength

approx 15cm

Arlesey bomb

AAA shot

▲ **Small roach deadbaits are ideal for big perch but if there are pike about use a braided hooklength.**

an open-ended swimfeeder packed with maggots and flavoured groundbait. Try experimenting: additives such as dried blood, worm extract (which you can buy from tackle shops) and red dye (red is a favourite colour of perch!) often work. Maggots help to keep small fish interested and these in turn attract big perch into the area where your bait is.

Just worm On smaller lakes, ponds and canals, a swimfeeder can cause too much disturbance. Instead, try fishing a worm on a straightforward link leger or under a waggler type float.

When waggler fishing, loosefeed maggots to keep the swim alive. If no takes are forthcoming, try twitching the bait back towards you by giving a couple of quick turns of the reel handle every few minutes. This often brings an immediate response from an otherwise suspicious perch which may have

Top perch waters

● **The River Thames** Particularly in its lower reaches, the Thames holds vast shoals of perch – some of them well over 3lb (1.4kg). Perch appear to be on the increase in this river system with good fish being reported from tributaries such as the Mole and Wey.

● **The Oxford Canal** Just one of a number of canals nationwide now producing perch in good numbers. Many matches fished here in the latter part of the 1990-91 season were dominated by perch catches with some big individual specimens reported.

● **Linear Fisheries** is situated next to the M1 at Newport Pagnall. Run by well-known anglers Len Gurd and Bob Baldock, these gravel pits have produced many good perch in recent seasons. The fishing is well managed and, with the majority of regulars tending to specialize in the more popular carp, tench and pike,

there is plenty of scope for the enterprising perch angler.

● **Leisure Sport Angling** group probably controls more gravel pit fisheries than anyone else. Many of these contain perch which have scarcely ever been fished for.

● **The Yorkshire Ouse** above Acaster contains a great many perch which average around 12oz-1lb (0.34-0.45kg), with the possibility of bigger fish. Most of the fishing in the city of York is free to holders of a NRA Yorkshire region licence.

● **The Scottish lochs** Anglers who head north of the border to fish for pike are missing out on some great perch fishing. Loch Awe in Argyllshire, Loch Ken in Dumfriesshire and Lochs Tay and Tummell in Perthshire all provide excellent perch fishing. Most of the fishing is free, but check with local tackle shops and land owners first.

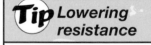

Tip Lowering resistance

Legering indicators such as swingtips, quivertips and monkey climbers either create too much resistance or don't allow enough freedom to a taking perch.

You can make a perfect lightweight indicator by cutting a 3mm strip of plastic from an empty shampoo bottle or similar container and forming it into a ring about 3.5cm (1½ in) in diameter.

Thread the ring on to the line when setting up the rod. It doesn't impede casting and, when the bail is off, allows fish to take line without feeling any resistance.

been eyeing the bait for some time, wondering whether to take it.

Spinning On large, deep waters spinning is a good alternative to the sit-and-wait approach – you can actively search the water for big fish. Patterns like the tried and tested ABU Toby, Atom and Reflex work well. It is important to retrieve the lure as slowly as possible – let it sink to the full depth before starting to retrieve.

Always use a wire trace. It doesn't put the perch off and is a good insurance against any unfortunate pike which might otherwise engulf the spinner and bite through monofilament line.

Live and dead fish baits catch their fair share of good perch. Unlike spinning – where an interested fish has to snap impulsively at a bait before it has gone – live and dead baiting allows an interested fish to inspect a bait thoroughly before deciding whether to take it. This means that you can't use a wire trace. If you are fairly certain there are no pike about, then you can get away with monofilament but if you aren't sure then use one of the new braided hooklength materials such as Kryston Silkworm, which is supple and reasonably resistant to a pike's teeth.

Livebaits should be lightly paternostered near a suitable ambush point – old lily roots, for example.

Deadbaits should, if possible, be freelined or lightly legered so as to minimize the resistance to a taking fish. Debris on the bottom such as dead leaves and twigs can cause the leger and bait to become buried. You can get round this by using a buoyant leger coupled with an air-injected bait. This helps to keep the bait and leger free of snags and prevents the bait from being obscured. (You can fish lobworms in exactly the same way.)

Deadbaits should always be freshly killed – small roach, rudd, perch or gudgeon of 3.5cm-5cm (1½-2in) are ideal. Never use a smelly old bait and avoid sea baits – perch do not like the taste of sea fish.

Hitting the bites

Perch have a habit of toying around with a bait – albeit in a fairly savage manner – which can make bites hard to hit. When floatfishing, for example, don't strike as soon as the float disappears. Allow the fish a couple of seconds to get the worm into its mouth, then take up any slack line and gently lift into the fish. Don't wait too long though, or else the fish may drop the bait or swallow the hook.

▶ Perch populations rise and fall frequently – it is part of the natural cycle of these fish. This is why even famous perch fisheries – such as the private, record-producing lake in Kent – only hold the headlines for a couple of seasons before a new venue hits the news.

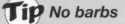

Tip No barbs

Some anglers don't like to use barbless hooks but Stewart says: "I always use a barbless hook when fishing for perch with worms. If a fish does take a bait deep down while you are waiting for a bite to develop, it makes the job of unhooking it much easier. I have lost very few fish as a result of barbless hooks."

▼ If you miss a lot of bites when fishing worm, don't worry – this is probably caused by small perch tugging the end of the worm. A big perch has a mouth like a bucket and usually doesn't mess around for long.

Swingtipping for bream

Swingtipping is enjoying a deserved revival as more and more bream anglers realize its advantages over quivertipping – and nobody does it better than matchman Sid Meads.

The swingtip is the most sensitive bite indicator ever devised for legering, and the man we have to thank is the late Jack Clayton of Boston, Lincolnshire, who invented it back in the 1950s. Swingtipping as we know it today hasn't changed very much since then – Jack's ingenious invention has withstood the test of time.

Different links

Jack and fellow Fenland matchmen did a lot of experimenting in the early days, until finally they settled on swingtips with nylon links, which are stiff enough to prevent tangles at the rod tip when casting, yet are sensitive enough to show the slightest of bites.

You'll have to scout around to find such swingtips nowadays, because most modern

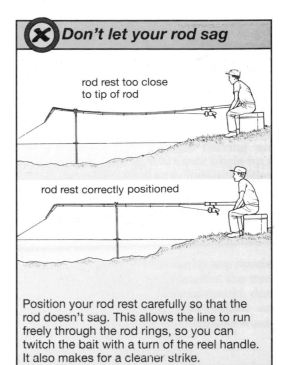

Don't let your rod sag

rod rest too close to tip of rod

rod rest correctly positioned

Position your rod rest carefully so that the rod doesn't sag. This allows the line to run freely through the rod rings, so you can twitch the bait with a turn of the reel handle. It also makes for a cleaner strike.

▼ *A bream angler waits expectantly for a bite on an Irish lough. Ireland is a mecca for anglers in search of a haul of bream, and one of the best methods there is to swingtip over a large carpet of feed. Sid Meads has won many Irish Festivals doing just that.*

ones have soft silicone rubber links that, though very sensitive, tend to make the swingtip flap about on the cast, causing tangles at the rod tip.

You can also get moulded rubber links, which make casting easier, but they aren't as sensitive as nylon ones.

Tip Forget the swimfeeder

Sid Meads prefers not to use a swimfeeder when swingtipping unless he really has to. The reason for this is that accurate groundbaiting is essential for success when legering for bream. Sid finds it easier to groundbait accurately by hand or by catapult, and easier to cast accurately with a bomb than a feeder.

With a feeder, one cast going astray can split your shoal, but if the odd cast goes astray with a bomb, no damage is done.

▼ *Ireland's rivers can be just as good for bream as her loughs. Here a happy angler returns a fighting fit Shannon bream. It fell to swingtipping, a method pioneered in England but used to devastating effect in Ireland over the years.*

Different lengths

Length of swingtip to use depends on the type of water you're fishing. The deeper the water and the stronger the flow or tow, the longer the swingtip needs to be. So carry a selection from 25-50cm (10-20in), to cover every eventuality.

The right balance

The key to success, as always, is balanced tackle, from rod to line, bomb, hooklength and hook.

Rods In the days before groundbait catapults you rarely swingtipped more than 30m (33yd) or so out because that was about as far as you could throw groundbait by hand. Swingtip rods then were usually 9-10ft (2.7-3m) long, which was fine. Nowadays, with groundbait catapults allowing you to fish twice as far out, you need a longer rod to pick up the line on the strike – one of around 11ft (3.3m) or so. Make sure it has a soft, through action, to absorb the shock of striking into soft-mouthed, deep-bodied bream.

Reel, line and bombs Choose a good fixed-spool reel with two spare spools. Fill the spools with 2½lb (1.1kg), 3lb (1.4kg) and 4lb (1.8kg) line. This is the start of getting the balance right. Generally, you want to use a ¼-½oz (7-14g) bomb to 2½lb (1.1kg) line,

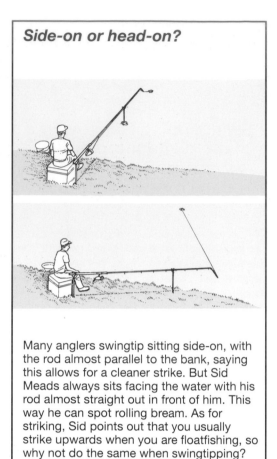

Side-on or head-on?

Many anglers swingtip sitting side-on, with the rod almost parallel to the bank, saying this allows for a cleaner strike. But Sid Meads always sits facing the water with his rod almost straight out in front of him. This way he can spot rolling bream. As for striking, Sid points out that you usually strike upwards when you are floatfishing, so why not do the same when swingtipping?

a ½-¾oz (14-21g) bomb to 3lb (1.4kg) line, and a ¾-1oz (21-28g) bomb to 4lb (1.8kg) line. Weather and water conditions and distance to be cast dictate which combination to use. Always go for the lightest bomb you can get away with – but remember, it needs to be heavy enough to get your bait to the desired spot and hold its position when you tighten up.

End tackle For the bomb link, use a slightly heavier piece of line than your reel line, to take the shock of casting. Make the link about 40cm (15in) long, so that you can twitch the bait (to tempt a bite) without shifting the bomb.

Go for a longish tail – about 1.2m (4ft) – because a slow-sinking bait is more attractive to bream and the longer the tail, the slower the drop after the bomb hits bottom. Don't try to go any longer with the tail or you'll have too much line to pick up on the strike.

If you're fishing a water that's not had a hammering, a juicy bunch of redworms or a pinch of breadflake on a size 10 or 12 hook can work well, with a big weight on the cards. But you need to use a 14, 16, 18 or 20 on most of our hard-fished waters, with smaller baits to match – three pinkies on a 20, a caster on an 18, two or three maggots or casters on a 16, or a small redworm tipped with a maggot or caster on a 14.

Plan of attack

Now you're tackled up, you're ready to catch some bream. Mix a small amount of

A SELECTION OF SID'S SWINGTIPS

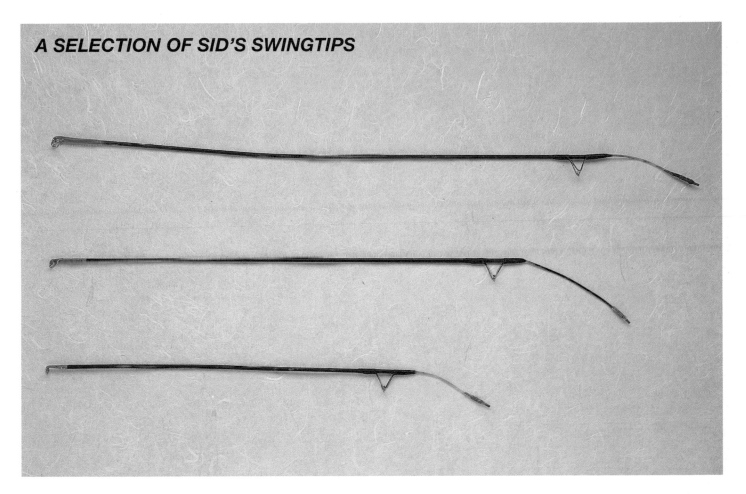

groundbait and add some squatts, casters and a few chopped worms – just enough so you can still squeeze the groundbait into balls that hold together in the air.

Let's assume you're fishing a Fen drain or slow river about 30m (33yd) wide and 2.5m (8ft) deep. Attach a shortish (25-30cm/10-12in) swingtip. Position the rod rests directly in front of you but angled slightly downstream or downwind so the rod is aligned with the bow of the line. Use a smooth overhead cast with the bomb hanging about 1m (3ft) below the rod tip and aim some 5m (5yd) short of the far bank.

Tighten the line so the swingtip hangs at a slight angle, just clear of the water. Then, if a bream swims towards you after taking the bait, you will be able to see the swingtip drop back.

Hang fire with the groundbait for a few minutes, just in case there's a shoal of bream out there already – you don't want to scare them away before you've even started.

If you haven't had any indication, put in five tangerine-sized balls – but not all down the same hole. Put the first three in a line across the back of your target area, then drop the next two slightly short, in a line towards you.

The idea is that when the bream move in they hang tight to the far bank. To keep them happy, let them stay there feeding on the first three balls of feed, while you take the odd fish from over the two balls you dropped short. These are the hungry ones that can't get into the main shoal and read-

ily accept your hookbait.

Only move into the main shoal once bites start to tail off. This is a crucial time. You must put more feed in to hold the shoal, but there's always the risk of frightening the bream away. So never overdo it at this stage. Try them with a single ball of groundbait only. If it doesn't spook them you've cracked it, and can put one in as and when you think they want it. If bites slow after you've put one in, leave it a bit longer before the next. Your main baiting area is the far side, on a three to one ratio – three to the

Groundbaiting for bream

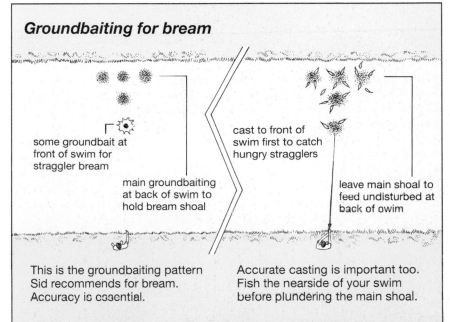

some groundbait at front of swim for straggler bream

main groundbaiting at back of swim to hold bream shoal

cast to front of swim first to catch hungry stragglers

leave main shoal to feed undisturbed at back of swim

This is the groundbaiting pattern Sid recommends for bream. Accuracy is essential.

Accurate casting is important too. Fish the nearside of your swim before plundering the main shoal.

main area, one to the near side. But remember – only ever one ball at a time.

Once you get into the pack, expect a few line bites – big, sweeping bites from fish hitting your line and leaving your swingtip out straight. Only through experience can you learn to distinguish liners from real bites. Even then, you still only get it right about half of the time.

The problem of liners is not the fault of the swingtip, which has one big advantage over the quivertip. Those little half-inch taps of the quivertip on hard-fished waters often mean a bream taking the bait and moving just enough to tighten the line. On feeling this the fish drops the bait. These are the bites you can hit on the swingtip. Hold the rod in the rest and at the slightest movement, move the rod forward with the bite. Sometimes you'll be amazed how those tiny half-inch bites turn into big sailaways. When this happens you will be hooked on swingtips for life.

► *On an easy water it saves time, if the edge is shallow, to scoop each bream out by hand. On harder waters, where you have to work for your fish, take no chances and net every one.*

▼ *Slabs, lumps, lunkers...call them what you like, slimy-sided bream are the favourite fish of the many anglers who have fallen under the spell of the sensitive swingtip.*

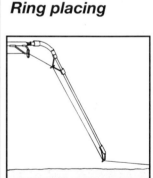

Ring placing

Sid likes swingtips with the top ring just below the link, to prevent tangles when casting.

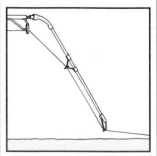

Other anglers prefer to have the top ring lower down, believing that it allows smoother casting.

Tactics for barbel

The barbel is often regarded with something approaching awe – as a tremendous fighter caught by the lucky few. But catching one may be easier than you think. Martin Hooper tells you how.

▼ *Chris Yates plays a big barbel among the thistle-down. A centrepin reel is favoured by many anglers because it enables them to give line immediately.*

To catch barbel you have to be familiar with their nature and feeding habits. They are a specialized fish – streamlined and with an underslung mouth. The torpedo-shaped body enables them to swim with ease in the fastest currents. The four mouth barbels on the upper jaw – two at the leading edge and two at the trailing edge – are used to detect food lodged among stones and gravel on the river bed. It makes sense, then, to fish for them on the bottom of the river.

Feeding the swim

It may sound obvious but you can only catch barbel if they are in the swim. It is no use fishing blindly in the hope that one may eventually turn up – you might have to wait forever! By feeding a swim you greatly increase the chances of an encounter.

Shallow clear rivers make it easier to spot your quarry but you can still use the same tactics on deep, coloured waters.

To get the the fish interested, feed free offerings within a tight area on to the bed of the river.

The simplest way – if the flow and depth are not too great – is to throw in a few samples. If the flow is such that the bait is washed out of the swim before it reaches the bottom, it's best to try a baitdropper or swimfeeder.

Load the dropper with samples of the hookbait and swing it out into the feed area. When it reaches the bottom a plunger releases the bait. Droppers have a limitation, though. If you try to cast too far they have a nasty habit of opening in mid-air –

◀ *The business end of an eight-pounder (3.6kg). The fish's sensitive barbels are used to detect particles of food.*

dispersing both the loosefeed and the fish. This is the time you should start using a swimfeeder.

By baiting regularly on each visit to a water, you can 'brainwash' barbel so their appetites are tuned into your attractor. Hempseed is one of the cheapest and most effective. Liberally laced with a few choice hookbaits – such as sweetcorn or luncheon meat – it forms an enticing patch on the river bed. If there are any barbel around in feeding mood then it won't be long before they move into your swim.

If the stretch you have chosen sees a lot of a certain bait, then the barbel become accustomed to eating it. If not, then pre-baiting is essential. It can take a considerable time to introduce the fish to a new bait.

The hardware

Barbel are one of the most fickle of biters and the most powerful of fighters. So you need to get your tackle right.

A rod of around 1¼lb (0.56kg) TC with a through-action is fine. There's no need to break the bank – any mass-produced rod will do, provided it meets the basic requirements.

The reel A barbel specialist would probably choose a centrepin reel. This type enables you to respond immediately to the demands of an accelerating fish. Giving line with a fixed-spool reel is done through the gears and is therefore less direct – you have to anticipate what a barbel is going to do next, and that isn't easy!

Line of around 6lb (2.7kg) b.s. is about right. Use forged heavy wire hooks.

To complete the set-up you need a big landing net. One of about 1m (3ft) across with big mesh – so that it doesn't get caught by the current – is ideal.

End rigs and tactics

There are all kinds of leger rigs but one of the most versatile is a three-in-one rig which incorporates sliding stops.

With the stops pushed well up the line it's a free running rig; hard against the boom it becomes a bolt rig; just pushed away from the boom it is a variable-length confidence rig. Within a matter of seconds you can change the rig to suit the mood the barbel are in on the day – giving you a much

▲ *Where the current is strong a baitdropper like this is the answer. It is ideal for introducing samples of your hookbait directly on to the river bed – where the barbel are!*

Tip The edge

On heavily fished stretches, prebaiting with a less common bait can often give you the edge – helping you to catch more and bigger barbel.

The lazy man's rig

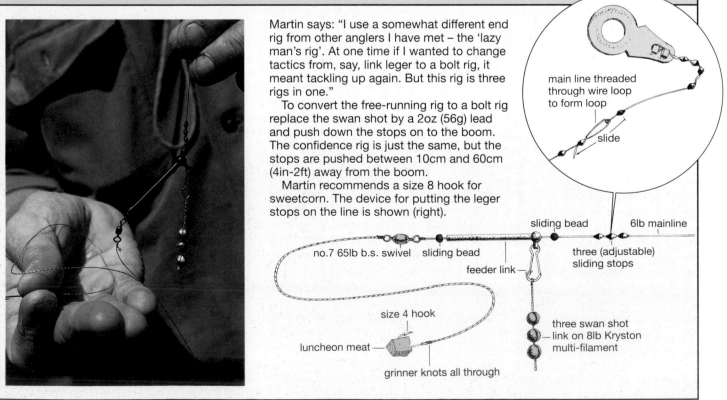

Martin says: "I use a somewhat different end rig from other anglers I have met – the 'lazy man's rig'. At one time if I wanted to change tactics from, say, link leger to a bolt rig, it meant tackling up again. But this rig is three rigs in one."

To convert the free-running rig to a bolt rig replace the swan shot by a 2oz (56g) lead and push down the stops on to the boom. The confidence rig is just the same, but the stops are pushed between 10cm and 60cm (4in-2ft) away from the boom.

Martin recommends a size 8 hook for sweetcorn. The device for putting the leger stops on the line is shown (right).

main line threaded through wire loop to form loop

slide

sliding bead   6lb mainline

no.7 65lb b.s. swivel   sliding bead

feeder link

three (adjustable) sliding stops

size 4 hook

luncheon meat

three swan shot link on 8lb Kryston multi-filament

grinner knots all through

Hooking luncheon meat

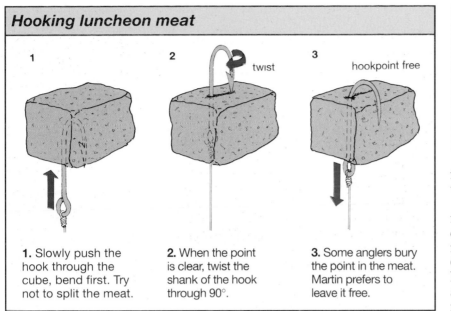

1. Slowly push the hook through the cube, bend first. Try not to split the meat.

2. When the point is clear, twist the shank of the hook through 90°.

3. Some anglers bury the point in the meat. Martin prefers to leave it free.

Tip A happy ending

Your end tackle is extremely important. Check your hook each time before you cast out. If there is any sign of damage then replace it. Hooklengths should be checked and dealt with just as ruthlessly. It's a horrible feeling when a fish is lost – even more so if the reason is through neglect.

greater chance of hitting bites.

A free running rig is the commonest choice when the barbel are their usual shy selves and you are fishing with one rod.

It's essential to hold the rod, feeling for bites with the line held between your finger and thumb. Bites are rarely savage, rod-wrenching affairs. This is particularly so with larger fish and on heavily fished waters. The bites are often tiny plucks – more akin to dace bites than anything else.

The bolt rig comes into play when fishing with two rods. Obviously, quick biting barbel are likely to be missed if you are trying to watch the ends of two rods at the same time. What's needed is a method where the

fish can take care of hooking itself. This is what a bolt rig does.

The bait is fished on a hair rig. When a fish picks it up it does one of two things. It either moves on to take the next piece of food, pricks itself then panics and bolts (hence the name of the rig) and, by doing so, hooks itself. Or it realizes its mistake and attempts to eject the bait – with the same result. This usually produces a fairly posi-

◀ *A simple, sturdy free-running centrepin such as this is ideal. Unlike fixed-spool reels, centrepins have no gears – making the contact between angler and fighting fish more direct.*

▼ *Martin Hooper stalking barbel on the Dorset Stour. Fish spotting in clear waters is made much simpler if you wear a pair of polarizing glasses and a hat to shade your eyes. It is easier to catch a barbel if you can see where it is.*

tive indication and gives you a chance to pull the hook home.

The confidence rig works on much the same principle as the bolt rig. The difference is that you should leave slack line to allow the fish to move away with the bait until it suddenly hits the stop. As its name suggests, this rig works best when the fish are feeding without a sense of caution. In clear water this is indicated by fish moving all over the swim trying to get as much food as possible before the others get it all. In coloured water if a lot of line bites are occurring without any fish being hooked, the chances are that they are feeding confidently too.

The advantage of this rig is that by the time a fish feels the hook it probably has it well inside its mouth. There is little chance of it ejecting the bait. With this method you should make no attempt to strike – if you do the likelihood of foul hooking is very high.

Picking swims

The more time you spend on the bank looking for fish, learning their habits, feeding patterns and preferred swims in times of low waters through to flood conditions, the greater are your chances of hooking up with a really big barbel. This is a much better general approach than feeding what merely looks like a good swim. If it looks good it was probably fished yesterday and may well be

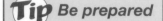
Tip Be prepared

When touch-legering a rod rest should be used only for the purpose its name suggests – to rest the rod on while it is not in use.

Often barbel bites are extremely fast and shy. The angler who puts the rod on a rest misses nearly every bite before he has even cleared the rod rest.

Always hold on to the rod and be ready at any moment to respond to the slightest twitch.

▶ *An angler plays a barbel on the Royalty fishery on the Hampshire Avon. Barbel exhaust themselves during a fight. Return them to the water as soon as they have recovered.*

fished again tomorrow. The fish will be hard to catch – if they are there at all.

The farther you get from the car park, and all the other anglers, the better are your prospects of a good day's fishing – and possibly of connecting with that elusive double-figure specimen.

▼ *John Watson cradles a big Wensum barbel. With its bronze, streamlined body and large fins it is easy to see why the barbel is such a powerful and handsome adversary.*

Guide to carp fishing

Carp are cunning, they grow big and fight furiously – it's not surprising they are so popular with anglers. But how do you catch a specimen? The successful specimen hunting family, Bryan, Jon and Stephen Culley, tells you how.

M irrors and leathers are varieties of the common carp *(Cyprinus carpio)*. The crucian carp *(Carassius carassius)* is a separate species which is related to the carp family (as are roach, bream and tench) but does not reach the same enormous size as the common carp – which can often grow in excess of 50lb (23kg). Whatever the size, carp provide excellent sport.

Where to go

The beginner should try a water with a large head of carp – where bites (or 'runs') are not too scarce. This will increase the chance of getting to grips with a fish before patience wears out. You will find that tackle dealers and anglers are only too happy to tell you about the carp waters you can fish in your area.

The more experienced angler may prefer the challenge of a water with fewer carp but of a higher average weight. These fish will be wary and more difficult to hook. If you are to get one on the bank you must be prepared to put in the hours.

Lakes are generally best for really big fish. Canals and rivers are neglected and can be worth a try; few of the carp in these waters have been caught before so they often fall to less sophisticated baits and methods.

Locating the fish

Finding the fish is the secret to catching them. Walk around the water looking for tell-tale signs. Small clusters of bubbles or dark patches of muddy water indicate feeding carp. Look out for fish capering about – leaping clear of the water, for example.

During daylight carp retreat to the cover of islands, lily beds, weedbeds and over-hanging or sunken trees. A bait cast tight up to these fish-holding areas will often produce runs.

On gravel pits it is worth trying a bait along the bottom of gravel bars. You can precisely pin down the location of these by careful plumbing with a float or by casting a lead and timing the drop.

◄ *Many carp-holding lakes are picturesque and tranquil – until a powerful fish grabs your bait and the action starts. Carp like the cover of heavy weed so look for them by features such as lily beds and reeds.*

Choosing the tackle

Before selecting your gear you should ask yourself a few questions. For instance, are you going to fish the margins or at long range, and is the water snaggy? And what size fish are you after? If in doubt, get advice from a tackle dealer or an experienced carp angler – especially one who knows the water you want to fish.

Rods You don't have to buy a special carp rod if you already have a through-action, 11 or 12ft (3.3 or 3.6m) rod with a 2lb (0.9kg) test curve. This is a good bet for most carp on most waters, especially at short to medium range. However, if you want, you can select a rod with a fast taper, tip action for fishing at longer range. Also, the further out you fish the heavier the weight needed to cast. So use a powerful rod, such as one with a 2½lb (1.1kg) test curve, when the weight is over 2oz (57g). Below that a 2lb (0.9kg) test curve rod will do and for close-in fishing with lighter weights use a rod with a 1¾lb (0.8kg) test curve.

Reels The reel should be of a sturdy, open-face design and have a spool with a line-holding capacity of at least 140m (153yd) of 8lb (3.6kg) line. It should lay the line evenly on the spool, so that a running fish is able to take line easily. A baitrunning feature is useful – it allows the fish to run without your needing to take the bail arm off.

Line Choose your line strength to suit the water – 8lb (3.6kg) is suitable for open waters but step up to 10 or 12lb (4.5 or 5.4kg) if there is heavy weed or snags.

Hooks A variety of carp hooks is available and choice is very much a personal matter. In any case hooks should be strong and sharp. Useful sizes range from 4s to 10s. Obviously, the bigger the fish, the bigger the hook.

▲ *Effective carp baits include: dog biscuits (1) which you must soak before use or they swell inside the carp; cooked peanuts (2); flavoured boilies such as strawberry oil (3), oceanic oils (4) and tropicana oil (5); milk concentrate (6); sweetcorn (7); chick peas (8). Breadcrust (9), breadflake (10) and luncheon meat (11) can work on waters not often fished for carp.*

◀ *Whatever their size, carp are hard fighters and good fish for getting beginners interested. This fine specimen was caught in the margins on floating breadcrust bait.*

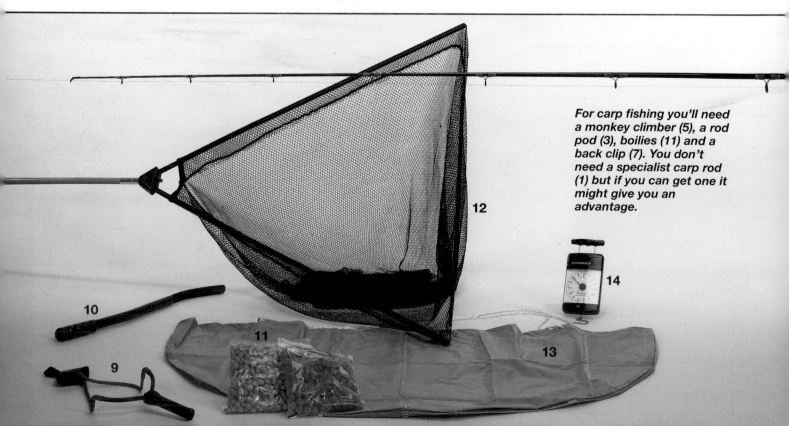

For carp fishing you'll need a monkey climber (5), a rod pod (3), boilies (11) and a back clip (7). You don't need a specialist carp rod (1) but if you can get one it might give you an advantage.

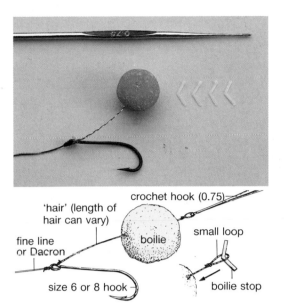

‘hair’ (length of hair can vary)

crochet hook (0.75)

fine line or Dacron

boilie

small loop

size 6 or 8 hook

boilie stop

▲ To make a boilie hair rig push a size 0.75mm crochet hook through the boilie. Tie a loop in the hair and draw it through the boilie. Put a stop in the loop and pull hair to tighten stop against boilie.

Carp baits

Boilies have an advantage over other baits in that smaller fish, such as bream and tench, are less likely to take them. You can buy boilies or make them at home. The range of flavours and colours is so wide that it is impossible to say which are best. You must experiment to find out which ones the carp on your water prefer.

Other good baits include breadflake and crust, luncheon meat, lobworms and sweetcorn (although the carp may be wary of these baits on hard-fished waters).

Dog and cat biscuits are good floating baits but soak them well before use.

Bite indication

The monkey climber works on a simple principle: that of the old-fashioned dough bobbin. The 'monkey' is a plastic cylinder free to slide up and down a vertical metal needle. The top of the needle is usually enlarged to stop the monkey flying off. The line passes between the climber and the needle. On a run the monkey climbs the needle as the fish takes line. It drops if the fish runs at you. When you strike, the line is freed from the indicator. Monkeys can be fitted with glowing isotopes for night fishing, and fished together with electronic alarms.

Carp rigs

Rigs for carp divide into two categories: those for bottom-feeding fish and those for surface feeders.

Hair rigs Most carp are caught on the bottom, with the bait on the hook or on a 'hair' (a length of fine line). A hair rig is effective because it leaves the hook entirely free – so there is a much greater chance of it catching in the fish's mouth.

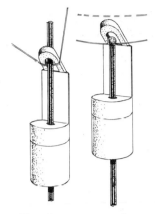

To set up your monkey climber, pass line between the loop and the needle. Leave the bail arm disengaged so that a running fish is free to take line. A run causes the monkey either to rise and hover on the needle or, if the fish runs towards you, to drop back.

▲ With a bolt rig it's important to back clip the line. This keeps tension in the line which helps set the hook. The line is wedged behind the clip (7).

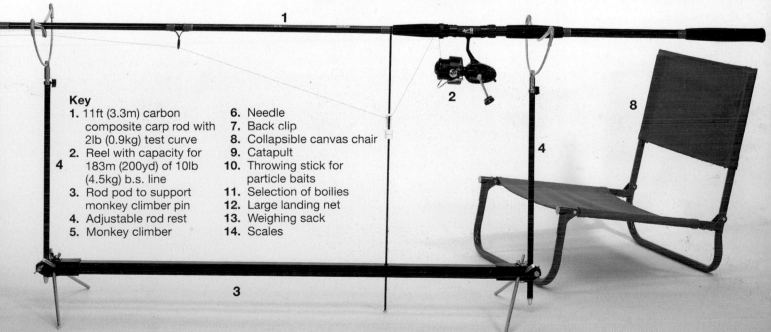

Key
1. 11ft (3.3m) carbon composite carp rod with 2lb (0.9kg) test curve
2. Reel with capacity for 183m (200yd) of 10lb (4.5kg) b.s. line
3. Rod pod to support monkey climber pin
4. Adjustable rod rest
5. Monkey climber
6. Needle
7. Back clip
8. Collapsible canvas chair
9. Catapult
10. Throwing stick for particle baits
11. Selection of boilies
12. Large landing net
13. Weighing sack
14. Scales

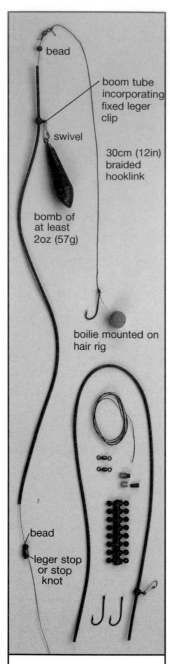

bead

boom tube
incorporating
fixed leger
clip

swivel

30cm (12in)
braided
hooklink

bomb of
at least
2oz (57g)

boilie mounted on
hair rig

bead

leger stop
or stop
knot

Anti-tangle rig

Anti-tangle booms let you
cast long distances
without the line tangling
and they help to keep the
line off the fish's back as it
is brought in. To prevent
tangles, make sure that
the length of the hooklink
is shorter than the length
of the boom. The boom
can be either stiff or
flexible.

▶ *Bryan Culley's patience
was rewarded with this
double-figure common that
fell to a simple hair rig. He
took it from a river – an
often neglected water for
carp but worth a try if you
are prepared to wait.*

Rigs for surface feeders

The **running bomb rig** (right above) works
on waters up to 1.8m (6ft) deep. The bomb
anchors the rig. Use binoculars to watch the
bait. A different coloured hookbait helps you
to pick out your floater from the loose feed.
On waters deeper than 1.8m (6ft) use the
controller rig (right below). This acts as a
casting aid rather than as a bite indicator.
So, when spotting bites, watch your
hookbait rather than the controller.

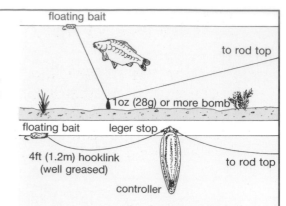

floating bait

to rod top

1oz (28g) or more bomb

floating bait

leger stop

4ft (1.2m) hooklink
(well greased)

to rod top

controller

Bolt rigs A hair rig is normally used
together with an anti-tangle bolt rig. Plastic
booms with a fixed wire clip are available
from tackle shops. A heavy bomb of about
2oz (57g) is clipped to the boom and the
boom is free to slide on the line over a short
distance.

It is in the nature of carp to suck in
morsels of food and blow them out again
before finally swallowing them. With the
hair rig, a carp sucks in the bait along with
the hook and as it blows it out again the
hook pricks the inside of the fish's mouth,
causing it to bolt. Line is pulled through the
boom as the fish runs. The stop knot comes
up hard against the boom and the fish
hooks itself against the weight of the bomb.
This self-hooking principle depends upon
the hook being free from bait.

Running leger rigs Some baits have to be
fished on the hook because it is not practical
to put them on a hair. (For example, lobworms won't go on a hair and bread will go
on but won't stay on.) These baits are normally fished on a running leger.

Surface rigs Fishing on the surface is one
of the most exciting ways of taking carp and
it always pays to throw in a few floating
baits during the day to see if the fish are
interested in feeding on the top.

Fishing for carp

Accurate casting and feeding is always
important. Find a likely fish-holding spot
and cast close to it. Encourage the fish to
feed by using a catapult, throwing stick or
bait dropper to present free offerings
around your hookbait. Sometimes it is possible to intercept margin-feeding fish by
dropping a bait right in the fish's path.

When carp fishing, patience is a virtue
but if you are not getting results and you
can see signs of fish in another part of the
water, don't hang about – move on.

Caring for carp

It is important to use a large landing net
with a soft mesh to protect the fish. Always
unhook your carp on grass or an unhooking
mat, weigh them in a net sling and then
photograph them and get them back into
the water as soon as possible.

Floater fishing for carp

Even the wisest and canniest carp seem irresistibly tempted by floating biscuits and cereals. When carp are feeding on the surface it's quick and exciting sport. Carp expert Bob James reveals the secrets of floaters and suspenders.

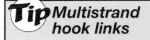

Tip Multistrand hook links

Multistrand hook links are the ultimate device for these really cunning carp. Once in the water the filaments separate out, making it very difficult for fish to see or feel.

Multistrand links used to tangle badly, but a newly invented gel, available in larger tackle shops, sets when applied to the link, leaving it semi-rigid. Within a minute of landing in water the gel dissolves leaving your link soft and supple again. Give them another chance!

O ne of the most successful but least used methods of carping is floater fishing. It requires little tackle, short sessions and must be *the* most exciting way of catching carp. It requires stealth and craft since the carp's reputation for cunning is well earned.

Can your nerve last?

Look for swims other anglers have neglected because of weeds, lilies or fallen trees. Since you are surface fishing these spots should not cause the same problems as bottom fishing, and they are just the places carp enjoy. Put a few floaters out in one or more such areas, then sit quietly in a place which allows you to keep an eye on them. It doesn't usually take long for carp to show some interest, but don't be in a hurry to cast. Let them eat a few first. Then, if they still do not look very confident, feed more loose offerings.

Once most of the freebies have gone and the carp are looking around for more, you can quietly introduce your hookbait. Don't drop it right on top of their heads – put it slightly away from them in some part of the swim where you can see them feeding.

If you've done everything right, your nerves are going to be tested to the full. This must surely be the most exciting moment in angling, as carp loom up on to your bait. If you can see the bait you must strike as soon

▼ *In warm months carp like to feed near the surface. Floaters such as pet food biscuits can make an irresistible snack for even the canniest carp.*

as the carp closes its mouth over it. If your bait is obscured wait for the line to move away and then hit it!

Bread and biscuits

Back in the 1950s when floater fishing began, bread was the popular bait, either as flake or crust. There are still many waters where bread works, although few anglers seem to try it now. Today there is a huge selection of surface baits from breakfast cereals such as puffed wheat, and nut hoops, through to animal feeds like trout pellets and dog and cat biscuits.

Just take a look along the shelves of your local pet shop. There are dozens of different biscuits of various flavours, colours and sizes. Most, if not all, will catch carp, and only by experimenting will you find the best for any particular fishery.

Biscuits can be used two ways, dry or soaked. Dry biscuits without cut patterns have to be drilled and tied to the hook. You

Preparing floaters

1. Soaking pet food biscuits in hot water makes them easy to attach to your hook, without having to resort to drilling each biscuit. However, pre-soaked biscuits are less buoyant and you may need more than one on your hook to keep it afloat.

2. Before draining off the hot water, you can add colouring and flavouring to your biscuits. If you have a hunch that carp like the taste of honey, or prefer the colour red, this is the time to put your ideas into practice.

3. Fixing your softened and dyed biscuits to the hook is now easy. It's probable that in tests, nine out of ten carp who could express a preference would prefer pet biscuits.

▲ *Carp take the biscuit when it comes to floaters. They gorge on pet food biscuits, wet or dry , bread crusts and a variety of other baits.*

can use as many biscuits as you like. Alternatively they can be soaked and then threaded straight on the hook.

While soaking it is a simple matter to introduce a flavour or colour, making your bait more individual. To do this, put 1½lb (0.7kg) of biscuits in a polythene bag. Then pour 150ml of water into a cup and add 10-15ml of the flavouring, as well as any colourings you want. Empty this into the bag, fill it with air, and shake it for a few minutes, until all the liquid is evenly distributed. Leave the mixture to stand for at least an hour, until you have a nice rubbery-textured bait.

When and where

Warm summer days are perfect for surface fishing. Often you can see carp basking, or slowly drifting around the upper layers in the warmth of the sun. If they are moving about, try to spot their route. It is likely that they have a regular patrol path, in which case bait placed to intercept them is far more effective than bait thrown to them. However if they are stationary use whatever drift or breeze there might be to work floaters out into their vicinity. This causes far less suspicion. Don't be put off if there is a ripple and the carp are not visible – these can be the best conditions of all!

Throw plenty of bait out so that it drifts right across the lake. Often fish start taking way out in the middle but then follow the floaters into the far margins, where great sport can be had.

During the warmer months fishing the night hours can be very productive. If there are any waterfowl present, don't fish areas

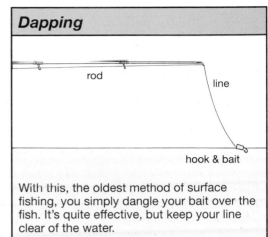
Anchored floater

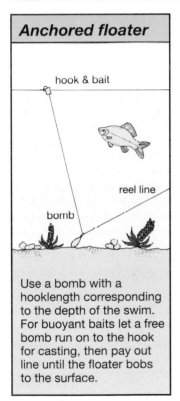

Use a bomb with a hooklength corresponding to the depth of the swim. For buoyant baits let a free bomb run on to the hook for casting, then pay out line until the floater bobs to the surface.

▲ **You do not need to be a millionaire to try fishing with a controller. You can go back to nature using a buoyant stick. However there is an excellent range of proprietary brands.**

you can't see. Don't risk hooking a duck or swan in the middle of the small hours – it won't be much fun for either of you!

Autumn can be excellent for surface fishing as carp often spend hours nosing around great carpets of floating leaves, especially in the downwind corners. Even in winter it is possible to catch carp near the surface on mild, sunny days. Conditions have to be spot on, however, and once the frosts have arrived it's rarely worthwhile.

Choosing tackle

Controllers A range of controllers will provide you with casting weight for summer fishing.

Rods You don't need to buy a completely new set of tackle for good results, but using the right rod and reel gives you a definite advantage. Since you will often be hooking fish at close range or near snags, a rod with a

1½-2lb (0.7-0.9kg) test curve with an all through action is ideal. If you use a rod that is too powerful or has a fast taper, either the hook hold will give, or worse, you may tear the carp's mouth. When stalking fish under trees or in overgrown areas a shortish rod, about 9-10ft (2.7-3m) long makes life easier. If the fish are feeding further away a 12-13ft (3.6-3.9m) rod copes far better.

Reels Fixed spool reels are excellent for distance fishing. Choose one that holds plenty of line and has a reliable clutch – be sure to set it before you start since takes can be very stubborn and leave no time for mistakes. For fishing the margins centrepin reels give unparalleled control. You don't have to pump to gain line on a heavy fish and there's no clutch to set wrong!

Line Choose your line carefully. In open water you may need to go down to a 6-8lb (2.7-3.6kg) line but near snags you need a line of around 15lb (6.8kg). In most cases you must judge for yourself but don't go lighter than necessary – leaving fish hung up or trailing yards of line about is not sporting.

Low diameter pre-stretched lines can help fool ultra-wary fish, but check carefully after each fight for marks or rubbing. Replace it straight away if it looks worn as much of its strength will be lost.

Hooks Fish in open water generally only take single biscuits and on light line, so size

Controller rig

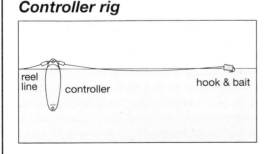

The controller, available commercially, has a piece of rig tube pushed through the swivel to stop tangles when casting. A 60-90cm (2-3ft) hook link seems to work best and doesn't make casting too difficult.

Anchored controller

With an anchored controller rig (right) the bomb is left running. This makes casting far easier, especially when fishing deep water. After casting pay out line until the controller surfaces.

This way of fishing a controller is particularly useful if surface drift is becoming a problem. The running lead will hold your mixers – or whatever bait you are using – in position.

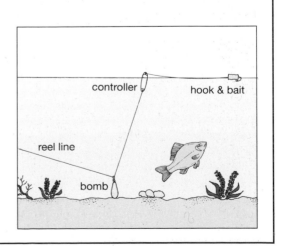

Beachcaster rig

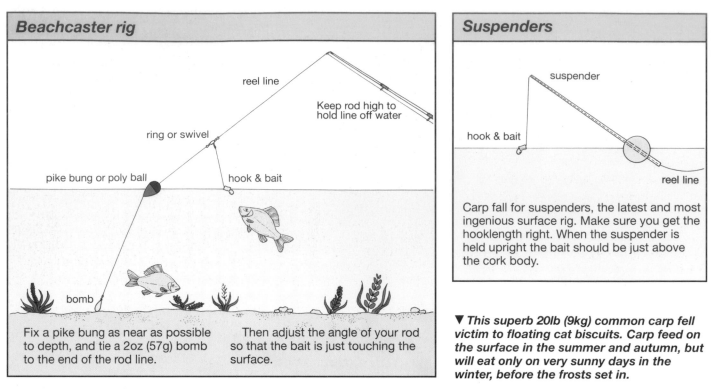

reel line

Keep rod high to
hold line off water

ring or swivel

pike bung or poly ball

hook & bait

bomb

Fix a pike bung as near as possible
to depth, and tie a 2oz (57g) bomb
to the end of the rod line.

Then adjust the angle of your rod
so that the bait is just touching the
surface.

Suspenders

suspender

hook & bait

reel line

Carp fall for suspenders, the latest and most
ingenious surface rig. Make sure you get the
hooklength right. When the suspender is
held upright the bait should be just above
the cork body.

▼ *This superb 20lb (9kg) common carp fell*
victim to floating cat biscuits. Carp feed on
the surface in the summer and autumn, but
will eat only on very sunny days in the
winter, before the frosts set in.

8s or 10s are best. As there is little buoyancy
in a single bait you require a medium wire
hook to stay afloat. Near snags, weeds and
lilies, carp are a little bolder, so go up to size
6s or 4s in thicker wire – you'll need the extra
strength in these conditions. Hair rigs are
very successful in catching carp. Tie a hair of
between 2.5cm (1in) and 6cm (2½in) to the
eye of your hook and attach your bait to it.
With a free hook there's a much greater
chance of catching the fleshy part inside the
carp's mouth when it strikes.

Dry mixers

To hook up dry dog food mixer biscuits, drill
a small hole then pass some 2lb (0.9kg) line
through it. Tie one end to the hook and the
other to the eye.

Pre-soaked mixers

Pre-soaked mixers are less buoyant, and
you may need two to float your hook. Leave
a gap between the bait and the hook point
to allow for good hooking.

Carp hooklengths

It's your hooklength that is going to take the strain when a big carp takes your bait. It's too late then to change your mind!

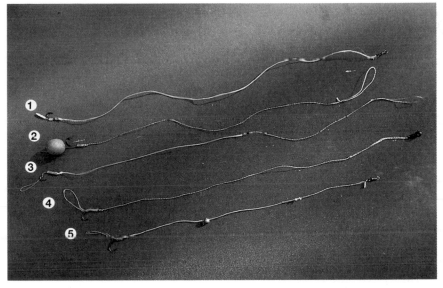

▲ *There's more than one way to string a boilie. 1. Multistrand line with boilie spike. 2. Braided line. 3. Combined braided and multistrand line to ease casting. 4. Braided line attached to main line with swivel. 5. Pop-up boilie rig with shot.*

Make the wrong choice of rod or reel and it probably won't be crucial. Make the wrong choice of bait and a hungry carp may still take it as a one-off. But if you make the wrong choice of hooklength, you're going to lose that big fish. Your line selection is crucial to landing a big carp successfully.

There's no point in choosing hooks inappropriate to the line you are using. As an extreme example, a size 2 hook with 2lb (0.9kg) line would make no sense. A size 2 hook shows you are expecting a pretty large fish, using a big bait – yet 2lb (0.9kg) line isn't going to hold up to the strain if there are any snags in the water. The most important thing is to balance your hooklength correctly with your chosen size of hook and style of rig.

What's my line?

It's no longer true that a high breaking strain line is automatically thick, inflexible and obvious to even the dullest of carp.

Modern monofilament line has a low diameter and is very supple – a quality to look for in a hooklength since it allows bait

Tip *Shock!*

When long range casting use a shock leader – a 4.5-6m (15-20ft) length of heavier line (10-15lb/4.5-6.8kg) – between the main line and hook link.

▼ *If a carp can put a healthy bend like this in your rod you need a strong hooklength to be certain of landing it.*

Equipment key

1-3. Dacron carp line – this stands up very well to any abrasion.
4. Multistrand line – thin and strong, strands separate in water making it hard for carp to spot.
5-7. Braided line – this gives strength and flexibility to a hooklength.
8. PVA string dissolves in water, and is used for accurate loosefeeding.
9. Anti-tangle solution to stiffen braided line.
10. Monofilament line.

to fall naturally. Line is also being improved constantly to ensure improved casting and less resistance when a carp takes your bait. Make sure you store it away from light, and wet it before you knot it, and it should give good service.

Braided line is an alternative to monofilament for your hooklength. This can be 10 or 15 times more supple than its equivalent breaking strain nylon counterpart. Braided line is particularly good for hard-fished waters where carp become extra sensitive in detecting the resistance caused by line as they play with the bait. Marvellous, you might think, but there must be a catch. And there is – braided line is quite a bit thicker than nylon. It is up to you to choose whether you think carp are

more spooked by the sight or by the feel of line.

Multistrand is the latest development. It consists of many strands of high strength micro fibres. Once in the water these strands separate, becoming almost invisible. Kryston Multi-strand is the pioneer in this type of line.

Colour of line There's some controversy today over the colouring of hooklengths, with some companies claiming black is now the worst possible colour for terminal rigs, since educated carp have learned to avoid it. Green or brown line is the current fashion trend, and if you have the money, Maxima Chameleon supposedly absorbs light rather than reflects it.

More than one boilie can be used on a hair rig. This set-up uses a braided hooklength which continues through the eye and is used as the hair as well. It is designed to entice big and greedy carp. A boilie needle is useful for threading boilies on to a hair.

A knotty question

The kind of knot you use is quite important in your choice of hooklength line. Different lines are now designed to give maximum strength with certain kinds of knots. For example, Drennan Carp Dacron is designed with a weave that works best with a grinner knot. It makes changing rigs easier if you incorporate a swivel link.

The other problem that will affect the strength of your line is abrasion. As line rubs against rocks or snags it frays, reducing the strength of the line considerably. If your hooklength has rubbed against any sharp surface, or is looking a little old and tired, dispose of it immediately. It could make the difference between a twenty and feeling fed up for a week! Anglers such as Kevin Maddocks replace their entire lines at least twice a season, and their hooklengths after any hard fight. It sounds expensive, but it's worth it to make sure you land the fish.

Tip Spiked hair

Among the hooklengths shown on page 189 there is a rig using a boilie spike (top). The plastic spike is attached to the hook and the boilie is then simply pushed on to it until the spike is buried.

The advantage is that boilies can be replaced simply and quickly.

The basic leger rig

Since legering is the most popular method of carp fishing, a standard carp leger rig is probably the simplest and most useful one to look at.

The hair rig diagram on page 192 shows a simple leger rig set-up (ignore the hair itself

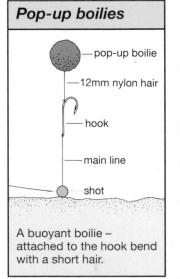

Pop-up boilies

- pop-up boilie
- 12mm nylon hair
- hook
- main line
- shot

A buoyant boilie – attached to the hook bend with a short hair.

▶ *Careful preparation of your rig before you go fishing means more chance of success. This angler is incorporating an anti-tangle tube into the rig to ensure there are no problems when casting using Dacron.*

Is it sporting?

After the novelty of catching big carp has worn off, some anglers choose to increase the excitement by catching big carp on light hooklengths. But this greatly increases the danger of breaking off on snags, leaving hooks in the carp. It's fun for anglers, but not for the carp.

Legering a hair rig

This is a simple set-up for legering with a hair rig. The rig incorporates a swivel linking the main line to the hooklength and the boilie is attached to the end of the hair.

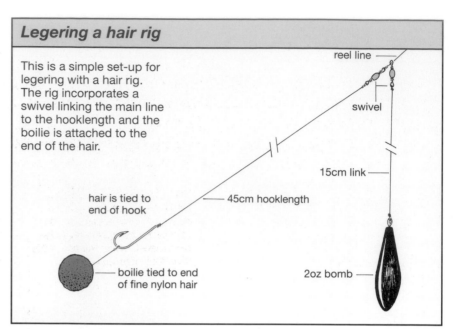

reel line

swivel

15cm link

45cm hooklength

hair is tied to end of hook

boilie tied to end of fine nylon hair

2oz bomb

for the moment). Most anglers use a link swivel to connect the main line to the hooklength. Very often it is the same strength line straight through – typically 8lb (3.6kg) line for most waters, 10-12lb (4.5-5.4kg) line for snaggy or weedy waters, and 12-15lb (5.4-6.8kg) line for very heavily snagged waters. A standard hooklength is generally between 30cm (12in) and 45cm (18in) long.

The leger weight (normally an Arlesey bomb or a pear lead) is on a link around 10cm (4in) long. The bomb can be attached straight to the main line, but it's better on a link because – if the weight sinks in mud – it's not going to drag the hooklength down with it.

The hair rig

Carp are wily creatures. They might not be quite as intelligent as some anglers make them out to be, but they do learn. When they became suspicious of bait with a hook in it, the hair rig was devised to keep them guessing.

Kevin Maddocks and Lenny Middleton studied the way that carp took boilies in a large aquarium. It was soon obvious that they went for every boilie except the one with the hook and line. Kevin and Lenny decided that the carp were probably taking the boilie back to their pharyngeal teeth, feeling the line on their lips and rejecting the bait.

The two anglers decided to try attaching the bait to a piece of human hair. Sure enough, the hair was so fine that the carp didn't detect it. Of course human hair isn't strong enough to hold a carp, so they then attached the short length of human hair to a hook; which was in turn attached to the main line. They found that the carp still took the bait.

Oddly, later research by anglers has shown that, in fact, the hair rig seems to work best because a suspicious carp repeatedly sucks in and blows out food as it investigates it. As it does this, the hook catches the carp's lips at an angle when a hair rig is used. Today, hair has been replaced by fine nylon line, though anglers like Andy Little use unwaxed dental floss.

◄ *If you have chosen and prepared your hooklength correctly there's no reason why you shouldn't land a nice carp like this.*

Advanced carp rigs

Peter Mohan's advice is to fish simply if you can. But in some circumstances you might need more complicated rigs to get the most out of your angling – so it's worth having a few variations up your sleeve just in case.

One of the greatest aids to success in modern carp fishing is knowing how to make up and use different rigs. In most carp waters, the standard running link leger method with a hair rig is all you need to catch bottom feeding carp.

However, in more difficult lakes where the fish are caught frequently and have become wary of baits on the bottom, experimenting with more advanced rigs can make

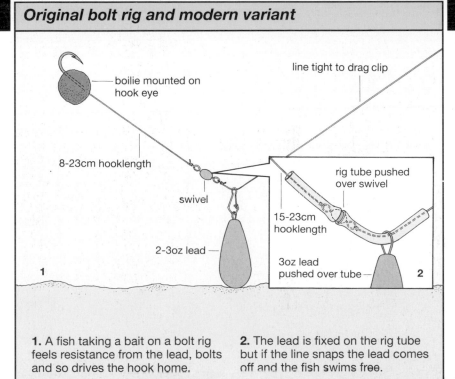

▲ Dawn is one of the best times for carp fishing. This solitary angler stands a fair chance if his rigs are right for the water.

Original bolt rig and modern variant

- boilie mounted on hook eye
- line tight to drag clip
- 8-23cm hooklength
- swivel
- rig tube pushed over swivel
- 15-23cm hooklength
- 2-3oz lead
- 3oz lead pushed over tube
- 1
- 2

1. A fish taking a bait on a bolt rig feels resistance from the lead, bolts and so drives the hook home.

2. The lead is fixed on the rig tube but if the line snaps the lead comes off and the fish swims free.

all the difference between blanking and catching big fish.

Knowing when to switch

It's no good using complex rigs and then forgetting all the other skills which help you catch. However modern your rig, it won't work if you are fishing in areas where the fish are not feeding, or if you are using a bait the fish won't take.

But how do you know when to switch to a different rig?

If most anglers on your water are catching more than you, if you get a lot of small bite indications which don't produce proper takes, if you are frequently losing fish because they come off, or if the fish you catch are hooked just outside the mouth – then it's time to change.

If you get lots of twitches, slacken the line

Tip Wallet wheeze

One way to save time at the waterside is to make up your rigs before going on a fishing trip. To keep them tidy and tangle-free a rig wallet is a fine idea.

so it lies along the bottom, making sure they're not line bites. If the twitches continue, try to make sure they're not caused by small fish (perhaps by trying a smaller bait – small fish often suck at a bait too large for them).

Bespoke rigging

When you're pretty sure you have a rig problem, you should think about trying a different set up.

Bolt rig For the original type of bolt rig use a fairly large long shank, down eye hook – a size 4 perhaps. Side-hook a boilie, leaving a gap of at least 3mm (⅛in) between the boilie and the hook point. If you don't do this the point will go into the bait when you strike

▶ *Is it a genuine rod-bender or a wad of weed? A helicopter rig often helps you to avoid snagging up in weedy waters.*

🐟 Lead free fish

Never use a permanently fixed lead.

If the line breaks above the lead a fish might be swimming around for months with an unwanted weight attached. Worse still, a rogue lead getting dragged around could easily tangle up in a snag and tether a fish to one spot until it starves to death.

▶ *Almost there! Many carp anglers never adjust their rigs, and wonder why fish come off – it's often because they are only just hooked outside the mouth.*

and not into the fish.

Use a hooklength of 8-23cm (3-9in) and attach the 2-3oz (56-85g) lead to the line by a running link. Fish this on a tight line held on the rod by a drag clip.

Modern variation This variation of the bolt rig is the semi-fixed breakaway lead method. The lead is fixed as far as the fish is concerned, but if the line breaks the lead comes off with the tube so the fish doesn't end up dragging a heavy burden around.

Bolt hair rig If neither of these methods is successful, try a bolt hair rig. Mount the bait on a hair tied to the bend of the hook instead of on the hook eye.

Anti-tangle rig You're bound to get into tangles sometimes, whether you are using a bolt rig, a bolt hair rig or even a standard hair rig. When trying these methods for the first time it is worth retrieving your tackle quickly a few times after casting, to see if the rig is tangled. If it is, try an anti-tangle rig.

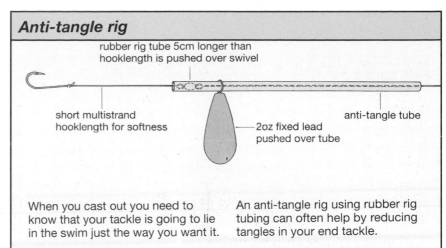

Anti-tangle rig

rubber rig tube 5cm longer than hooklength is pushed over swivel

short multistrand hooklength for softness

anti-tangle tube

2oz fixed lead pushed over tube

When you cast out you need to know that your tackle is going to lie in the swim just the way you want it.

An anti-tangle rig using rubber rig tubing can often help by reducing tangles in your end tackle.

▼ *If you land a decent fish like this one, make a note of the hook's position in the mouth – you may need to adjust your hooklength.*

Weed-free whirlybird

You may suspect that fish are rejecting your baits because the nylon line used for the hooklength in your rigs is too stiff, causing the fish to feel it over their lips. In this case try braided hooklengths or multistrand, which are much softer and can be used with all types of rigs. However, since they are so soft, these hooklengths are prone to tangling and you are likely to require an anti-tangle rig.

Helicopter rig Not all waters have clear bottoms. Some have a few inches of dense blanket weed in which the bait gets buried, making it hard for the fish to find. The helicopter rig – so called because the hooklength and bait revolve round the line during the cast – is especially good for this type of water. It is also a good anti-tangle rig.

A light hair rig type of hook is best for the helicopter rig and a soft multistrand hooklength goes some way towards preventing the bait being ejected by wary fish. The rig tubing helps to prevent tangles caused by the multistrand looping round the main line during the cast.

The hair rig can be tied to the bend or the eye of the hook. Better still, buy a hair rig fixing tube from a tackle shop and push it over the point of the hook. This enables you to have the hair coming from any part of the hook.

If you are fishing in snaggy areas or in heavy weed with a helicopter rig it's best to use light line on the bomb link. If the lead gets caught in a snag, the line breaks and the lead is lost, but you should be able to save the rest of your tackle and get any fish away from snags without difficulty.

Tip Keep it simple

Use the simplest rigs for as long as you can – even freelining can still work on some waters.

Only get into the more complex rigs when you are sure they are necessary on difficult waters.

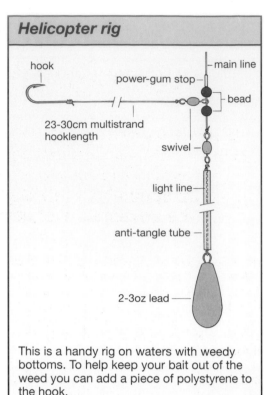

◄ *Top carp angler Ritchie McDonald carefully displays a handsome thirteen pounder (6kg).*
   Note the fish's grin – the carp's very sensitive, protractible lips are one reason why soft hooklengths are effective.

▼ *Advanced rigs are only effective if you combine them with sound angling methods.*

Helicopter rig

hook — power-gum stop — main line — bead — swivel — light line — anti-tangle tube — 2-3oz lead — 23-30cm multistrand hooklength

This is a handy rig on waters with weedy bottoms. To help keep your bait out of the weed you can add a piece of polystyrene to the hook.

Made-to-measure

Since advanced rigs are fairly complicated and include several attachments, make sure everything is secure before you cast, and that all the bits are in the right place.

Each time you catch a fish, note carefully where the hook is positioned in the mouth. If the fish is hooked just outside the mouth, you need to lengthen your hooklength by 2.5-5cm (1-2in) so that the hook will go further inside the carp's mouth.

Altering the length of the hooklength can also help you to get better takes from twitchers – these are often fish which have taken a hair-rigged bait inside their mouths leaving the hook still outside! Try shortening the hair as well.

Very short hairs On hard-fished waters many anglers now use rigs with hairs of only about 12mm (½in) between the edge of the boilie and the hook. They are often best for those wary fish that constantly mouth baits but don't take them.

This mouthing of baits happens quite a lot on most waters but when you can't see the fish you tend to forget what's happening. It's easy enough to see carp when they're taking every floater on the water except yours with the hook in it – and it's very frustrating. But at least you can see them doing it – you know what's happening and you can try to do something about it.

With legered baits all the action is underwater but it shouldn't stop you from trying different methods when you're not catching any fish. If you don't fancy donning a frogman suit to find out what the problem is at the business end of your line – a few rig adjustments might just do the trick.

Float fishing for specimen carp

In any branch of angling, flexibility is a great boon. In carp fishing, sticking blindly with the leger can sometimes lose you good fish. Big carp specialist Chris Ball runs through the advantages of using the float.

At a guess, of all the methods which catch carp, float fishing is very much the least practised. It has never been fashionable, nor has it been given a fair trial by many modern day carpmen. All too often it's discarded as a waste of time, only capable of catching small fish.

It's now time to take off your blinkers and face up to the truth. There are situations that cry out for the float, which is, after all, the most effective form of bite indication so far devised. True, it can be of great use when the target is small carp, but used properly, it's a technique that most big carp anglers would do well to master.

Where and when

Obviously, if you're fishing a water where the carp are only ever caught behind a gravel bar over 100m (110yd) out from the bank, a float is not going to be much use to you. However, there are many waters where the carp patrol close to the margins, providing excellent opportunities for catching them close in. That's when the superior bite detection of a float scores.

Proof of the pudding

"Several winters ago I discovered some big carp hiding in the remains of an old lily bed in the shallow margins of a lake. I threw them a few boiled baits and as I watched, they cautiously began to mop them up. Because the water was crystal clear, I decided to freeline my boilie.

"It wasn't long before a big mirror began to show interest. When it was within an inch of the bait, its movements caused the silt on the lake bed to puff up – obscuring the fish's mouth and the bait. All this time I am sure the line did not move, but I decided to strike anyway. The line came back minus the hook – a bite-off!

"The next day, I went back, but this time armed with float tackle. A big mirror – the same fish I think – again approached the hookbait. Again the silt puffed up as the fish sucked at the boilie. The float dipped slightly and I struck. After a tense battle, I landed a fine 19lb (8.6kg) mirror carp, perfectly hooked – another success to the float..."

▼ *Carp put up a real scrap on float tackle, and as bite detection is so good, it's the first choice for carp close to the margins.*

In some cases, anglers actually cast much farther than they need – a bit of stealth would show the fish feeding under the rod tip. This is the key   you can't stomp up and down the bank, setting up a bivvy and so on and expect to catch carp in the margins. The quiet approach is essential.

Observe the water carefully. Even if the depth close to the bank is greater than visibility allows, carp often swim in the top 60cm (2ft), disappearing only when they sense food – or an angler. Watch for tell-tale clouds of colour in the water as the carp root around for food.

Other fish can produce the same effect, especially tench, but more often perhaps you realise, it is carp that are responsible. Sometimes the observation can be quite accidental. You may be fishing at range, but if you have remained quiet for a few hours, the carp may not notice you as they patrol

Tip Water edges

Watch for any disturbance in the margins – it often betrays a big fish. Keep your eyes peeled, stay quiet and you often find the culprit is a carp.

round the edges of the bank.

Don't ignore these fish. Make a note of where you see them and take some float fishing gear with you next time you plan to fish the same swim. If you bait up the area where you saw the carp before, this holds the fish, so you can present the bait to them. Catching a fish you have fooled by stealth is one of the greatest pleasures in fishing.

Carp float fishing gear

The right gear for the job

An Avon-type rod **(1)** with a test curve of 1-2lb (0.45-0.9kg) and a through action is essential for float fishing. You also need a reliable reel **(2)**. It doesn't need to have a tapered spool, but one like this is good for both float fishing and legering. Terminal tackle includes a variety of floats **(3)**, strong, forged hooks **(4)**, swivels **(5)**, split shot **(6)** or tungsten putty weights, and some pre-tied supple hooklengths **(7)** or braided line **(8)** to tie them on the bank.

What you need

If you've read this far, you're convinced that it might be worth at least giving it a try, so what tackle do you need?

A rod of around 10-11ft (3-3.4m), with a test curve of 1-2lb (0.45-0.9kg) and a nice easy action is essential. You are generally fishing close to the bank – a fast taper or heavy duty model does not have the necessary flexibilty to absorb the sudden lunges of a fleeing carp at short range. This also means you don't need a carbon fibre rod. Glass-fibre and split cane are just as good.

Reel choice is fairly wide. A reliable fixed-spool reel does the job – and there are plenty available. A centrepin also performs admirably, keeping you in direct contact with the fish, and giving you fingertip control over the amount of pressure you put on the fish.

Lines and hooks are mainly a question of common sense and bait size. However, it is important to use balanced tackle. Don't team a small, fine wire hook with 10lb (4.5kg) line, and size 2 hooks (or bigger) don't go with 4lb (1.8kg) b.s.

For smaller carp, 4-6lb (1.8-2.7kg) line straight through to a size 8-10 hook is ideal. For bigger specimens, line strength needs to be 8-12lb (3.6-5.4kg). Use one of the specialist supple materials for your hooklength, through to a hook size which

▲ *You need to be stealthy to creep up on carp in the margins. But as long as you don't put them to flight, you can catch some big carp on light float fishing gear.*

▼ *The author, Chris Ball, poses with a fine float-caught common before returning it carefully. Note Chris's large landing net which is essential for fishing any water where you might catch big carp.*

depends on the fish and the bait.

Whatever tackle you use, look for solid reliability and strength. fishing in the margins soon finds out any weak points in your terminal tackle!

Floats are often a personal choice, but whether you use peacock quill or clear plastic waggler-type floats, they should not be too large – you've no need for a 3SSG float.

Baits and rigs

Of the many baits available, two stand out as consistent performers – sweetcorn and boilies. For smaller carp particularly,

sweetcorn is a great fish catcher, though its attraction for other species means you might end up with a mixed bag. Straight from the tin, it is a convenient and reasonably cheap bait to use.

Boilies catch carp of all sizes. They are a versatile bait too, since you can buy or make them any size from 10-20mm or bigger. Sweet, fruity flavours and fishy ones are very successful. You don't need to make your own, either. Shelf life boilies have the definite advantage that you can keep them in your tackle box until you need them.

One bait you should not ignore when you

Chris's rigs for carp

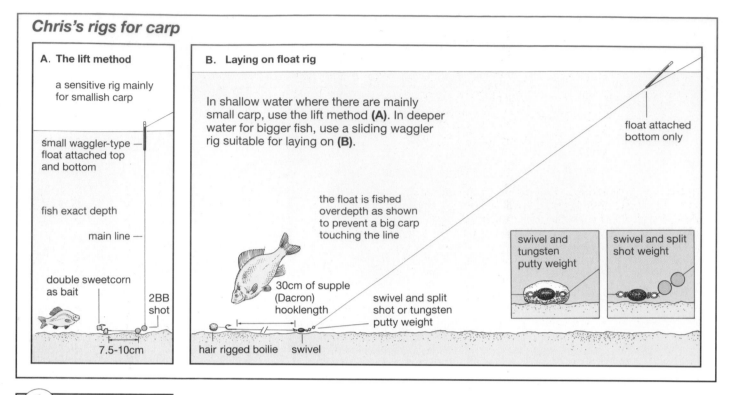

A. The lift method

a sensitive rig mainly for smallish carp

small waggler-type — float attached top and bottom

fish exact depth

main line —

double sweetcorn as bait

2BB shot

7.5-10cm

B. Laying on float rig

In shallow water where there are mainly small carp, use the lift method **(A)**. In deeper water for bigger fish, use a sliding waggler rig suitable for laying on **(B)**.

the float is fished overdepth as shown to prevent a big carp touching the line

float attached bottom only

30cm of supple (Dacron) hooklength

swivel and split shot or tungsten putty weight

swivel and tungsten putty weight

swivel and split shot weight

hair rigged boilie   swivel

Tip Soft spot for sweetcorn

When you are using sweetcorn on the hook, make sure the hook point remains well clear or you risk bumping fish off on the strike.

Alternatively, you might try fishing two or three grains of corn on a standard hair rig.

can see your quarry in shallow water is breadflake. Its use is in no way limited to other, smaller species, and it can be deadly, as well as very cheap.

If your target is mostly the small fish shoaling in shallow water, fish the lift method with your float attached top asnd bottom and sweetcorn on the hook. All the shot needs to be 7.5-10cm (3-4in) from the hook with the float set at the exact depth. Fished in this way it is a highly sensitive method of bite detection.

For bigger carp, it's best to present a boilie on a hair rig with a supple hooklength

such as Dacron or a multistrand. These fish are usually very wary of line – just touching it as it hangs from the float can spook them. To combat this, and the potential problem of line bites, set the float considerably overdepth and draw it well clear of the bait.

Used well, these techniques help you catch more fish close in. You might also find the excitement of float fishing addictive.

▼ *A float with sweetcorn hookbait, fished tight up against a lily bed, proved the downfall of this lovely, streamlined 10lb (4.5kg) wild carp.*

Basic pike kit

Pike are Britain's supreme freshwater predatory fish. But – tough as they look – they can be easily killed or injured by inexperienced anglers, using incorrect tackle.

Piking is sometimes thought of by newcomers to the sport as an addition to a day's fishing. They take along an old boat rod and put a mackerel in the water 'to see what happens'.

This is exactly the **wrong** attitude to pike fishing. Pike frequently swallow hooks deeply and if your tackle is not up to the job and breaks – leaving the hook deep in the fish – they can suffer an agonising death. Always avoid deep-hooking pike.

There are three main ways of fishing for pike: livebaiting, spinning and deadbaiting. Arguably, anglers new to pike fishing find deadbaiting the easiest method of catching, but some specialist tackle is needed in even a simple deadbaiting kit.

The right rod

Your rod needs to be quite sturdy. Ideally you should choose a 2¼lb test curve rod. Most types of carp rod can be used, but

Basic pike kit key

1, 2. A 2¾lb TC Ryobi 'John Wilson' pike rod. This two-piece rod is 12ft (3.7m) long and is fine for 10-15lb line. Quality pike rods are not cheap – but can handle most conditions and most fish.
3. Specialist **fixed-spool reel**, designed to catch specimen fish. Get one with a good drag system to cope with the sudden rush of a large pike.
4. Pike slider float.
5. Pencil deadbait float.
6. Wire trace, complete with **snap-tackle**.
7. Treble hook guards – these reduce accidents.

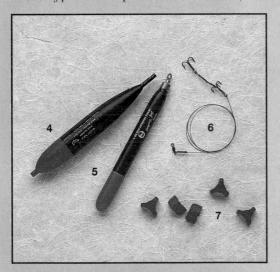

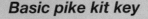

those with a soft action are inadequate for casting heavier baits long distances. A 10ft (3m) stepped-up carp rod is fine – but better still is a 10-12ft (3-3.7m) pike rod. The rod shown here has a 2¾lb test curve. This might sound about as responsive as a tree, but good pike rods, such as this, have an excellent tip action. They can handle casting big baits and landing large pike.

A robust reel

The pike fishing reel should be of a more robust, heavier design than those used for general coarse fishing. A fixed-spool reel, deep spooled and loaded with 10-12lb (4.5-5.4kg) line, is the easiest kind to use.

Open-faced reels are better than closed-face reels for piking – pressure from big fish makes the line bed-in with a closed-face reel. Specimen reels are a little more expensive than match and light float fishing reels, but offer greater flexibility and strength.

Specialist floats

If you intend to leger using a float, or to suspend your deadbait in the water, you need specialist pike floats. A sliding pike float is suitable for both a suspended rig and a bottom fished rig. When using large pieces of deadbait, such as herring or mackerel, make sure you get a sliding float big and buoyant enough to suspend your deadbait.

▲ *Pike are partial to smelt (shown here), roach, mackerel or half a herring. Try twitching your deadbait along the bottom to simulate a wounded fish. Pike prefer slow, easy targets.*

A pencil deadbait float – held in position by a stop knot and bead above the float – is also excellent for legering.

Line and snap-tackle

Your reel line should be 10-12lb (4.5-5.4kg) bs and must be connected by a swivel to an 18-20in (45-50cm) cable-laid wire trace of around 20lb (9kg) test. Pike bite through normal line, and are then left with treble hooks embedded in their bodies.

▲ *Gotcha! Playing a pike, even a large one, should be easier – and safer for the fish – with correct tackle.*

Attach the deadbait to the line by using two size 8 treble hooks connected together by 3in (7.5cm) of the wire trace. This is called snap-tackle. Attach the herring, mackerel or other chosen bait to the two hooks. To make doubly sure the bait is attached securely – if you are casting a long way – you can tie the fish to the snap-tackle rig around its tail.

Pike usually swallow whole fish head first, so keep the hooks as far back, near to the tail, as possible. This way the pike is less likely to swallow the hooks deeply. A deep-hooked pike is a dead pike unless you can get the hooks out very carefully.

Ideally, with barbed treble hooks, you should leave the barb on the point to which the deadbait is attached and file or squash the barbs on the two points that are to catch the pike. It makes them easier to hook, and they suffer less damage if they swallow the bait deeply. The occasional fish throwing your hooks is a small price to pay for these advantages.

Gags and forceps

Now you've hooked your first big pike – what do you do with it? A large, soft, knotless mesh landing net helps you bring the fish to the bank. To unhook it, 8in (20cm) straight artery forceps are best.

If you feel you must, you can use a pike gag to keep those powerful jaws open while you unhook your fish. Old pike gags are fairly barbaric instruments, but if you cover the sharp ends with rubber sleeves, cloth or cork they should not do too much damage to the pike's mouth.

◄ *Forceps are the ideal means of unhooking pike. Today's 'fish friendly' anglers, such as John Wilson, do not use a pike gag. A leather glove can protect your hands.*

Unhooking pike

Unhooking pike can cause needless stress to both angler and fish. Kevin Smith tells us how to keep our heads ...and our fingers!

Beginner specimen-hunters don't need to be afraid of unhooking a pike – this predator's 'freshwater shark' reputation is ill-deserved. The pike won't bite off your hand, nor pull drinking dogs into the water! It does have a fine set of teeth, though, rows and rows of them. It uses these to clamp on to – and then keep hold of – its prey. All you need do is to follow a few basic rules and buy the right equipment to avoid a nasty nip.

Pike kit

Before setting off in pursuit of pike, make sure your tackle box contains the following equipment: a good pair of forceps at least 20cm (8in) long; a special pike disgorger – available from all good tackle shops; and either a carp sack or a piece of foam large enough to lay the pike on.

In addition you may find a tough glove is useful; it should fit the left hand if you are

▲ Author Kevin Smith with a 22lb (10kg) pike which he unhooked and returned to the water with the minimum of fuss. Kevin says the most important points to remember are: keep calm, have the right equipment with you and don't be afraid to ask experienced anglers for any help you may need.

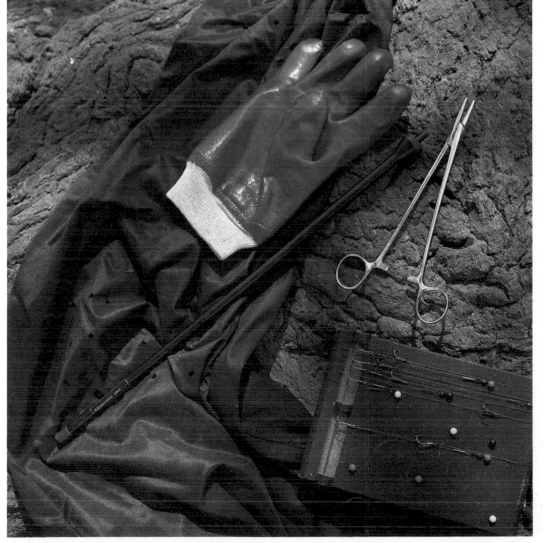

Dealing with deep hooking

Very occasionally every angler is going to run against a difficult deep hooking situation. At these times – says Kevin Smith – you'll need a commercial disgorger – such as the John Roberts Deep Throat or the Drennan pike disgorger.

To use them, slip the wire trace into the channel which is cut in to the head of the disgorger, and push firmly down on to the hook.

This pushes the hook out of the tissue and the disgorger's shaped head prevents it from catching up again.

Sadly, should you find yourself totally unable to remove snap tackle, it is best to kill the pike.

◄ A pike unhooking kit – from left to right, a sack to lay the pike on, an optional glove, a deep hook disgorger and long forceps.

right-handed. Using barbless trebles and prompt striking also help the job of unhooking.

Dentist's-eye view

Probably the most popular rig for catching pike is a deadbait snap-tackle rig using two treble hooks. To release a pike from this rig the fish is first laid gently on the wetted carp sack. If it starts jumping about, steady the fish by covering its head with your hands. Always have your unhooking equipment at-the-ready alongside the sack.

Kneel over the pike on the mat. Its lower jaw should be facing to the left if you're right handed. If you feel you need to use the glove, now is the time to put it on your left hand.

Slip two fingers along the bottom of the gill cover and into the V-shaped slit under the jaw. Make sure your fingers are properly in – just the tip isn't enough.

Now lift the pike's head. This should cause the pike's mouth to open. If not, lower the head and repeat the action.

You now have a dentist's-eye view of the jaw cavity. If the bait is in the way remove it with the forceps. A prompt strike should ensure that the hooks are in the mouth. Keeping hold of the trace (if possible ask a

friend or fellow angler to hold it) use the long forceps to remove the top treble from its hold. Take care that the first treble doesn't catch again while you deal with the other.

Don't panic!

Don't panic if one or both trebles are out of sight down the pike's throat. Pull **very gently** but firmly on the trace until the hooks are visible at the throat entrance. The pike's gut is surprisingly flexible and it does return after unhooking. Still keeping a firm hold of the trace, pass the forceps through the gill-slits and carefully clamp them on to the shank of the treble.

Next, invert the hook. If you're using barbless trebles this operation is surprisingly easy. Be firm at this point if the treble is a little stubborn. Finally, push towards the mouth opening – the hook should come out. Barbed trebles may need to be given a good push after the hook is inverted.

This combination of two trebles on a trace is, in fact, the most difficult one to remove. You can make life easier for yourself by using a single treble trace or a single large hook and treble combination.

Remember, use barbless hooks and don't be afraid to ask for assistance from more experienced anglers.

That old gag

The pike gag, a nasty tool for forcing a pike's jaws open, is still used by some anglers. The one shown is a semi-humane gag, the sharp points replaced by balls. Older gags have pointed ends, cover the points with cork.

▼ *Even when a pike has not swallowed the hook deeply a pair of forceps is a good idea. When fishing for pike ALWAYS strike swiftly – before it has a chance to swallow the bait. As Kevin says, it is possible to unhook deep-hooked pike, but it is more difficult and dangerous for the fish.*

Deadbaiting for pike

Deadbaiting is a highly successful way of catching pike because these fish, like many other predators, are active scavengers as well as hunters. Neville Fickling outlines the basics of this method for all seasons.

▼ *Neville Fickling, one of the most successful and respected pike anglers and authors in the country and a former British pike record holder, carefully returns a double-figure beauty to her watery home. The specimen fell to what is probably the most widely used method of all – deadbaiting. Correct handling and unhooking of pike is vital – put them back as soon as you can.*

D eadbaiting – using a dead fish, or part of one, as bait – is probably the most widely used method for catching pike and accounts for a great many double-figure specimens every year.

Sometimes pike can ambush live prey but often they have to give chase. Dead fish, however, are free pickings; there's no chase, which means the pike expends little energy in acquiring a meal.

To enable them to locate dead as well as live fish, pike have a highly developed sense of smell and keen eyesight. To be a successful deadbaiter, therefore, you must know how to exploit both of these senses by presenting a deadbait that is both encitingly smelly and highly visible.

Different deadbaits

A variety of dead fish, both freshwater and sea, are acceptable. The most popular sea species – because of their easy availability and high oil content – are herring and mackerel. Generally, use them whole up to about 15cm (6in) long, or as half-baits when larger. Sardines, pilchards, sprats and horse mackerel (scad) are also very popular. Less commonly used, but also very effective, are sandeels, garfish, whiting and red mullet.

Freshwater deadbaits can be any species easily caught on rod and line, but the most commonly used ones are roach, rudd, dace and eels (in sections). Also popular are smelt (a migratory fish) and rainbow trout.

Obtaining deadbaits

You can buy sea fish and rainbow trout from fishmongers and some tackle shops sell pre-packaged, ready frozen sea fish deadbaits. Frozen fish make just as good deadbaits as fresh ones, so have a ready supply in your freezer. Wrap and freeze them in polythene bags, individually or in small batches.

The same goes for freshwater fish baits. Rather than wasting time and even risking total failure trying to catch them on the day you go piking, have plenty in reserve at home in the freezer.

Choice of deadbaits

Your choice of deadbait on a particular venue depends on whether the pike there have been fished for extensively. Smelt and mackerel generally catch pike from any water, unless the pike have been caught many times on these baits. Then a change bait is well worth trying.

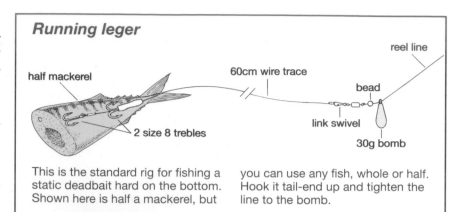

Running leger

reel line

half mackerel

60cm wire trace

bead

2 size 8 trebles

link swivel

30g bomb

This is the standard rig for fishing a static deadbait hard on the bottom. Shown here is half a mackerel, but you can use any fish, whole or half. Hook it tail-end up and tighten the line to the bomb.

To fool wary pike, you can modify the smell of a deadbait by injecting it with different flavours and fish oils. Likewise you can buy deadbaits dyed different colours, to ring the changes and tempt a cagey pike.

Tackle for deadbaiting

Deadbaiting requires tackle capable of handling baits weighing 100g (3½oz) or more. You need to use a rod with a 2-3lb (0.9-1.4kg) test curve and a good quality, robust fixed-spool reel loaded with 11-15lb (5-6.8kg) line.

Always use wire traces. Good quality

Wobbled deadbait

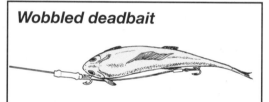

Put a bend in the deadbait before hooking it on (head-end up) to make it wobble on the retrieve like a sick or injured fish.

▲ *This set-up is one of the most effective means of bite indication when fishing a static deadbait. You cast out the bait, tighten the line, open the bail arm and trap the line in the white plastic clip. When a pike runs with the bait, the line pulls free of the clip and the orange ball drops – setting off the blue alarm.*

▶ *A small roach deadbait ready to be cast out. It's worth experimenting with different sizes of baits, but it doesn't necessarily follow that the bigger the bait, the bigger the pike. Small baits have proved the downfall of many big pike.*

Vaned float

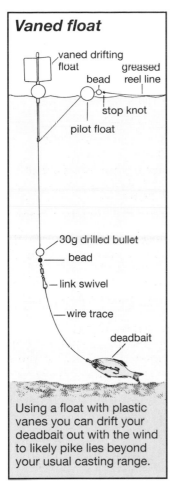

vaned drifting float

greased reel line

bead

stop knot

pilot float

30g drilled bullet

bead

link swivel

wire trace

deadbait

Using a float with plastic vanes you can drift your deadbait out with the wind to likely pike lies beyond your usual casting range.

▼ *Sea fish deadbaits can work very well for pike. It pays to stock your freezer with a variety of both sea and freshwater deadbaits, so that when one fails you can try another. On hard-fished waters, pike soon wise-up to baits.*

traces of about 60cm (24in) long, fitted with pairs of size 8 or 6 treble hooks, are readily obtainable from tackle shops (they are called 'snap tackles'). One hook from each treble holds the deadbait. You can slide the top treble up or down the trace, according to the size of the bait.

Last but not least, never go piking without a pair of long-nosed artery forceps for unhooking your catch, and a good-sized landing net.

Deadbaiting tactics

There are two successful deadbaiting techniques – static and mobile. Which one you use depends very much on the mood of the pike, and that is something you can only determine on the day. But once you have the tackle and know-how to fish the various basic static and mobile techniques, you are ready for every eventuality.

Static deadbaiting

Static deadbaits have caught many big pike over the years. Apart from its visibility, the big attraction of the static deadbait is the scent trail it gives off. This is why it can pay to try half a dead fish rather than a whole one – it greatly increases the scent trail. Alternatively, puncture a whole deadbait several times so that more body juices are released underwater.

The key to static deadbaiting is to have good bite indication so that the pike has no time to turn and swallow the bait and become deep-hooked. Plenty of weight – around 30g (1oz) – is needed to anchor the bait so a tight line can be kept to it.

Running leger This is the simplest static rig, with the bait held fast to the bottom (see *Running leger* diagram).

Popped-up deadbait This is a variant of the running leger rig. A foam stick is inserted into the deadbait to make it hang in the water off the bottom, where it is more easily seen by pike (see *Popped-up deadbait* diagram). It is especially effective over a weedy bottom or deep soft mud, both of which can hide a bait.

Suspended deadbait This is a more complicated but very effective rig. It uses a pilot float sub-surface to suspend the deadbait above the river or lake bed (see *Suspended deadbait* diagram). Again, this presents a highly visible bait and one that won't get lost in weed or mud.

Suspended deadbait

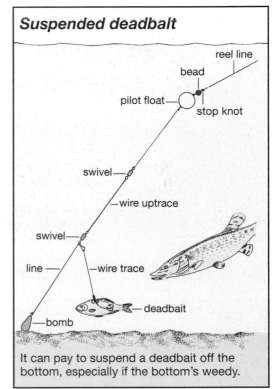

reel line

bead

pilot float

stop knot

swivel

wire uptrace

swivel

line

wire trace

deadbait

bomb

It can pay to suspend a deadbait off the bottom, especially if the bottom's weedy.

Popped-up deadbait

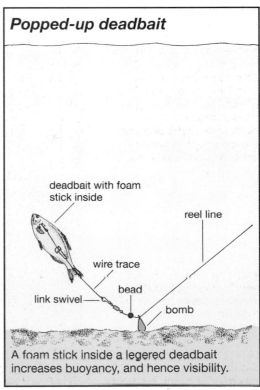

deadbait with foam stick inside

reel line

wire trace

bead

link swivel

bomb

A foam stick inside a legered deadbait increases buoyancy, and hence visibility.

Drifted deadbait

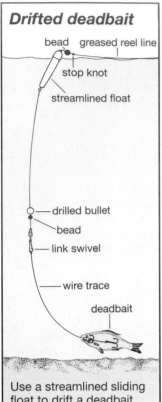

bead greased reel line

stop knot

streamlined float

drilled bullet

bead

link swivel

wire trace

deadbait

Use a streamlined sliding float to drift a deadbait just off the bottom more slowly and at closer range than with a vaned float.

Static deadbaits can take time to work, but on a good day it is possible to get as many as a dozen runs from pike of all sizes. Only pike in waters where they are very well fed show little interest.

Mobile deadbaiting

With a moving bait you are playing not only on the pike's highly developed sense of smell and sight, but on the sensitivity of its lateral line to vibrations.

Mobile methods include wobbling a deadbait through the water, using a float to drift a deadbait out to likely looking lies, and trolling.

Wobbled deadbait For wobbling, the deadbait is mounted head up on the trace and retrieved in an enticing manner. The amount of bend you put in the body of the dead fish determines how much it wobbles through the water (see *Wobbled deadbait* diagram).

Drifted deadbait Sometimes it is impossible to cast your deadbait directly into the spot where you expect a pike to be lying, either because it is a little too far from the bank or because a reedbed or other obstacle is in the way. A drifting float can be the answer to the problem, provided the wind

▼ *The reward for picking the right swim, using the right tackle and presenting a deadbait correctly – a pike for the net.*

direction is in your favour and the wind is not too strong (see *Drifted deadbait* diagram).

Drifting is useful anywhere when you want to search out likely looking areas of water rather than just fish your bait in one particular spot.

Vaned float A more difficult technique to master but one that allows you to fish a deadbait at extreme range – 100m (110yd) or more from the bank – uses a vaned float to 'sail' the bait through the water (see *Vaned float* diagram).

Trolling On very large waters you can often locate pike only by extensive searching. A proven method on such waters – Loch Lomond in Scotland, for example – is to troll (tow) a deadbait behind a boat. Like the vaned float, this is more a specialist technique than a beginner's method.

Spinning for pike – the lure of success

Barrie Rickards, who began spinning forty years ago, and still catches many big pike, shares some of his secrets for successful piking.

Spinning's tops

Fishy folklore maintains that you can't catch big fish on spinners. But Britain's record 45lb 12oz (20.3kg) pike was caught on a spinner – and in two and a half years Barrie Rickards has caught no less than 25 pike over 20lbs (9kg) by spinning.

Many anglers are unaware just how successful spinning for pike can be - possibly because of a few ingrained notions which are hard to budge. In particular it is necessary to dispense with two fallacies concerning lure fishing. First, while it is correct to say that the *average* size of lure-caught fish is smaller – about 7lb (3.1kg) – you do get plenty of big fish. By and large, you also get *more* fish.

Secondly, it is also true that spinning is more successful in summer and autumn than in the depths of winter. However, win-ter spinning can be very successful.

Choosing rods and reels

The rod you choose should be around 9ft (2.7m) for bank fishing. This is a good compromise since it overcomes two ever-present problems in pike fishing that create contradictory demands on the length of the rod. First, marginal reeds and rushes are a fact of life so a rod needs to be about 9ft (2.7m) long to reach over them. Secondly, overhanging trees also seem to be a year-round problem, so the rod can't be too long or it could well catch in the branches.

When boat fishing, or casting on small streams or drains, a 6ft (1.8m) rod may be ideal. Carbon rods are lighter if you intend to carry them all day, and a telescopic version – permanently fitted up with reel line – is invaluable.

Rod strength is important. You don't need a powerful deadbait throwing rod – nor do you need one with a through-action. A

▼ *Pike – when they are in a feeding mood – seem completely unable to resist a spinner. This pike has struck instinctively at a barspoon spinner.*

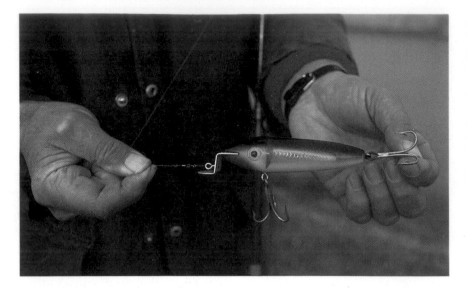

▲ *The term spinning is used to describe all forms of artificial lure fishing and not just fishing with revolving blade spinners. This is a plug – excellent for simulating a fish that is struggling in the water.*

they won't cast as far as a fixed-spool reel, but they are more accurate. A multiplier is not difficult to use and half an hour's practice serves to put a reasonably competent angler on the right road – with only a few tangles to follow.

If you are a right-handed angler – and therefore wish to hold your rod in your right hand while playing the fish – get a **left-hand wind** multiplier. Don't believe any one who says it doesn't matter. Using a left-hand wind outfit makes the whole action sweeter, smoother and much more efficient and keeps your right hand free for casting. Right-handed anglers cast better and more accurately using the right hand – you can't hold the rod *and* wind-in with just one hand!

One of the great advantages of using a multiplier is that the moment the lure hits the water you are in action, fishing smoothly, alert right from the start. Many pike strike the split second that the spinner hits the water – so be ready.

stiffish rod with a tip action and a 1¾-2lb test curve is excellent.

Anglers are spoilt for choice with fixed-spool reels. Almost any decent reel or brand suits perfectly well. There's no point in choosing a heavy reel – one that takes 100yd (90m) of 15lb (6.8kg) line is fine.

Multiplier reels are a pleasure to use –

▼ *A good selection of lures. On the top is a row of buzzers, the second row are spoons, while those on the round log nearest the bottom are spinners of various types.*

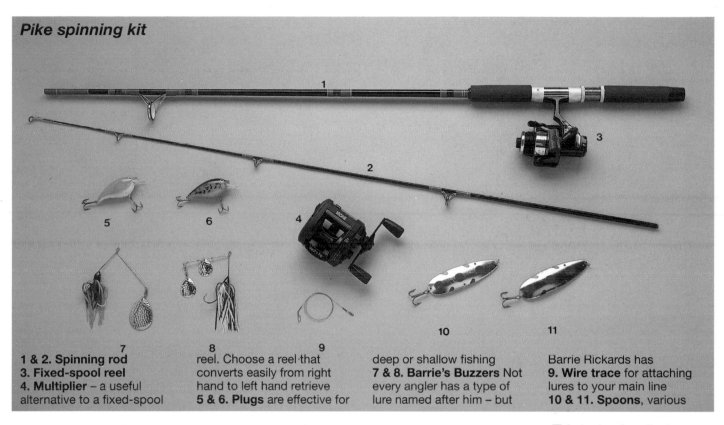

Pike spinning kit

1 & 2. Spinning rod
3. Fixed-spool reel
4. Multiplier – a useful alternative to a fixed-spool

reel. Choose a reel that converts easily from right hand to left hand retrieve
5 & 6. Plugs are effective for

deep or shallow fishing
7 & 8. Barrie's Buzzers Not every angler has a type of lure named after him – but

Barrie Rickards has
9. Wire trace for attaching lures to your main line
10 & 11. Spoons, various

Choosing line

Line for spinning can vary from 10 to 15lb (4.5 to 6.8kg) b.s. Wire traces should be 12in (30cm) long. Never use 6in (15cm) traces – a pike of 15lb (6.8kg) upwards can swallow lure and trace in one gulp. Choice of wire varies – try softer, supple varieties, but avoid very fine wires which tend to be stiff and difficult to twist by hand.

Put a swivel on one end and a link swivel on the other. Strengthen the exact point where the overlap of twisted wire ends with a blob of Epoxy resin Weed slides easily over the blob – but make sure it is a *blob* as a smear catches just as irritatingly as a knot.

Special extras

When you are spinning, line twisting can sometimes be a problem, particularly when using barspoons. However, you'll probably find that anti-kink vanes are rarely necessary. If you are using barspoons extensively, then fit a Wye lead at the top of the trace. This effectively stops the line spinning and as a bonus gives extra casting weight.

Landing nets are a vital piece of equipment for the keen pike spinner. Get a 75cm (30in) diameter round net. Avoid

micromesh nets – hooks get caught in them and may take up to half an hour to pull free, which is bad news for the poor fish. Try a knotless 12-25mm mesh net that is soft and knitted.

A backpack for carrying flask and food and warm clothes, including gloves in the winter, is also essential!

▼ *Spinning for pike is a particularly successful method during the summer months, when the water is clear. The shiny colours show plainly and the spinning action makes the lures strikingly obvious to hungry pike.*

Tip Buzzing along

Buzzers are the latest type of lure to reach the market, and they contrast strongly with more traditional lures in that they do not resemble wounded fish in any way. Pike can detect from some distance away the commotion buzzers create in the water when being cast and retrieved.

Barrie Rickards seldom uses anti-kink devices when spinning – except a Wye lead. But some pike anglers, such as Barrie's frequent fishing partner, Ken Whitehead, find an anti-kink vane is invaluable.

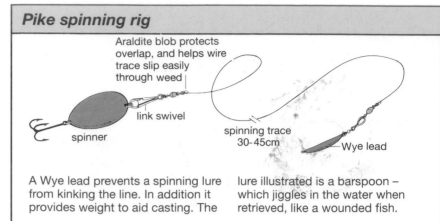

Pike spinning rig

Araldite blob protects overlap, and helps wire trace slip easily through weed

link swivel

spinner

spinning trace 30-45cm

Wye lead

A Wye lead prevents a spinning lure from kinking the line. In addition it provides weight to aid casting. The lure illustrated is a barspoon – which jiggles in the water when retrieved, like a wounded fish.

▼ *This pike was fooled by the wobbling action of a typical spoon.*

Down to action

All the equipment mentioned is vital if the pike spinner is to enjoy piking. Good technique is worth nothing if the angler is uncomfortable and operating inefficiently.

The actual casting and retrieving is the least of your worries. Even so, there are a number of things to be wary of.

Don't get into the bad habit of 'casting round the clock'. Try to work out where the pike might be and cast accordingly. Just which lure you choose to use depends very much on the season and on the conditions you find in your swim. In many cases only experience will tell you what to try. You need to take into account water clarity, snags and weeds and the depth of water the fish may be feeding in. The lures themselves perform in various different ways – a spinner has a small blade that spins, a spoon wobbles on retrieve but has no blade and a plug closely resembles a fish and can do a variety of things on retrieve. Change lures frequently until you find the winning combination of style, size and colour for the day. This can be critical. The slightest change in depth, retrieve style or colour of lure can make a 'fishless' water productive.

In general, try a steady, slow retrieve, and in winter keep as deep as possible. During summer come up to the top with surface lures and try more varied depths as well. Vary the retrieve from steady to erratic only when the former fails.

Impossible swims?

Seek out seemingly impossible swims where no one has fished before – often a good fish lurks there. By using single hook buzzers you can fish among trees and in the middle of lily beds. If you suspect the location of a good fish, spend half a dozen casts nearby – but not actually too close to its lair. The pike will hear the repeated splashes and, by the time you throw the spoon to it, will be really curious and ready to strike.

In short, think before acting; be mobile; and be versatile. And above all, go spinning when you expect the pike to feed, not when other methods have failed.

Drift float fishing for big water pike

There's no doubt that if you can get your bait out to features beyond normal casting range, you'll catch more pike. Jon Culley explains how a drift float can help you do just that.

I n an unfished water, pike feed without inhibition whenever they are hungry and wherever there is food. However, as with many other kinds of fish, they soon learn to avoid feeding in areas where they have been caught frequently.

On many large hard-fished waters, such as reservoirs and big pits, the pike learn to stay out of normal casting range. They come into the margins only rarely, usually at dawn and dusk, spending the rest of the time near distant drop-offs, islands and other pike-holding features.

▼ There are several designs of drift float. Each type must include certain characteristics though. It must have a curved vane to stop it spinning instead of drifting, the top ring must come away on the strike, and the vane must be highly visible, even at distances of up to 200m (220yd).

Big pits drifter

So, if you can get your bait out beyond the farthest cast, preferably near some feature, you are going to waste less of your fishing time and put more fish on the bank. Drifting the bait lets you fish in the middle of big waters, where the big pike feed without fear.

You can use any fairly standard pike gear for this type of fishing. However, a rod with a test curve of 2 ½-3lb (1.1-1.4kg) and a fast taper to set the hooks at long range can make life easier. A long rod also helps here. The reel must have a large capacity – at least 200m (220yd) of 12lb (5.4kg) line – for long drifting.

There are two main techniques which involve drifting your baits – the first uses a drift float and the second a balloon. Each has its advantages and you should learn to use both, so you can cope with a variety of venues and conditions.

Blowing in the wind

Drift floats are blown along by the wind, dragging a bait behind them. They have a small sail or vane to catch the wind. This is attached to an ordinary floating body. They come in many forms, the best of which have

Balloons are litter too!

When you have finished ballooning for the day, remember that you must round up your balloons. Go to the far bank and collect the balloons you have released. On a very windy day, you might have to do this regularly to stop them blowing away.

Littering a venue can only help get fishing banned. If you can't be bothered to tidy up, or the water is too vast for you to find your balloons, don't fish with them.

a spherical buoyant body, with a stem or mast for the vane. The vane must be curved in shape or the float tends to spin as it is blown along.

A drift float is designed to tow the bait out with the wind, suspending it at a chosen depth. The vane is usually painted in some highly visible colour, giving good bite indication over a great distance.

The body is a poly ball or something similar. Some makes of float come with a variety of sizes of body, so it's easy to change the buoyancy to suit the conditions and size of bait you are using.

The line is attached top and bottom which helps prevent the line from sinking. A sunk line can hinder or even stop a drift.

The top eye of the float should come adrift during the strike, leaving the float attached bottom end only. That way the vane does

not get in the way of the strike – if it did, setting the hooks at long range would be even more difficult.

To start a drift, you only need to cast to where the wind begins to ruffle the water. The wind then carries the float with it. Make sure you pay out the line in as straight a line as possible – a big bow in the line causes drag.

As it drifts, the bait works pretty much like a trolled bait. The live or deadbait is dragged along – past pike on the lookout for an easy meal. The bait is prevented from swimming along the surface by a ½oz (14g) drilled bullet on the trace.

When your float has drifted as far as you want it to go, or it has reached the feature

Grease your line

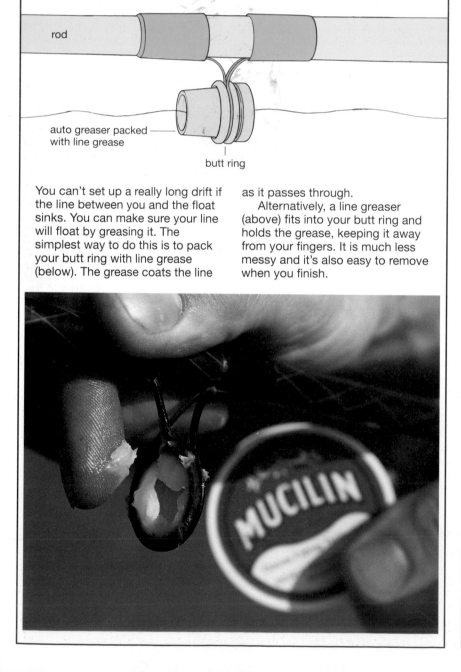

rod

auto greaser packed with line grease

butt ring

You can't set up a really long drift if the line between you and the float sinks. You can make sure your line will float by greasing it. The simplest way to do this is to pack your butt ring with line grease (below). The grease coats the line

as it passes through.

Alternatively, a line greaser (above) fits into your butt ring and holds the grease, keeping it away from your fingers. It is much less messy and it's also easy to remove when you finish.

A drift float rig

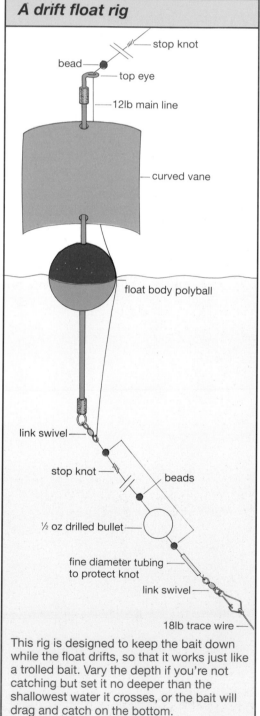

stop knot
bead
top eye
12lb main line
curved vane
float body polyball
link swivel
stop knot
beads
½ oz drilled bullet
fine diameter tubing to protect knot
link swivel
18lb trace wire

This rig is designed to keep the bait down while the float drifts, so that it works just like a trolled bait. Vary the depth if you're not catching but set it no deeper than the shallowest water it crosses, or the bait will drag and catch on the bottom.

Ballooning for big pike

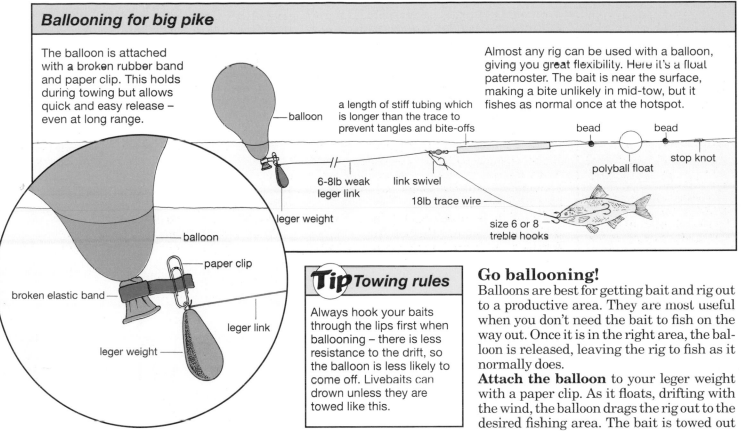

The balloon is attached with a broken rubber band and paper clip. This holds during towing but allows quick and easy release – even at long range.

balloon

a length of stiff tubing which is longer than the trace to prevent tangles and bite-offs

Almost any rig can be used with a balloon, giving you great flexibility. Here it's a float paternoster. The bait is near the surface, making a bite unlikely in mid-tow, but it fishes as normal once at the hotspot.

bead   bead

stop knot

6-8lb weak leger link

link swivel

polyball float

18lb trace wire

leger weight

size 6 or 8 treble hooks

balloon

paper clip

broken elastic band

leger link

leger weight

▼ *An angler prepares to cast a big deadbait on a drifting rig. Drift floats are ideal for a big, apparently featureless water such as this, as they allow you to search large stretches of water to find the fish.*

Tip Towing rules

Always hook your baits through the lips first when ballooning – there is less resistance to the drift, so the balloon is less likely to come off. Livebaits can drown unless they are towed like this.

you want to fish, close the bail arm. You can then float fish as you would normally do, but at longer range!

If bites do not follow, work the bait back slowly – takes can even come during the retrieve. Next cast, try to get your float drifting along another line and eventually you'll find the pike.

Go ballooning!

Balloons are best for getting bait and rig out to a productive area. They are most useful when you don't need the bait to fish on the way out. Once it is in the right area, the balloon is released, leaving the rig to fish as it normally does.

Attach the balloon to your leger weight with a paper clip. As it floats, drifting with the wind, the balloon drags the rig out to the desired fishing area. The bait is towed out very close to the surface, and the whole arrangement generally travels much faster than a drift float rig.

This means that while you *can* get takes on the way out, the bait isn't really fishing until it reaches your chosen spot. For this reason ballooning is best when you want to fish a specific area beyond casting range, whereas fishing a drift float is ideal for

Big pike waters

Drift floats are very useful on the following big waters.

- **A1 Pits, Notts** Six pits – pike over 25lb (11.3kg).
- **Abberton Res., Essex** Pike over 30lb (13.6kg).
- **Attenborough Gravel Pits, Notts** 30lb (13.6kg) pike.
- **Broadlands Lake, Hants** Pike over 35lb (15.9kg).
- **Damflask Res., Yorks.** Pike to 34lb (15.4kg).
- **Hollowell Res., Northants,** Many doubles, pike to 20lb (9.1kg).
- **Linear Fisheries, Bucks** Pike to 30lb (13.6kg).
- **Lochs Lomond and Awe, Scotland** Huge pike over 35lb (15.9kg).
- **Stanford Res., Leics** Pike to 30lb (13.6kg).
- **Startops and Wilstone, Tring Res., Herts** Pike to over 30lb (13.6kg).

searching large areas of water.

Ballooning really scores over drifting when you need to be versatile with your rigs. You can tow anything – from a float paternoster to a simple freeline rig – behind a balloon. With a drift float you are restricted to float fishing.

Unfortunately, you can't cast with a balloon set-up. You can only drop it in at the edge of the water, or it'll fall off! A gentle breeze may struggle to push the balloon along against the drag of the line and bait so close to the bank. When this happens, tie another balloon to the first for extra dragging power.

When the wind is strong and gusting, you might find that the balloon keeps coming out of the paper clip. Partly filling the balloon with water slows it down and stops it blowing away on its own.

You must also make sure that the line is peeling freely off the spool. If it is catching anywhere, this can impede the drift causing the balloon to come free.

Once your bait is in the right area, close the bale arm and wait until the line tightens up. This gets rid of the bow that usually forms in the line. Wind down, and when the balloon starts back towards you, release it with a firm sweeping strike. This pulls the balloon out of the paper clip, leaving the rig in place.

The balloon moves much more quickly across the water when it isn't held down by your rig, so it's easy to spot if you've done it right. If you don't manage to release it first time, repeat the strike until you're sure the balloon has come off, leaving the bait where you want it.

Put the rod in rod rests and attach a bobbin or drop-off bite indicator. You're now fishing much as you would if you had cast normally, but much farther out.

These methods may seem complicated at first but once you've tried them, you'll see how easy they are. You'll also notice that you're catching more big fish on large waters than the other anglers who all fish within casting distance.

▼ *John Watson cradles a 30-pounder (13.6kg) from Martham Broad. Drift floats are ideal for fishing a broad from the bank when you can't find the fish close-in.*

Float fishing for pike from boat and bank

John Watson's view is that simplicity is what counts in catching pike. A couple of simple float rigs are all you need to cover almost every baitfishing situation effectively.

Take a look at the pike tackle in any tackle shop and you cannot fail to be impressed by the sheer number and variety of pike floats. Some of these are of little or no use, being more of a trap for the angler than the pike.

For John Watson, Norfolk specimen hunter, simplicity is the key to pike fishing.

He uses only basic rigs and end gear, and the number of big pike he's caught over the years speaks for itself. Avoid complication for its own sake and you not only cut down on tangles, you land more fish too!

Many of the ready-made sliding floats, self-cockers and floats with transparent bodies can work very well, but not significantly better than the simple poly ball in a variety of sizes. For most forms of pike float fishing except drifting over long distances, a plain poly ball is simplest and is often all you need.

▼ *It's a good feeling when you've safely boated a fine fish like this 18-pounder (8.2kg). A boat gives you the freedom to try a roving float or a float paternoster in the hotspots of a water from very short range.*

Tip Bite off!

With a float paternoster a pike sometimes grabs both the bait and the main line in its mouth. When this happens it may bite through the main line. To stop this some anglers use an up-trace. This extra length of wire is attached to the swivel above the bomb link so the pike cannot bite through it.

John Watson does not use an up-trace. He sets his paternoster at an angle so the bait never gets close to the line. Make sure you keep the line tight between the rod tip and float when you do this or it won't work.

A variety of pike floats

Most pike floats can be used for a float paternoster and roving float rig. They include: **(1)** simple pike bungs; **(2)** sliding and bottom-end only floats; **(3)** self-cocking floats, with and without vanes for drifting and visibility; and **(4)** John Watson's preferred option – the poly ball. Use drift floats **(5)** only for drift float fishing.

Why use a float?

A pike float serves two main purposes – as an indicator and as a controller.

As a controller, a float can help you position the bait accurately by allowing you to see where it is and letting you drift it into position. It also acts as a buoyancy aid, whether it's out of sight or being used as an indicator.

As an indicator, it shows you where the bait is and when a fish has taken it. Float fishing is a highly sensitive method of bite detection, and is probably the best way of avoiding gut-hooked pike.

However, the indicator is only as sensitive as the technique involved. For the float to work, your rig and methods must work well too.

Floating pike baits

Apart from drift float fishing there are two main methods of fishing with a float. You can either fish a bait that's free to move, or use some form of weighted float rig to anchor the bait in a certain area.

A free-swimming bait can, to a certain extent, be guided to where you want it to fish. Use the current on a river to drift the bait past various features. Or, on still waters, use the drag caused by the wind to move the bait over a wide area.

The rig is simple. The bait and trace are suspended by a sliding poly ball, held at the right depth with a bead and stop knot. The line must be greased to keep it on top of the water, and you can add a weight if the bait keeps rising to the surface.

A float paternoster is best if you need to anchor the bait in a certain spot. It keeps the bait in a pikey-looking area, while allowing it as much movement as possible, especially with a livebait. The float can be used as a visual indicator, or merely to keep the bait off the bottom (in which case the float fishes below the surface).

Livebaits and deadbaits

You can use these techniques with success either livebaiting or deadbaiting. With only slight modifications, the rigs are effective under almost all circumstances.

With a livebait on a roving rig, make sure that the poly ball you choose is big enough. Otherwise the bait pulls the float under and keeps it there. The odd brief dip below the

surface is fine, but you don't want the float staying out of sight for half a minute at a time, or you won't know when you've got a run.

With baits up to 3-4oz (85-115g), a 25mm (1in) diameter float has enough buoyancy to keep the bait afloat. For bigger baits – there's rarely need to go over 6oz (170g) – a

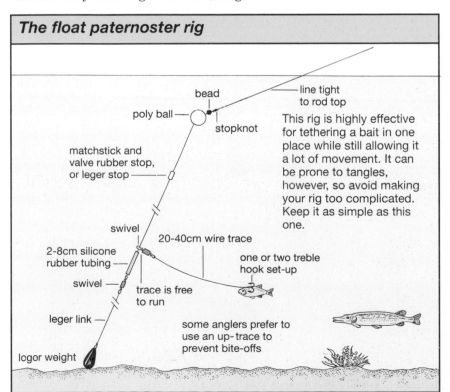

▲ *A simple sliding float rig fooled this pike into taking a roving deadbait. In the absence of any distinct features, a roving bait often finds the pike long before the pike find a static deadbait.*

The float paternoster rig

bead
poly ball
stopknot
line tight to rod top

matchstick and valve rubber stop, or leger stop

swivel

20-40cm wire trace

2-8cm silicone rubber tubing

one or two treble hook set-up

swivel

leger link

trace is free to run

some anglers prefer to use an up-trace to prevent bite-offs

logor weight

This rig is highly effective for tethering a bait in one place while still allowing it a lot of movement. It can be prone to tangles, however, so avoid making your rig too complicated. Keep it as simple as this one.

Increased visibility

Sometimes when fishing at long range, a poly ball can become hard to spot. That's when a more visible float is very useful. The type above features a vane similar to the feathers on a dart. This makes the float stand out at a distance and helps it to drift freely in the wind.

Tip Poly balls

Most float fishing for pike is carried out at short range, and so a poly ball is perfectly visible, in addition to being cheap, easy to use and very versatile.

If you want to use really large baits, one poly ball may struggle to keep them afloat. In these circumstances, you can either use an expensive float, or use two poly balls in tandem!

38mm (1½in) diameter float is right.

Tethering a livebait in a good looking spot calls for a float paternoster. It stops the bait from simply lying doggo on the bottom, while allowing it a great deal of freedom to move. Since it is the struggles of the bait which attract the pike, the more movement the better.

A roving deadbait rig can easily be set up using the simple float rig described earlier. This allows you to search the water with your bait, rather than just relying on the smell of the bait to attract the fish. You can fish the deadbait horizontally or vertically – pike don't seem to mind. For ease of casting you should hook it head down.

For a static deadbait you can use either

The roving float rig

bead and stopknot

poly ball

swan shot or weight

swivel

30-40cm wire trace

one or two treble hook set-up – to suit the size of bait

This is the simplest float rig for pike but it is very effective nonetheless. The weight above the swivel is only necessary if the bait keeps floating to the surface.

▼ The author with a beautifully-conditioned predator from the Norfolk Broads. It took a dace deadbait on a roving float.

the float paternoster rig, or a modified roving float. Fish the paternoster exactly as you would with the livebait. Like the roving deadbait, it can have the advantage over legering and freelining that the bait is off the bottom – visible to any pike cruising around. The bait therefore appeals to two senses – sight and smell – and not just to smell.

You can easily modify the roving or free-swimming rig to keep a deadbait static on the bottom. The deadbait is attached at the end of the trace as before. But instead of fishing underdepth with the bait suspended, the float is set overdepth.

The optional weight or swan shot that you may need to keep a livebait from rising to the water's surface now becomes essential to keep the deadbait in one place. Plumb the depth carefully, and set the weight so it sits on the bottom.

This float leger rig uses the float as a bite detector. Provided you keep the line tight between rod and float, it will remain close to the surface – away from the wind but above any heavy weed or snags. Keeping the line tight also prevents pike from swallowing the bait without your seeing the bite – and so reduces the chance that they might gut-hook themselves.

With these basic float rigs you can cope with almost every situation. You don't need to invest in expensive floats unless you want to – all you really need is the good old poly ball. So stick to the basics and enjoy your piking!

Index

Page numbers in *italics* refer to illustrations

Acknowledgements

Photographs: Heather Angel 149; Angling Press Service (Bill Howes) 99(c), 176(t); S&J Bailey 55(b), 172(b), 182(c), 193; Chris Ball 125, 199(b); Ian Christy (Eaglemoss) 163(t); Bruce Coleman Ltd 26(c); Eric Crichton Photos (Eaglemoss) 67(t), 68(t), 126; John Culley 184(b); John Darling (29(t), 138, 170 (t); Andy Dawson (Eaglemoss), 14(b), 24(t), 39(l), 40, 41(b), 42(t), 45(l), 160(cr); Neville Fickling 90(t), 142(tr), 150, 205, 206(c); Peter Gathercole 155, 157(bc), 169)b), 171; Carl Geddye (Eaglemoss) 51(c), 53; Jim Gibbinson 165, 166(t), 167(b); Nick Giles 92(tl); Jens Ploug Hansen 29(b), 31, 60(b), 88(b), 99(b), 100, 111(b), 122(b), 123(b), 144, 176(b), 209, 212(b); Mike Helliwell 19; Neil Holmes 71, (Eaglemoss) BC, 46, 70, 73, 74(b), 75, 77–80, 105(c), 154, 161(b), 166(c), 195, 202(tl); Trevor Housby 17, 38(t), 60(t), 107, 120(b), 132, 159(b), 172(t), 173, 192, 208, 217, Bob James 37, 177(c), 185; Dennis Linley 38(b), 128, 161(t), 194(tr,b) (Eaglemoss) 6, 66(t), 67(c), 72, 84(t), 86(tr), 108(b), 152; Patrick Llewelyn-Davies (Eaglemoss) 74(t),156(tr,bl), 198; Kevin Maddocks 134; Graham Marsden 18, 33, 61(b), 62(t), 81, 115(b), 174, 189, 191(b), 197, 215, 219(t); Bill Meadows (Eaglemoss)156(br), 158(t), 196; Mike Millman 23, 27(b), 82, 85(b), (Eaglemoss) 24(b), 114(br), 178(b), 179; Natural Science Photos 94(b), (T. Davies-Patrick) 200, (R. Forsberg) 89(r), (P&S Ward) 51(b), 57, 62(b), 109, 110(bl,br), 111(t), 115(t), 122(tr), 159(t), 162(b), 170(b), 188; Martin Norris (Eaglemoss) 12, 13, 14(t), 39(r), 43, 44(t), 87(t), 88(t), 108(t), 117(b), 175, 190, 201, 211, 218; Janet Oddy 11, 65; Andy Orme 55(t), 56, 163(b); Tom Pickering Back flap; Barrie Rickards 119(tr), 121; Bill Rushmer 36; Kevin Smith 15, 28(b), 30(tl,tr,cl), 35, 47(b), 61(t), 69(b), 76(b), 83(t), 93, 95(t), 97, 98, 101, 102, 104, 110(tr), 112, 113(tr,br), 114, 116, 117(t), 118, 119(cr,b), 122(tl), 124(tr), 130, 136, 140, 153, 177(b), 178(t), 186, 187, 191(t), 203, 204(t), 213, 214; (Eaglemoss) 95(t), 96, 105(b), 106; John Suett (Eaglemoss) 9, 20, 21, 23 (inset), 25, 26(b), 48, 50, 52, 83(b), 84(b), 85(t), 86(tc), 120(t); Steve Tanner (Eaglemoss) 22(tl), 89(cl,inset), 90(bl), 182(t,b), 183, 184(tl); Bob Taylor (Eaglemoss) 27(c), 41(t), 54, 69(t); Mick Toomer 142(tl); Jim Tyree 3, 42(b); Alain Urruty 34, 68(b), 91(t), 92(tr,cr,bl), 113(bl), 114(bl); John Watson 146, 168, 180(b), 216, 219(b), 220; Ken Whitehead 110(tl), 180(t); John Wilson 16(b), 22(tr), 28(t), 30(cr), 44(b), 45(r), 47(t), 49, 58, 59, 67(b), 90(br), 95(b), 103, 123(tl), 148, 158(b), 169(b), 162(c), 164, 169(t), 181, 199(t), 202(tr,b), 204(b), 206(b), 207, 210(b), 211(b); Stuart Windsor (Eaglemoss) 123(tr), 124(cr,bl), 157(tl,bl), 167(t), 194(tl), 210(t), 212(t); Shona Wood (Eaglemoss) 66(b), 76(t), 91(b).

Illustrations: Peter Allen 130; Craig Austin 135; Peter Bull 15(t), 16–8, 28, 32(tl,tr), 36–7, 40–1, 46, 49, 50, 56, 57, 59, 75, 78, 102, 107, 118(r), 122, 134, 136, 138, 140, 142, 144, 146, 148, 150, 152, 157, 170, 171, 173, 174, 175, 187, 188(tl,tr), 191–3, 195, 196, 200, 206–8, 214–5, 219–20; Michael Cooke 32(bl), 34, 70–1, 74, 88, 90, 96, 100, 118, 127, 131(tr), 139(t), 141(t), 143(t,b),145(t,b,inset),149(t,b,inset),151(t,b,inset), 162, 166, 167, 168, 176, 178, 179, 188(c,b); David Etchell 20, 21, 128; Mei Lim 124, 212, Linden Artists (Mick Loates) 131(b), (Craig Warwick) 22, 132; Mick Loates 129, 133, 137, 139(b), 141(b), 143(c), 145(b), 149(b), 151(b); Richard Smith 147(b).